To Shane, with support... for *continued*
to put up with CU

*[handwritten signature: Richard Blythe]*

# A GLIMPSE OF
# WHAT'S
# BEYOND

## The story of Colchester United's rise to the second tier of English football and their momentary view of the Premier League.

### By RICHARD BLYTHE

**Published by Richard Blythe**
richard.blythe2@yahoo.co.uk

ISBN 978-0-9934131-0-0

**Printed and bound by**
**Sudbury Print Group Ltd**
www.sudburyprintgroup.co.uk

# CONTENTS

# INTRODUCTION

Nobody said being a Colchester United fan was meant to be easy. Nick Hornby wrote a well known book about the trials and tribulations of being an Arsenal fan. Oh how my heart bled for him! He was never likely to receive much sympathy from those who follow an unfashionable club because it represents the area of their upbringing, their family seat, the fulcrum of their life.

A football club should choose you, and there is a small band of people who were chosen by Colchester United. We have reverse snobbery down to an art form. We look down on those who acquire their football club by applying the same values employed when buying the latest designer trainers. Thus, if you are well adjusted, you receive a football club into your heart by nothing more than an accident of geography. You have to accept it, warts and all. In no sense is it a commercial transaction. It is an affair of the heart.

The sort of football fan I imagine to be represented by Nick Hornby looks for a football club that they can wear as a fashion accessory. It has to be big, glamorous and successful. These fans can be seen at Colchester`s railway station every Saturday, or whatever day Sky TV has decreed for that week. No doubt the same is true at the stations of market towns up and down the country.

If you are a fan of a small club this is infuriating. It is like being denied invitations to the best parties. It takes you back to your school days. I imagine that Nick Hornby and those like him were the popular kids at school. Invited to all the coolest parties, an adoring girlfriend on each arm and a windowless social diary. Colchester United fans were the nerds. Keen on IT and German progressive rock. We were the overweight asthmatics standing outside the games lesson with a note from mother. We did not have many friends but we remained loyal to those we did have. We were not bullies and we did not cheat at conkers. We did our homework if it interested us. If not we studied the solar system and considered the artistic attributes of black and white photography.

In short we had the right values and if we liked football we supported our local club. We sat resplendent atop the moral high ground. And were we happy? Of course we weren`t! Not for us the glory of domestic dominance, a residency on Sky TV, European travel, multi million pound transfers, celebrity players as famous as the Queen and with a greater income. No, it is our lot to endure relegation to some strange world called non-league, to be reminded of Mr Bean when considering the physical co-ordination of our centre half, to lose 8-0 at the home of some East London barrow boys. To be a Colchester United fan you must travel to Humber side and discover that not only has your best and only coveted player left you, he has actually signed for that day`s opposition. Do not expect your ex players to show respect when scoring against you. Oh no, their past is quickly forgotten in that moment of joy.

You will make headlines only when you are thrashed at some muddy and unheard of North Eastern outpost known only for breeding an annoying form of dog. You must accept that your manager will probably leave if he gets a few good results and go to your richer, and more glamorous, local rivals. On the rare occasion when headlines are made for the right reason by a spectacular opening day result you must learn shoulder shrugging when the manager and the entire coaching staff decline the team bus home and prefer the employment of the bigger club you have just vanquished.

Being a Colchester United fan is hard, and the chosen few are measured by their quality not their quantity. No bandwagon has ever been seen within 15 miles of either Layer Road or the Weston Homes Community Stadium.

I was chosen on Saturday 1st April 1967 when at the age of six I walked with my brother the 500 yards from my home to Layer Road Football Ground to watch the mighty U`s dispatch hapless Walsall 5-1. In my young mind I probably thought that this was just the beginning of a lifetime of 5-1 wins, the start of an unshakeable trajectory to the very pinnacle of the game. The only question was whether the first European Cup win would come before or after my first team debut as the free scoring centre forward destiny had in store for me.

It was April Fools` Day and, sadly, things have not quite panned out that way either for me, or the club. The near 40 years between my introduction and August 2005 saw many ups and downs. To be precise, it saw two promotions to the third tier of the English game, and three demotions back to the fourth. It saw the utter humiliation of relegation to the Conference in 1990, a rebirth in those humble surrounds, some cup runs and three days out at Wembley. Mostly however it was neither up nor down. It was flat.

That all changed in the 05/06 and 06/07 seasons which will forever be a golden period in Colchester United`s history, a period which made all the suffering worthwhile. What follows is the story of that period. It starts with the arrival of a Reading legend in February 2003.


**NB Quotations in bold italics and indented are taken from recent interviews with the author. Quotations in the ordinary text are from the time.**

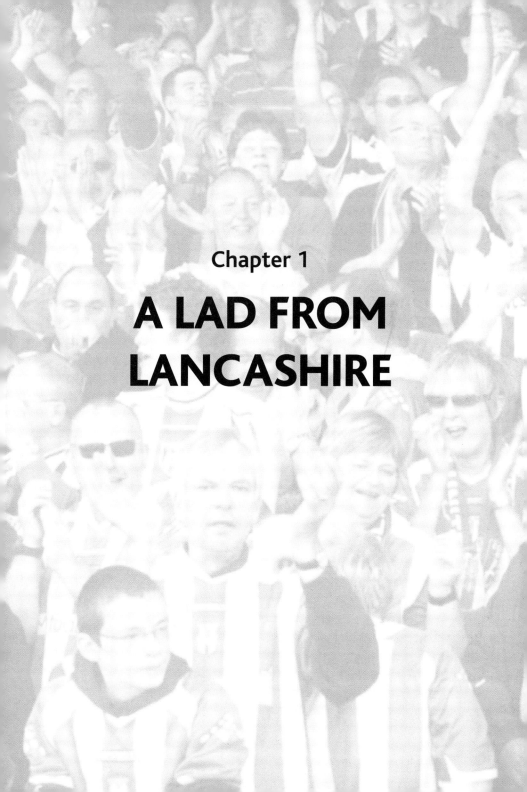

## Chapter 1

# A LAD FROM LANCASHIRE

# Chapter 1
## A LAD FROM LANCASHIRE

Philip John Parkinson was born on 1st December 1967 in Chorley, Lancashire. Soon after he started school, the family moved to Cheshunt in North London. Then, when he was eight, they moved to Stockton on Tees in County Durham.

His moves up and down the country continued when his football career started as an apprentice at Southampton, and he takes up the story,

*"Lawrie McMenemy was the manager of Southampton, and he was a Gateshead boy. Through him, Southampton had a school of excellence in Gateshead, which I attended. This is how I came to join Southampton. Leaving home at sixteen and moving to the other end of the country certainly hardens you up. Dave Merrington, who later managed Southampton, was the youth coach, and he was a hard task master. He taught us discipline, and was a big influence on me.*

*I was a dedicated pro, but I was never quite able to make the break through at Southampton. The closest I got was being a substitute in a First division game against Leicester, when Matt Le Tissier scored a hat trick and I didn`t get on. I left 12 months later."*

Now aged 20, and with first team opportunities impossible to come by, Parkinson realised he would have to take a step backwards to move forwards. He therefore left the First Division club to return to the north with Third Division Bury. He had been recommended by Merrington to his former Burnley teammate Martin Dobson, then in charge at Bury. Signed for £12,000, Parkinson was finally given his Football League debut.

*"Bury was a great education for me. Like me, Dobson was a midfield player, and I thought he was a very good manager. His number two was Frank Casper, and they were a good management team. I went straight into the first team, and I thrived. There were some old heads in that dressing room, like the ex Man United players Sammy McIlroy and Mark Higgins and the late Noel Brotherstone. You couldn`t help but learn from players of their experience."*

Parkinson quickly established himself in Bury`s midfield, helping to consolidate them as a mid table Third Division club. He was soon a fan`s favourite, as the following responses from Bury fans testify, "he would tackle anything that moved", "never gave less than 100%", "Parky had a strange gait and ran awkwardly almost bow legged but he was a fierce competitor. Not the most gifted ability wise but he more than made up for it in commitment"

Another Bury fan remembers him being sent off for fighting at Brentford with Micky Hurlock, an equally combative player. The two continued to swap punches in the tunnel!

Female Bury fans saw other qualities in the young Parky, one remembers him as being "rather cute"

*"Bury is a nice family club and I had four good years there. I still have friends in the area. Sam Ellis took over as manager and he was quite a character. His organisation of the team, his preparation for matches and his thoroughness are things which have stayed with me. You didn't always like playing for Sam, as he could be tough. But he was honest, and he was the sort of manager you appreciated after he had left. We reached the Third Division play offs under him which was a great achievement for a club of Bury's size. He then left for Manchester City."*

Parky's commitment to the cause was demonstrated in November 1988, when Bury were drawn away to non-league Guisborough Town in the FA Cup First round. The part timer's home was considered inadequate to stage the tie. It was therefore transferred to Ayresome Park, the former home of Middlesbrough. Parkinson missed his brother's wedding to play, and scored the only goal of the game. He then rushed away to attend the reception, which was being held by coincidence in Guisborough! One can only wonder at the welcome he must have received from any local football fans.

This must have completed a surreal day for Parkinson, who had earlier witnessed Guisborough's Ray Hankin being sent off for dissent. It had followed the Referee's decision to book him for not wearing a captain's armband!

For the 1990/91 season Ellis's assistant Mike Walsh had taken over as manager. With Parkinson a stalwart in midfield they again reached the play offs, where they suffered the agony of losing to local rivals Bolton Wanderers, 2-1 on aggregate.

The following season was to be Parkinson's last at Gigg Lane, and it did not end well. It is often the case that a team which loses in the play offs suffers a hangover in the following season. In the midst of financial crisis Bury finished 21st, and were relegated. Parkinson had missed a large part of the season through injury. After a heavy defeat at Huddersfield, manager Walsh commented that Parky on one leg would have played better than the rest of the team!

*"I met Aidan Davison during my time at Bury. He was looking for digs when he came to the club, and I had a friend who was looking for a lodger. We were both single lads from the North East, and we became good mates. However, Aidy could never get in the first team because Gary Kelly was such a good keeper and never got injured. Aidy eventually moved on in search of first team games, but we stayed in touch, and this would later be a great benefit to Colchester United."*

Although Parkinson had loved his time at Bury and made many firm friends, he had no ambition to play Fourth Division football at that time.

*"I was out of contract, and my friend Craig Maskell was at Reading. We had been at Southampton together. The Reading manager was Mark McGhee, and at the end of the season he had been talking to Craig about the sort of midfield player he felt they needed. Craig said he thought I would be ideal, and Mark remembered me from when Bury had played Reading. I signed for Reading just in time for pre season in July 1992."*

By 1992 Reading had been taken over by publishing magnate John Madejski. They had ambitious plans but it did not take much of Madejski`s multi millions to bring Parkinson to Berkshire. Mark McGhee paid Bury £37,500 to bring the combative midfield player south. It proved to be money well spent.

*"Mark McGhee and Colin Lee were a superb managerial team. In my first season we just missed the Division Two (third tier) play offs and the next season we won the title."*

Parkinson was twice named player of the year during his 11 years with the Royals. He was a key member of 93/94 side which won the Football League Division Two title and finished as runners up in Division One the following year. Due to the streamlining of the Premier League the runners up had to play off for promotion, and heartbreakingly Reading were edged out 4-3 by Bolton after extra time. Clearly, Bolton were establishing themselves as Parkinson`s nemesis.

*"I was injured for that game, and had to watch as we were 2-0 up and then missed a penalty. From that position we lost 4-3, otherwise I think I would have become a Premier League player. We had a hungry group of young players who wanted to*

*improve, and we'd had a great time. Despite losing Mark McGhee, we'd carried on the momentum built up during the previous season and we just fell at the final hurdle."*

Parkinson had watched while manager Mark McGhee left Reading for what seemed a more attractive job at Leicester City, soon after Reading's promotion from Division Two. Could it be that a seed was planted which would influence future events?

Reading slipped back to Division Two in 1998. However in 2002 they returned to Division One under Phil Parkinson's captaincy. Now 34, his playing career was winding down, but he was rewarded with a testimonial year by Reading. The highlight was a benefit match against an England XI which included Paul Gascoigne, John Barnes and Chris Waddle in front of 20,000 fans.

*"Terry Bullivant made me captain at Reading, and I enjoyed that responsibility. I think it is good preparation for being a coach and a manager. You are the link between the players and the manager and coaches, and, now I'm a manager, I can see how much help a good captain can be both on the pitch and in the dressing room."*

Parkinson's committed style of play and loyalty ensured that he would always be a fan's favourite. He made over 400 appearances for Reading, and his standing amongst the club's faithful was confirmed after his retirement. A fan's poll selected him in the club's best ever eleven. He was voted their best central midfield player with 60.3% of the vote.

*"The first time I played against Colchester was in February 1999 at Layer Road. I was Reading's captain and Geraint (George) Williams was captain of Colchester. I scored the equaliser that day with my left foot, which was a rarity.*

*Two years later I remember us playing at Layer Road in the penultimate game of the season. We were third and the second promotion spot was between us and Kevin Watson's Rotherham. Jamie Cureton had put us in front, but Barry Conlon equalised before Colchester won it with a penalty. Rotherham won which put them five points above us with only one game left. So we went into the play offs, where we lost to Walsall in the final. Not such a happy memory of Layer Road! In fact I played there four times, and the time I scored was the only time we got anything. This taught me how Layer Road could be a difficult place for away teams to visit.*

*It was while I was at Reading that I took an open university degree in Social Science. I actually started to take some courses while I was at Bury, but they got interrupted when I was transferred. Correspondence study through the OU made sense, because there was always the chance that I might move on from Reading.I did it for six years.*

*Football can take over your life, and doing something like this gives you a different perspective. I think it helped me to grow on a personal level. I also think it has helped me when going for jobs. Chairmen can see on your CV that you`ve spent time doing something different, and I think it helps to set you apart. I remember Peter Heard being very interested in this.*

*Alan Pardew had become manager of Reading and in 01/02 we got back to Division One as runners up to Brighton. I made 33 appearances in the league that season, but I was coming to the end. I didn`t play in the first team in 02/03."*

When a manager joins a new club it is normally struggling. Colchester United were no exception in the late winter of 2003. When the final whistle blew at the U`s home match against Blackpool on January 25th, it signalled more than the end of the match. It was the end of Steve Whitton`s nine years at the club, three and a half of them as manager. United had lost 2-0. The team seemed without spark. They had not won for seven games and had dropped to third from bottom of Division Two. Crowds had been dipping below 3,000. The natives were decidedly restless, and so was the Board.

The north easterly blowing through Layer Road that dull afternoon was an ill wind for Steve Whitton. He was summoned to a meeting and his career in the professional game was over.

With small crowds, and playing in a ramshackle stadium, unable to generate income outside match days, Whitton had been hamstrung by budgetary constraints throughout his time as manager. He was asked to compete with big city clubs like Bristol City, QPR and Cardiff and it had eventually overwhelmed him. His cause had not been helped by a home defeat against non league Chester in the First round of the FA Cup.

He said "I am very angry about being asked to go, because I know what sort of job myself, my staff and my players have done. They have all performed above themselves. I am very proud of the job we all did, but it has taught me a lot. When I was playing, I never imagined that managing Colchester United would be like it was.

"It is a unique club, very well run but I`m sure there is not another like it. If I do pop up again as a manager I hope it is with a club where I have a chance."

Whitton has not worked in football since.

Football can be a ruthless and cut throat business. One man`s tragedy can be another`s opportunity. The mantle was handed over on a caretaker basis to assistant manager Geraint

Williams. He was a friend and former team mate of Whitton. With Whitton's blessing and recommendation he applied for the permanent job and the team's performances under he and temporary assistant Mick Stockwell made clear it was a strong application.

The team's fortunes were transformed. There were good away draws at Stockport and Cheltenham, a home win over Mansfield and a spectacularly good 2-1 win at Ashton Gate against high flying Bristol City. This had seen the team rise from 22nd to 18th.

"Whatever happens next I gave it a good go" said Williams, referring to his application for the manager's post.

One might have thought that Steve Whitton's chilling final words would put off prospective new managers, but there were over 65 applicants for the job. No doubt these would have included the usual smattering of eccentric applications. Or perhaps some like the one submitted to Middlesbrough owner Steve Gibson from the applicant whose only qualifications were experience on the football manager video game and leadership of an under 11 team!

Names such as former England international Graham Rix, Dagenham's highly rated Garry Hill, Nigel Clough (then of Burton Albion) and former Danish international Jan Molby were being linked with the Layer Road vacancy.

Peter Heard was well connected in the game. Colchester born in 1938, he had qualified as a Chartered Surveyor, and with a partner had founded Churston Heard. This had grown to become the largest independent commercial property agency in the UK.

At the age of 16 a riding injury stopped him playing football, and he took up refereeing. He reached the upper echelons of the non-league game, and also officiated over professional clubs in the South East Counties League and the Football Combination.

He had been a Colchester United fan from boyhood, attending his first matches in the mid 1950's, when he would stand on the terrace between the Main Stand and what was then the Clock End. He takes up the story of how he became more than just a fan of Colchester United,

*"We had been doing some work for James Bowdidge, who was then the Chairman of Colchester United. The club were very short of money and James had not been able to secure planning permission for a new stadium. They were in the Conference and had just missed promotion back to the Football League. Knowing of my interest in football and Colchester United, James took me for a very nice lunch in Mayfair, where I was asked to "invest" £25,000 in the club and join the board. I suppose you could say that it was a very expensive lunch! It was the beginning of fifteen interesting years on the inside of professional football.*

*I found a club in some chaos, both administratively and financially. I soon became the majority shareholder. Gordon Parker chaired the club for me until I took the chair in 1998."*

Peter Heard`s interest in football went beyond the U`s. Described by former FA Chief Executive David Davies as an "FA and Football League bigwig for a generation", he had served at a number of posts in the inner sanctum of football, including as an FA and Football League board member. He was Chairman of the latter for a spell, and he sat on the disciplinary tribunal which banned Rio Ferdinand for eight months for missing a drugs test, thereby causing the England defender to sit out the Euro 2004 competition.

In 2001, when top referees turned professional, Heard was asked by the Premier League and the Football League to become the first Chairman of the Professional Game Match Officials Board.

He had a lighter side however. He was known as the originator of many nicknames within the FA including, "Captain Birdseye" for Ken Bates and "Mr Five Agendas" for David Dein, (a reflection of his roles with Arsenal, UEFA, the FA, the Premier League and the G14 organisation). Heard has also been credited with the name which attached itself to former Premier League Chairman Dave Richards, he became known as the "lollipop man" for his ability to change his opinion on any issue as fast as the lady on the zebra crossing turned her lollipop.

He took over as Chairman in 1998, following the club`s victory over Torquay in the play off final at Wembley which secured promotion to Division Two and said, "I hope to lead the club to further progress in the League and to spearhead our progress to a new stadium". Eventually his "investment" would be around £2 million. With such small income streams, it was this kind of accumulated injection that had been necessary to keep the club alive and reasonably competitive.

Heard had a refreshing attitude to being the owner of his local football club,

"A football club is only there for its supporters, neither I nor anyone else has a divine right to own it. The club belongs to the community and any Chairman of Colchester United is simply the custodian".

Phil Parkinson relates the story of how he took his first steps into football management,

*"I was starting to take my coaching badges, and Alan Pardew was talking to me about becoming reserve team manager. I had been doing some coaching informally at Reading, mostly with the reserves. Then one evening, out of the blue, Alan rang me and said the Colchester Chairman had rung John Madejski wanting to speak to*

*me about becoming their manager. I had not been applying for jobs, and I was not being contacted by agents about jobs, so it came as a complete surprise.*

*I believe someone at the FA or the League, whose wife worked at Reading, had mentioned my name to Peter Heard. I suppose this lady must have told her husband that I was moving into coaching, and in this way my name reached Mr Heard.*

*I did my homework on Colchester by ringing around a number of contacts in the game, and I paid to watch two matches with the crowd. I saw them win at Bristol City, and I stood on the Layer Road terraces when they beat Mansfield.*

*My first interview was with Mr Heard alone at his office in London. Then there was a second interview with him, which was also attended by the other directors and Marie Partner. As a player I had always prided myself on fitness and professionalism, and I wanted that to come over to the board along with the modern and progressive methods I wanted to employ. I must have impressed them, as later that day, which was a Sunday, Marie rang me. She said they would like to offer me the job, and could I start tomorrow! In fact I was due to attend a funeral that day so I managed to get it put off by 24 hours, but of course I said yes. I had no doubt that the job was right for me at that time."*

Peter Heard remembers how Phil Parkinson joined Colchester United,

*"Steve Whitton was a nice man who had worked hard as our manager for a few years. However, in 2003 the results had gone haywire. Peter Powell was a Director who unlike me had an office in Colchester. We called Steve into Peter`s office and told him, sorry but it`s come to an end.*

*John Nagle was the Head of Media at the Football League. He had connections with the town of Reading, and he recommended Phil Parkinson to me. He said there were signs that Phil wanted to move into management. I spoke to Reading`s owner John Madejski, and to their Chief Executive Nigel Howe. Mr Madejski is a very decent if somewhat laconic man, and it seemed clear that Reading thought highly of Phil, but at that time had no suitable vacancy to move him into. They were very accommodating and said that we could interview him.*

*We were inundated with applicants, but in Phil`s case it was us approaching him. He came to see me at my office in London. I liked him. I thought he had leadership qualities although he had no experience of managing. I arranged for him to meet the rest of the board. The other applicants we gave serious consideration to were Steve Parkin, who had been successful at Rochdale, Stewart Robson, who had played for*

*Arsenal and was coaching at Southend and, of course, Geraint Williams.*

*You have to be very careful when appointing a manager. Some come with high profiles which does not mean they will be good managers. Others can be very good in the boardroom but no good with players.*

*The board were not unanimous about Phil. Some wanted Geraint Williams. Marie Partner, our Chief Executive, felt that she could work with Phil. This was influential, as she would be working with him on a day to day basis. I was the majority shareholder and so could make my wishes prevail, but I was very keen that a new manager should have the support of everyone. On a previous occasion, we interviewed Steve Cotterill. I had wanted to appoint him but other board members didn't like him. They thought him "cocky". I allowed myself to be persuaded to go with Mick Wadsworth, and that led to the worst seven months I had as Chairman. This time I was determined to get my own way. I talked the other board members round. We took Phil on, overlooking the fact that he had no experience. It was a gamble. We did not set him any targets or tell him that we had any particular expectations. We just took a punt."*

So Peter Heard became aware of this well thought of young coach at Reading. Heard knew that this coach was ambitious, a 100% trier and held all the necessary coaching qualifications. He had also taken the trouble during his playing career to acquire a degree in Social Science, which somewhat set him apart from his team mates!

Geraint Williams looks back to the difficult day of Steve Whitton's departure,

*"Steve worked extremely hard and did a good job to keep the club in League One. I think he was unlucky to be sacked. After we lost at home to Blackpool we knew there was unrest and we were called to go down to the ground. Steve said, "It`s ok, if anything was going to happen we`d be called to Peter Powell`s office in the town." Almost immediately the phone rang and we were told to go to Mr Powell`s office! Steve said, "we`re gone", and so it proved, at least for Steve.*

*When Steve said he`d been sacked, I said that I`d go as well. He said, "If they offer you anything, take it". I said, "No, we came together, we`ll leave together". He told me I`d done all I could to help him, I`d worked my socks off and been honest throughout, and he wanted me to take anything that was offered. That was how I came to be caretaker manager, and then assistant to Phil Parkinson."*

Professional footballers tend to have a lot of spare time. They are encouraged to rest in between games and training sessions. Many take this to mean a resting of the mind, as well as the body. Some during the less enlightened 80`s and 90`s, drank to excess, knowing that the calories would be burnt off at the next day`s training. The intellectual pursuits of the stereotypical footballer would not go beyond The Sun and the card school. Phil Parkinson seemed to be from a different mould.

It would therefore have been a valid question to ask how such a relatively bookish individual could relate to the average professional footballer, let alone get him to strain every sinew in furtherance of a common cause. Could a man used to spending time in libraries and lecture theatres expect to convince a sportsman that humble Layer Road was the right place for him to maximise his short career. How could such a person exude the charisma necessary to engage fans?

Let us look at it from Phil Parkinson`s perspective. Although playing less now, he was still an important member of the 02/03 Reading first team squad. They had recently moved into a £50 million 24,000 capacity stadium and seemed destined for the Premier League. He was starting to coach at Reading, and was very well thought of by manager Alan Pardew. If Pardew was sacked, or moved on to greater things, Parkinson would have every chance of being fast tracked to the manager`s chair. Alternatively, he might then have followed Pardew to one of the biggest clubs in the land.

It is hard to assess why tumbledown Layer Road would form part of such a person`s career plan. Nevertheless, when contacted by scoop-searching BBC Essex, Parkinson confirmed that he was in touch with Colchester United. He made the shortlist with Parkin, Robson and Geraint Williams, the latter leaving the local press in no doubt that he would like the job permanently, "Football is like a well oiled circle" he said when describing the interaction between players, coaches and fans.

Perhaps it was that metaphorical clumsiness that cost Williams the job. Or perhaps Peter Heard knew a pied piper when he interviewed one. Whichever is true, a press conference was called on Tuesday 25th February 2003 to announce the appointment of a manager, who would just over three years later deliver the greatest achievement in Colchester United`s sixty nine year history. The reaction of most U`s fans was "Phil who?"

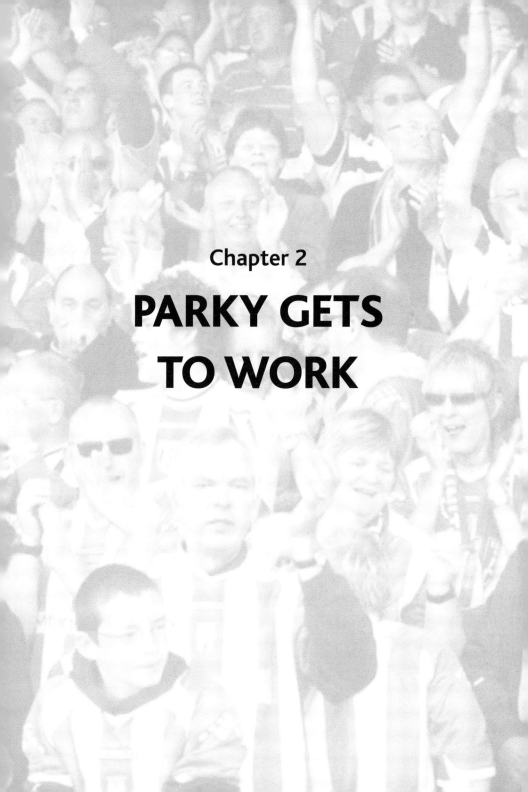

Chapter 2

# PARKY GETS TO WORK

# Chapter 2
## PARKY GETS TO WORK

At his first press conference as a manager, Parkinson was unsurprisingly upbeat. He said "I feel honoured to be given the job. It is an opportunity that I couldn`t turn down."

Although he had played little at Reading in the 02/03 season, he thought enough of his abilities to not rule out a return to the field. "Playing is an option that I want to leave open", he said.

Despite Whitton`s negativity, Parkinson seemed to believe the necessary foundations were in place.

"I rang around and did a lot of homework. I have watched the team play, and I know that I am taking over at a stable club, It is not a case of me making drastic changes. I believe the players already here are good enough to keep us in this division. I know supporters like to see players playing for their shirts. As a player myself, I like to perform with passion, and that`s what I will be looking for the lads to do here".

Peter Heard said, "He came highly recommended. He`s a strong leader, and I was very impressed the first time I saw him. I felt there was a rapport and he was somebody I could work with, and his enthusiasm and energy I found somewhat infectious"

The club was run on a very tight budget, which Steve Whitton had found increasingly restrictive. Going into the 02/03 season, four seasons had passed since promotion from the fourth tier, and some supporters were growing restless with the Board`s thriftiness and apparent lack of desire to progress. It did not appear that the arrival of the new manager would see any loosening of the purse strings.

Peter Heard was asked if more money for players would be made available to the new manager, "Phil Parkinson`s predecessor had a budget and that same budget is with Mr Parkinson" was his reply.

Managers usually bring their own support staff when they take over at a new club but it was Parkinson`s first job and he would have to mould the staff into his way of working, which he had not even established himself. He could not know how enthusiastically they would accept him. In particular, Williams attitude would have been a concern, since it may be presumed that he thought he could do the job at least as well as Parkinson.

This is a familiar problem faced by new managers at Colchester United. When Steve Wignall took the job in 1995 he found Steve Foley, Micky Cook, Tony English and Steve Whitton in various posts and everyone one of them had applied for the job he was taking!

So, under Parkinson Micky Cook would be remaining as Director of Youth Football and Brian Owen as First Team Coach/Physio and scout. The most speculation however surrounded the future of Geraint Williams. Would he continue the Assistant Manager role after he had tasted the top job? A good relationship between the manager and his assistant is vital at any club. Williams and Steve Whitton had been team mates in their playing days. Parkinson did not know Williams.

"I`ve had a good chat with Geraint" said Parkinson. "He is obviously disappointed but I will be looking to him for a lot of support as I bed myself in"

So looking back now what were Parkinson`s first impressions of the club?

*"I must admit that I was shocked about the very small budget and by how little the players were earning compared to the lads at Reading. Despite this, I had no hesitation in accepting the job. I was confident that I could get something out of the team, and I had got on well with Mr Heard. I liked his honesty and I felt I could work well with him. I felt the same about Marie and the other board members Peter Powell and John Worsp. I think if you have good straight forward and honest people around you, it gives you a chance. I certainly had that at Colchester.*

*I registered as a player for emergencies. I had been playing in the reserves at Reading so I was fit, and I think I could have done a decent job playing, but Mr Heard was insistent that being manager was difficult enough on it`s own and I should concentrate on that which was probably the right thing.*

*I did not know George Williams at all. Initially, I was going to bring in a number two, and this had been sanctioned by the board, but I took some advice from one of my former managers. He said the people there might be the best ones to help you. I asked George if he wanted to stay on and work with me, and he said he would. He came over as a very honest fella, and as I got to know him he impressed me as a "straight down the line" type of bloke, and he is now a good friend.*

*Brian Owen is a great character who has worked with me at Bradford. He was a straight talker, and had a good eye for a player. We had Paul Dyer scouting and working only for expenses. Mickey Cook and Adrian Webster were working with the young players until Joe Dunne took over Mickey`s role. All the staff seemed willing to buy into the methods I wanted to employ. They seemed to accept me very quickly.*

*Nothing had been said to me as to what the board`s expectations were in terms of league position, either long or short term. I don`t remember having any long term targets myself. All we were concentrating on was staying up, as we were in a bit of trouble."*

Parkinson faced his first match less than a week after being appointed. Port Vale would provide the opposition in front of a Layer Road crowd of 3,581. The Valiants were one place behind the U`s, and only separated on goal difference, so this would be an interesting first test.

The fans seemed to sense immediately that Parkinson`s arrival heralded the dawn of a much needed new era for the club. Whitton and Williams had been popular figures, but they did not hold back in welcoming the new man. The sombre atmosphere of the Blackpool match was gone, and optimism was everywhere. The cynics pointed out that this kind of atmosphere had been felt many times before, and it was normally followed by the sound of puncturing balloons and celebrating away fans.

Not on this occasion however. The only sound was that of steel crashing through ceramics as the men from the potteries were put to the sword. Karl Duguid set the tone in the fifth minute with a crunching tackle on Carragher, for which he was booked. Despite the outcome, Parkinson probably liked what he saw from the future U`s captain, and perhaps saw something of his own committed style. Maybe he would not have to play himself?

Two minutes later the first goal of the Parkinson era was scored. And what a spectacular start, Gareth Williams volleying in from 25 yards. Parkinson leaped skywards, further endearing himself to the fans, who appreciate a manager obviously having feelings similar to their own.

Another goal from Gareth Williams and one from Joe Keith, either side of half time, put the U`s firmly in control. Vale pulled one back, but this made little difference to the celebrating home fans as they hailed Gareth Williams` third goal in the 72nd minute.

This was the first time a U`s player had scored a hat trick for nine years. In fact, Gareth Williams was technically not a U`s player. He was on loan from First Division Crystal Palace, having been signed by Steve Whitton. He had scored in the previous game under Geraint Williams, and would score in the next one at Northampton.

The lack of a regular goal scorer had played a large part in sending the U`s into relegation trouble. The leading scorer upon Parkinson`s arrival had been penalty taking full back Joe Keith. Goal scoring is probably the most difficult, and sought after skill in the game. Leading exponents of the art do not come cheap, which explains why Colchester United spend large periods of their history without one.

Whitton had acquired Williams on a temporary basis from Palace in an attempt to address this suffocating problem. It was therefore ironic that he only started scoring after Whitton`s departure. It was also Parkinson`s good fortune. Peter Heard might have echoed Dwight D Eisenhower`s words "I would rather have a lucky General than a smart General". Parkinson however would go on to prove that he was both.

Phil Parkinson had innovative long term plans for Colchester United. He was, however, in no doubt that the short term had to be his first priority; there was a relegation battle to be won,

"My ideas are for the future. For now, I have to keep the spirit and build on that. I am coming in to take over a team that has been on a good run. I would be a fool to make wholesale changes. Short term, my aim is to keep the team in this division, and my first goal will be to raise the professionalism of the club."

There was no time to rest on laurels after the highly encouraging start against Port Vale. On the following Tuesday the U`s had to entertain the Cobblers of Northampton. Saturday`s win had seen them rise to 17th with a four point cushion above the relegation zone. Tuesday would be another must-win game, as Northampton were second from bottom. It was another great chance for the U`s to put some daylight between themselves and trouble.

A clearly confident Colchester ran out 2-0 winners, with Gareth Williams scoring again and Scott McGleish rounding things off. Parkinson was ecstatic about the start his team had made under him.

"Six goals and six points in two games is a dream start for me. The lads gave me everything and the clean sheet was very pleasing".

That result took the U`s to 41 points and 15th place. With twelve games left it also effectively meant the division`s bottom two sides could not catch them. They now only had to worry about 21st and 22nd, the other two relegation spots.

As fans we had to avoid being carried away by these two results. They were, after all, home games against struggling sides. Up next was a very tricky game at play off chasing Oldham. It was a grim afternoon. Is there any other kind at Boundary Park? It is truly one of the coldest, most exposed, and most forbidding places on the planet. Rumours that Captain Scott used to train his ponies there might be exaggerated, but at 526 feet it is the second highest football ground in England and Wales. Now this is not likely to impress the fans of Club Bolivar as they giddily stare down from the 11,932 feet Estadio Hernando Siles, but U`s fans have not yet had to travel to La Paz on a chilly Tuesday night!

It is said that Mount Olympus was "not shaken by winds nor ever wet with rain, nor did snow fall upon it". There is no danger that any of this might be said of Boundary Park, Oldham! The sort of serenity with which the Gods looked down from Mount Olympus is rarely on offer to U`s fans at Boundary Park. It is not one of the club`s happier hunting grounds. Points are seen about as easily as urban badgers

The deep depression extended into the Colchester dressing room at the final whistle. The U`s had been seen off 2-0. Central defender Alan White had been seen off just before the break, sent off for a "professional foul".

This was however the only set back suffered by Parkinson`s troops in their first eleven games together, a run which banished all fear of relegation. His first four home games were all won. There was a fantastic 3-0 win at third placed Cardiff and a 4-0 win at Chesterfield. He had made his first signing. Johnnie Jackson had arrived on loan from Tottenham providing some much needed strength on the left side. He had also appointed a new first team physio in Stuart Ayles. Brian Owen would continue multi tasking as a physio, coach and scout. Ayles would also be carrying out the role of fitness coach, employing modern techniques for achieving and monitoring fitness.

By the time Luton came to town on 21st April Parkinson`s first mission of staying up had been accomplished. He was able to play an experimental side, including the young Greg Halford making his debut. As experiments go however it was not entirely successful, as the Hatters rattled in 5 goals without reply!

When remembering the dark days of January, Parkinson, the Board and all the fans could afford to be satisfied with the final position of 12th with 58 points. This looked like something to build on and was three places higher than the previous season. It was the U`s highest finishing position for twenty three years.

Between 1st February and 19th April the U`s had played fifteen games, winning eight and losing only one. This was promotion form! There was no question of the new manager having to play. It is however a little known fact that Parkinson did lace his boots in anger during his time at the U`s. He played 45 minutes for the reserves against Millwall. Parkinson continues the story of his early days at Layer Road,

*"It wasn`t long before I realised that the club had fallen behind the times somewhat and needed a change of culture. I thought there was a drinking culture. That might have stemmed from the non-league days where people gather together for a drink after games but the game had moved forward.*

*I`m not being derogatory to Steve Whitton, who did a terrific job to keep them in the division for a number of years, playing some good football in the process. He had his own way of creating a spirit, but I wanted to go a different way. I wanted to "rip it up and start again", and any players who didn`t want to buy into that would have to move on.*

*I felt we needed to do a lot of work on fitness and conditioning, so I brought in Stuart Ayles as physio and fitness coach. He was recommended to me by Paul Turner who had been physio at Reading. He was exactly what the club needed, because as well as being qualified as a physio he also had a sports science background and I didn`t have the budget to pay two people!*

*It was clear to me that getting a club like Colchester moving was going to take an incredible work ethic from the staff and Stuart impressed me with his willingness for hard work. He thought nothing of working from seven in the morning until ten at night.*

*He formulated fitness programmes for the players to follow during that first summer, and we had them in during the summer to monitor them. This was a bit of a culture shock, but to be fair the players bought into it pretty well. They wanted to improve.*

*By way of example, I remember being very impressed with Gavin Johnson as a footballer, but I used to look at him and think he could be in better shape. Not being in the best condition can lead to injuries, and he used to pick up a lot of niggling injuries. He took my criticism on board and knuckled down, and he had two more good seasons with us. In 04/05 he made 44 appearances and scored 10 goals from midfield.*

*Stuart worked long hours over that summer, building a gym near the astro turf pitches at Layer Road. There`s no way that the building of a gym was in his job description, but he did it anyway. It was badly needed so we had somewhere to do weight training. This was an example of how everyone behind the scenes was prepared to go the extra mile, and that was so important.*

*I don`t remember any difficulties in getting the players to accept my methods. We had some good wins when I first arrived, and this always helps as players start to believe in what you are saying. There were some good professionals at the club, people like Dugy and Kemi and I bedded in quite quickly.*

*We finished the season very well and stayed up comfortably. Then in the summer I started to bring in big changes with the sports science and fitness programmes. Some of the players were monitored all the way through the summer. The rest just came in for a couple of test days. It was a case of making sure they were doing the work they needed to do in order to be fit for when pre season started.*

*Most players want to improve. They want to be in a disciplined environment and be part of a successful team, and anything they see which gears them towards that they should buy into. If they don`t, they don`t stay at the club."*

So, even in the summer, things were going to be different at Layer Road under Parkinson. The players were subjected to VO2 testing. VO2 max is the maximum capacity of an individual`s body to transport and use oxygen during incremental exercise. V meaning volume and O2 meaning oxygen. The individual exercises on a treadmill or cycle while ventilation, oxygen and carbon dioxide concentration are all measured. In layman`s terms, the test measures physical fitness. Parkinson had the players tested at the end of the season and sent them away with a fitness programme to adhere to. They had to return in early June to make sure they were keeping to it, and were then re-tested at the start of pre season training in July. The sports science expertise of Stuart Ayles was bearing fruit!

Peter Heard remembers Parkinson`s early days as a breath of fresh air running through the club,

*"On his first day he went to meet all the staff. He didn`t call them in, he went to wherever they were. That included the kit manager who was doing the washing and he even wanted to know all about that!"*

The new manager made equally good first impressions on the man who had wanted his job. Geraint Williams says,

*"I enjoyed my spell as caretaker, and I wanted to be the permanent manager. However when Phil came in it soon became clear to me that I wasn`t ready for it. He had prepared himself for a few years to be a manager. I was good at working on the training field but Phil was also heavily into developing all staff and the player`s nutrition and conditioning. When I saw that, I could see he was the right man for the job at that time. We didn`t know each other although we had played against each other, which he remembered better than me.*

*Phil and I had some teething problems in the early days. I wasn`t sure how much input he wanted from me. He wasn`t sure how much input I could give. I was concerned that we weren`t connecting as well as we might, and after a few months we had a frank and open discussion about it. I told him that he seemed so "hands on" that I wasn`t sure he wanted anything from me except to do his bidding. He made clear that he wanted my opinions and initiatives. From that moment we really hit it off.*

*I would be left to organise the training and take the sessions. Phil would often be travelling to watch the opposition or potential signings. Brian Owen and Paul Dyer helped him with that. Brian is football daft. Football being "more important than life and death" is a Bill Shankly saying, but it might just as easily have been said about Brian Owen. Phil would take some training sessions, and if I was taking them he would usually be there watching, although he might have only had a few hours sleep since getting back from a scouting trip.*

*Phil made the club so much more professional. Sometimes he had to push for things that would achieve this. He was very persuasive, and probably got things approved by the club that previous managers would have liked but couldn`t make happen.*

*When Phil came in as manager, I had just taken us out of the bottom four and his only aim was to avoid relegation.Ultimately however, he was clear that he wanted promotion and I completely bought into that. He made you believe that it was possible, despite the financial restrictions at the club.*

*Stuart Ayles was cut from the same cloth as Parky in terms of his work ethic and his boundless enthusiasm. The weights room summed up the work ethic which was at the club at that time. Stuart built it and sourced some cheap materials and equipment. Phil pushed for the money and it got done."*

*"It was Marie Partner`s job to manage Phil on a day to day basis",* says Peter Heard, *"That was not easy because he was so enthusiastic about everything. He would forever be ringing her up with ideas, sometimes late at night. But it was all good stuff. He wanted to do well and his passion transmitted itself both upwards towards us at board level and downwards to the players. He was never that interested in money for himself."*

As the curtain came down on the 2002/03 season there was a feeling of real optimism around Layer Road. With the introduction of simple things like ball boys and goal music, there was a new sense of urgency. The feeling during home matches was one of gathering momentum. If the U`s were attacking and the ball went out of play, Parkinson wanted it returned immediately. Spare balls were strategically placed around the pitch, and via a keen ball boy were into the waiting Colchester player`s hands in a split second. If it was a throw to the opposition the ball boy was still keen, but perhaps not quite so keen!

What could this bright young manager do with a team after a full pre season to prepare them? The club had been promoted to Division Two, the third tier of English football, in 1998. Since then the only aim had been survival. League positions had however been steadily improving, and with a new professionalism pervading the air, with modern methods of nutrition, conditioning, match preparation and recovery being employed by a highly qualified modern coach, how far could the club go? The days of waiting to return to the fourth tier, of calculating every August the number of points required for survival, of looking downwards, and of being tipped by every pundit for relegation, could these days be over?

Twelfth position was bottom of the top half! From that position it was possible to look up and see the promotion positions in the far distance. Beyond them lay a fabled land occupied by a species of club that Colchester United could know nothing of. There were experiences of which Colchester United could not even dream. If the hardship could be endured, there lay fortune. These broad sunlit uplands were then called Football League Division 1 and they were beckoning.

There were a few problems however. Amongst them was the little matter of money. This particular resource was somewhat scarce at Colchester United. It meant that almost all other resources were equally scarce. In football the word "ambition" translates directly into the word "money" and vice versa.

Colchester United had a little ambition, but it had to be tempered with reality. If Phil Parkinson had been asked in May 2003 how long it would take him to deliver second tier football to Colchester one wonders how he would have replied. He might have referred to concentrating first on the impossible, as miracles take a little longer. What is telling however is that the question was never put by journalists, and the issue was never even raised with Parkinson by the board.

Neither the club nor its fans expected a top half finish in 02/03. Finishing in the automatic promotion or play off positions was the stuff of fantasy. Nevertheless, expectations do not stay the same. Another top half finish was the minimum requirement for 03/04.

# Chapter 3

# AIMING HIGHER?

# Chapter 3
## AIMING HIGHER?

Colchester United Chief Executive Marie Partner had nicknamed Phil Parkinson "airwick", as she felt he had been a breath of fresh air through the club. She said "Phil's commitment to Colchester United has been second to none, this man does not sit still for one minute, going to games every day, twice a day, continually introducing new ideas"

Parkinson did not stop just because it was the off season. In the summer of 2003 he took the UEFA Pro-Licence course, the game's highest coaching qualification. He passed the course in the company of established names like Bryan Robson, Sam Allardyce and Steve McClaren. He was now qualified to coach and manage in the Premier League and the Champions League.

For now, however, Parkinson's focus was Football League Division 2 and Colchester United. He had a vision for how he wanted his team to play, and it was all about pace and momentum. He knew he had to re-vamp the forward line.

Gareth Williams had returned to his parent club. Adrian Coote, who had been signed by Steve Whitton for a record equalling £50,000, had never really found his way at the club, and had been hampered by injuries. He would be released early in the 03/04 season. Kevin Rapley had also been released.

The U's financial circumstances were such that new players could rarely be considered if any transfer fee was involved. They also had to fit within the club's strict wage structure. This meant established Division Two players were often outside the club's compass. Colchester managers had to look at reserve teams for potential new recruits. This might be reserve teams of clubs at the same level, or even the level below. Over the years they had found that this type of player often arrived with a chip on his shoulder and something to prove. They arrived determined to succeed, and often did. They did not expect a long contract, so if the move did not work out the club's financial outlay was modest.

In the summer of 2003 there were small signs that the club was shopping at a different store. In July, Wayne Andrews arrived from Oldham, where he had enjoyed a good season in Division Two, scoring goals for Ian Dowie. Then, on the same day in August, Craig Fagan and Rowan Vine signed. Both were strikers on loan deals. Fagan joined from Birmingham City and Vine from Portsmouth, both then of the Premier League. Vine had the added bonus that he had spent the previous season on loan at Brentford in Division Two where he had been successful. Fagan had also picked up useful Division Two experience during a loan spell at Bristol City. Andrews and Fagan had both scored against Colchester during the 02/03 season! The characteristic shared by all three was pace.

So, in a few short weeks, the club had signed three strikers, two of whom could be described as established in Division Two while the other was highly promising, having Premier League pedigree. They also still had Scott McGleish. There were few changes in defence or midfield, however, as Parkinson seemed satisfied with those areas although he did sign Phil Hadland and Andy Myers. Hadland was a 23 year old winger who Parkinson had known at Reading. Myers was an experienced defender who had made eighty four appearances for Chelsea in the 90s before being sold for £800,000 to Bradford City. His career had somewhat lost direction, and he arrived at Layer Road looking for a new start.

Despite what had been said, it was hard to escape the conclusion that the club had such faith in its new manager that coffers previously locked tight were seeing the light of day. However, Peter Heard is firm that Phil Parkinson had no budget increase. It just seems that he had a flair for persuasion and for making a small budget go a very long way.

Peter Heard describes how the club ran under his stewardship,

*"We had monthly board meetings. I always made our managers sit through all these, because I thought it important that they understand the whole structure of the club. At most clubs if the manager attends board meetings at all, it is only to report on football matters and then leave.*

*My managers always had to adhere to budgets, and it was Marie's job to make sure they did. In football I found that you only go wrong when you say yes. Not when you say no. Often Phil would want to sign a player, and it would transpire that he could not be fitted within the budget. Phil soon learnt that this meant it went no further, which he readily accepted, perhaps because he understood how the club worked from top to bottom.*

*Another of my quirks was that I always expected my managers to come and see me after a game. Win, lose or draw I liked to have a report. I never went into the dressing room, except once in the summer when they were being re-decorated and I wanted to see how that was going. The dressing room was the manager's domain. Equally, if a player came to me behind the manager's back, I would always tell the manager so that he could deal with the matter. Otherwise I thought the manager's position would be undermined. I rarely made statements to the media. I thought that was the manager's job. This was my style, and over time it seemed to work quite well.*

*Phil, Marie Partner and the in house accountant, Janie Gregory, had to prepare financial projections for me. We would project what our overheads (meaning our expenses excluding players) were going to be. We would then look at player costs.*

*The received wisdom was that a squad needed 21 or 22 players. I thought any club with more than that in their first team squad was getting it wrong. From there you could assess what the players as a whole were going to cost. We would then project the likely income, which was largely gate money, although there were also funds from the FA and the Football League. Projecting income can be difficult with transfer fees and cup runs, you can never assume anything will come from those sources, and with the cup 50% goes to the opposing club anyway.*

*If there was a shortfall between income and expenses, I would make it up. If it was more than I could afford Marie, Janie and Phil had to go back to the drawing board. I was never very interested in the budgets other clubs were working to. Some seemed to have no budgets at all! At Colchester the simple rule was, if we couldn`t afford it we didn`t do it. That avoided a lot of the troubles that other clubs got themselves into.*

*There was never any conscious decision to increase the budget so that we could afford certain players. The budget was dictated by what we could afford. I never allowed it to be dictated by the financial aspirations of incoming players. Sometimes Phil was able to land players even though we would not meet their demands. He could be amazingly persuasive and persistent with players. He would get cross if they wouldn`t sign, and he would refuse to take no for an answer. He didn`t get every target, but he would keep on and on at them and usually they would sign in the end.*

*I had certain rules of thumb. I would not give more than a one year contract to players over thirty unless they were a goalkeeper. Sometimes this caused ructions but I wouldn`t yield on it.*

*I took a lot of persuading that the players needed an overnight stop for an away game. Sometimes it was unavoidable, but generally I would maintain that a player`s preparation is better for being in his own bed. Also, I was haunted by hearing about a vital match at Torquay when we were battling to stay in the league. It was one of the last matches of the 1989/90 season, so it was before I was on the board. Apparently some of the players tied sheets together so as to escape out of a hotel window, and they went drinking until the small hours. They lost 4-1 the next day, and we went down shortly afterwards. Any danger of that sort of thing was avoided by travelling on the day.*

*Sometimes there would be disagreements about the need for an overnight stop. I remember once being unpopular because I made them travel on the day for a match at Preston which is a pretty long way. With my tongue in my cheek, I would* even argue that Hartlepool could be done without an overnight stop. I would say it's on this side of the country, straight up and down! I was well known for this. On occasions other Directors would offer to pay for an overnight stop, which would undermine my position, but generally I think my approach to expenses was the best one because it meant our budget went further."

Parkinson looks back on his early days at Layer Road,

"I really wanted us to put teams under pressure at home. I wanted us to play a high intensity type of game, and introducing the multi ball system was part of this. I am very disappointed that the authorities have stopped it. It quickens the game and improves the spectacle. Football should be a fast, forward moving and attacking game. With modern stadia the ball often goes into a lot of empty seats and takes ages to return. The system is allowed in the Champions League, but not in our league, which is ridiculous.

We tried to use the slope at Layer Road to pin teams in early in the game with a high energy high octane type of football, using the quality we had in the team. I thought this type of game would work well at Layer Road where the dressing rooms were tight and the crowd was close to the pitch. The ground only needed to have 3-4,000 in to have a good atmosphere, and we tried to use these things to our advantage. By this time there were very few grounds like Layer Road and the atmosphere was different, and I think this could upset some teams. If you could get teams on the back foot early they often never recovered.

I did the UEFA pro licence during that first summer. A lot of the benefit of those courses is in the people you meet. I did it with some high profile people and made some useful contacts. We went to Inter Milan and studied their whole structure.

George and I quickly established a method of working. He is a very good coach and would take most of the training sessions, although I would usually be there overseeing it. Straight after the warm up, he would take them into playing this high intensity game and he really enjoyed that. I tended to take the set pieces and team work sessions.

Of course, I would often be travelling with Brian Owen to watch games and players. If it was "up north" I might not get in until 3am so I would ring George and ask him to organise the content of the training. I always knew he would do it brilliantly. This was how our working relationship evolved. George's main strength was on the training field, whereas I enjoyed watching videos to analyse the opposition and potential signings, and travelling miles to find the players who would fit into how we wanted to play.

That first summer at Colchester was a great education in the business of signing players. I remember getting more and more stressed out because I couldn`t get players signed. There is an art to it, but there are no courses you can go on. Now I understand that it can be a hard slog. You have to network and make relationships with agents, managers and others in the game.

You have to be patient and understand that sometimes the players who are willing to sign early in the summer may not be the best available. The better players often wait while clubs compete for them. However, waiting can also be better for the clubs, because as the summer goes on wage demands often reduce.

I was tearing my hair out at times, and I had the local press on my case telling me about all these players that Southend were supposedly signing. Eventually I was able to make three great signings for the club.

I had been keen to sign Tony Carrs from Oldham. While I was trying to persuade him he mentioned that Wayne Andrews was out of contract at Oldham, and as he lived in St.Albans he was interested in moving to a southern club. I watched DVD`s of Wayne playing and I could see he had that raw pace to get in behind defences, and I spent hours talking to him about how we wanted to play, and trying to persuade him to sign.

Finally he agreed, and it was all arranged that he and his agent would meet Marie Partner at Layer Road to complete the paper work. Except for this, it was all settled and I had gone on holiday. I phoned Marie from a beach in Devon to make sure it had all happened and she said no, he wouldn`t sign! A deer had been running loose on the M25 and there was a three hour tailback. He had eventually arrived at the ground, but he said I can get up to Oldham as quick as this and it had put him off!

In the end I was able to persuade him that deer don`t escape on the M25 everyday, and we helped with some personal issues he had and he signed. I couldn`t get Tony Carrs though. He went to Huddersfield.

Another player I was chasing was Tony Capaldi, who was a young full back at Birmingham. While I was watching him, Craig Fagan caught my eye. Then the next night I saw Bradford reserves playing Blackburn reserves, because Aidan Davison was then at Bradford and he recommended one of their players. I didn`t fancy that player, but I noticed a young midfielder playing for Blackburn called Neil Danns. So that was a productive trip although it was more than a year before we got Danns to Colchester.

*I spent the whole summer working on the Fagan deal. Again, it was one of those where you had to be patient. He signed just before the season started, as did Rowan Vine. I managed to get Vine from under Wally Downes` nose at Brentford where he`d been on loan. I remember Wally saying that he`d gone to Colchester for extra money, but we only paid Vine and Fagan £1,000pw between them, which for two forwards of that quality was amazing. All three players had great pace and energy, which was what I was looking for."*

The U`s travelled to Barnsley on the opening day. All football fans go into a new season thinking that nothing is beyond their team. Positive words are flowing from the club about how well new players have settled, and how well the squad has responded at pre season training. Normally there have been convincing wins against local amateur sides, and plucky displays against bigger clubs in friendlies.

Often the optimism of opening day has evaporated by 4.50 pm, to be replaced by a steely resignation to a tough season ahead. U`s fans had been buoyed up by the tremendous form shown at the end of the 02/03 season and the healthy sprinkling of new signings. However, reality came crashing in on a hot day at Oakwell.

Despite Fagan and Vine making their debuts, there was little attacking threat from Colchester as they went down 1-0, Joe Keith missing a chance to earn a point from the spot. On the following Friday, Swindon came to town as the home campaign got underway. Again there was only one goal in it, and again it was not scored by Colchester. Two league games without a goal was not the start U`s fans had been hoping for from their new frontline.

Things started to look up on the attacking front when Colchester travelled to Port Vale. Wayne Andrews was now available, having completed a suspension imposed while at his previous club. Scott McGleish scored twice, and there was a debut goal for Andrews. Unfortunately, sloppy defending meant these were not enough even to earn a point!

Parkinson said, "Someone told me I`d learn what management is all about when I lose three on the bounce" He was learning! He felt it had been a disjointed start to the season, due to Fagan and Vine arriving only shortly before it started, and due also to Andrews` suspension.

The League table may not mean much after three games, but nevertheless it did not make pleasant reading for Colchester fans. They were only being held off the bottom by goal difference, and now faced the considerable challenge of much fancied, and so far unbeaten, Brristol City. The fans were asking if the end of last season had been a false dawn. Was it to be another relegation fight?

In fact, this difficult looking game was the beginning of an eight match unbeaten run. Bristol City were beaten. So were Brighton, Wycombe, Peterborough and Bournemouth.

At the beginning of this run Parkinson decided to strengthen the defence. Liam Chilvers had previously enjoyed a successful spell on loan at the U`s from his parent club Arsenal. Steve Whitton had brought him in. He had been the third youngster in a short period loaned to Colchester by Arsenal, following the popular Graham Barrett and the less successful John Halls.

Chilvers was not entirely green, having previously done well on loan at Northampton and Notts County. He had also spent half a season on loan in the Belgian League with Beveren, but had been played out of position and not enjoyed the experience, despite playing with future stars Yaya Toure and Emmanuel Eboue. Then came his first loan spell with the U`s, just in time to see Steve Whitton sacked. By this time it must have been clear that he had no future at Arsenal, but perhaps the terms of his Highbury contract were too good to give up, as he turned down a permanent contract at Northampton, preferring instead to remain an Arsenal player, albeit on loan at Colchester, for the second time. He obviously enjoyed life at Layer Road, staying for the whole season.

This eight game run saw the new forward line click. During it Vine, Andrews and McGleish all scored three. Unusually for Colchester United, competition for places up front was fierce. When McGleish was injured, Fagan came in and scored a spectacular overhead kick to help win the game at Peterborough.

All the glory did not, however, go to the forwards. The team had given up only seven goals in those eight games, all of which had been close affairs. There were three draws and five wins by one goal.

There had been set backs. For example, Myers had been sent off at Wycombe but the team still won. Parkinson had talked of how he wanted to hear rallying calls going around the pitch if things were going wrong, and there was no doubting that the new manager had injected a resilience that had not always been present before.

Club captain Scott Fitzgerald said, "The manager set out over the summer to create competition for places, and I think he has met his aim. The fear factor means you work that bit harder, and strive to reach higher standards to ensure you stay in the team".

The U`s finished September in a lofty 6th position and it came as no surprise when Parkinson was named as the Division Two manager of the month. In accepting the award Parkinson was quick to heap praise on his players. He must have been delighted with the contributions made by players he had brought to the club. He was also coming to appreciate the talents of the players he had inherited. None more so than 25 year old Karl Duguid. Already in his ninth year at the club, and in a signal to the future, Duguid was named as team captain for one match in September in the temporary absence of Scott Fitzgerald. "Whatever is happening in the game Dugy is always working at his maximum and inspiring players around him" said Parkinson.

Unfortunately, one good month does not a season make. The unbeaten run unceremoniously ended with a 3-0 defeat at Notts County`s Meadow Lane. In the following weeks the U`s found it difficult to maintain their September form. To the turn of the year results became inconsistent. Despite rising to 3rd at the end of October following a fine win at Wrexham, the U`s had dropped out of the top six by the beginning of January.

2003 finished badly with a 2-0 defeat in front of over 15,000 at second placed QPR. Karl Duguid was sent off and the experienced Andy Myers hobbled away with a back injury. He would not play for Colchester again.

The new year was hectic at Layer Road. In its first two months the club played fifteen games. Only seven of these were league games. When he had taken the job Parkinson mentioned how much he would like success in the cup competitions. This perhaps reflected how difficult he thought it would be to bring League glory to Layer Road. He would also have known how much the Colchester public enjoy a cup run.

The club had been starved of cup success in recent years, despite having a well known pedigree for it. To make matters worse, the fans had seen many a cup campaign ended ignominiously by non-league opposition. The all time nadir came in 1998 when they travelled to the north eastern village of Bedlington to play the Terriers in the First round of the FA Cup. Few knew where the place was, let alone what league they played in. As historians debated whether the U`s had ever met such lowly opposition in a competitive fixture, the goals started to flow but not from the Essex boys. The match was played on a quagmire and the U`s were taken to the cleaners, 4-1 the final score.

The LDV Vans Trophy is not a competition title to conjure up romance or glamour. It is never shown in silhouette underneath stirring classical music and interspersed by ancient footage showing men doing silly things in the latest fashions of the day. It is played for by teams in the bottom two divisions of the Football League. In its early stages, it usually conjures nothing for Colchester United except a long journey to play in front of a meagre crowd.

It is a competition with something of an identity crisis. It has never been quite sure whether it is a Cup, a Trophy or a Shield. As well as the LDV Vans Trophy, it has also been known as the Assosociate Members Cup, the Freight Vans Trophy, the Sherpa Vans Trophy, the Leyland Daf Cup, the Autoglass Trophy and the Auto Windscreen Shield. In a break from matters automotive, it is currently called the Johnstone`s Paint Trophy. Most fans know it as the Paint Pot. They pay it no more attention than that can of emulsion you used on the utility room in 1997,which has resided on a shelf in the garage ever since.

The difficulty of what to call it does not matter however, because no-one knows what it looks like, where it`s kept or quite why it exists. The early rounds are attended only by hen pecked husbands with no interest in the latest misfortune to befall Dot Cotton`s offspring.

In the latter part of 2003 the U`s had been quietly making progress in what was then called the LDV Vans Trophy, with line ups which had the flavour of experiment about them. It was an early example of how Parkinson could keep fringe players interested, and provide young players with invaluable experience, and thus keep a fully motivated squad. Game time given to Greg Halford in the first two rounds of the LDV would pay dividends in the future.

By 10th February they found themselves in the two legged area final. This is known as "the two games from Wembley stage" and it is no time for experiments. This was especially so, as the opponents were those lovely people from south Essex who do unspeakable things with crabs. Dame Helen Mirren is reported to have described Southend as "The armpit of England." It is a mid size town with no fewer than nine railway stations, an airport and the longest pier in the world. To Colcestrians these things reflect the natural human aspiration to get away from the place.

In fact the final was to be played at Cardiff`s Millenium Stadium that year due to Wembley having become a very expensive building site.

It is in the latter stages of the many named competition that its raison de`etre becomes clear. A "day out at Wembley", or in 2004, the Millenium Stadium. The day when a famous stadium is descended upon by the inhabitants of some distant market towns, where the local club suddenly discovers twenty or thirty thousand fans it never knew it had. Indeed, it is on these days that the sport of Association Football discovers tens of thousands of people who would not normally attend a match anywhere, for they are not fans of the club or the sport. They are there for the "day out" and because it is not difficult to get a ticket.

The competition also gives modest professional players a chance to play at a national stadium, and in front of the sort of attendance that would motivate Wayne Rooney.

Although Colchester`s league fortunes were fading in Division Two Southend were struggling in Division Three at this time. A large and expectant crowd therefore assembled at Layer Road hoping to see their side make progress towards Cardiff. Despite a stunning opener from Thomas Pinault the U`s were surprisingly outplayed and beaten 3-2. Parkinson said the performance had been so poor that he was pleased to be only one goal down.

The second leg was played at Roots Hall on 17th February, only 48 hours after Colchester had played a big FA Cup match at Bramall Lane Sheffield. This scheduling was not appreciated by Phil Parkinson, who doubted that a big club would have to put up with it. The U`s would need all their energy to overcome the deficit incurred in the first leg. Once again Colchester scored early to put the sides on level terms, but Drew Broughton`s goal in the second minute of first half stoppage time had the Shrimpers booking Welsh bound jalopies and charabancs.

The First round of the FA Cup had brought Colchester into contact with its past as Third Division Oxford came to town managed by former U`s boss Ian Atkins, and with popular ex keeper Andy Woodman beween the sticks. They were seen off 1-0 to set up consecutive ties against non-league opposition.

In the previous ten seasons Colchester had been dispatched from the FA Cup by non-league clubs on no fewer than six occasions. Aldershot and Accrington Stanley had at least been heard of. Indeed they were both ex League clubs. However they were now non-league, and that was enough to set the hearts of U`s fans a flutter. They watched these games through hands clasped to their faces with the sort of fatalism displayed only by England fans watching a penalty shoot out.

Phil Parkinson had no time for any of this. There was a new air of professionalism under his tutelage and the plucky part timers were put in their place. Unspectacularly, and in the case of combative Accrington only after a replay, but put in their place nonetheless.

Colchester were drawn away at First Division Coventry in the Fourth round and further progress looked unlikely. However a fine performance at Highfield Road earned a replay, and one of those classic FA Cup nights at Layer Road. A brilliant individual performance by Rowan Vine was enough to light up an already electric atmosphere, and it was "Mr Blue Sky" for Coventry. Vine`s hat trick sent them packing and Colchester into the Fifth round for the first time in 25 years.

The Coventry games soured forever the relationship between the manager and one of his players, as Phil Parkinson relates,

*"We trained at Rushden on the way up to Coventry. I took Rowan Vine to one side and told him he would be on the bench. I explained that I wanted to have Joey Keith on the left and try to be a little more compact, bearing in mind we were playing a Division One club. He couldn`t accept the decision. We got a good draw and I wanted to attack them in the replay so I brought Rowan back. He scored a hat trick and we won.*

*I said to him "look Rowan, what I did worked. I wanted to be solid away and maybe get a draw and you ended up the hero in the replay but you can`t accept the decision?" Our relationship was never the same afterwards. He was a young, impetuous lad and he really wanted to play through the middle, but we had Wayne,*

*Craig and Scotty McGleish so I usually played him wide left where he could cut in and use his right foot. In his eyes, he was being played out of position, and it had cost him his place in a big cup game."*

After this the Fifth round draw at Premiership chasing Sheffield United did not seem that daunting. However, to say the timing was not ideal would have been an understatement. 2pm on a Sunday sandwiched between the LDV ties against Southend. It was an opportunity for U`s fans to renew acquaintance with that nice Mr Neil Warnock. The man who had stirred the natives at Home Park Plymouth into giving the travelling fans a fine game of head the golf ball seven years earlier. He, who having been sent from the dug out, took up residence on the terraces from where he could coach dubious tactics to his players. Such as that inspiring tactic of hurling a long throw into the opposition`s box in the dying minutes of a promotion play off, after the throw in has been caused by Colchester putting the ball out of play to allow a Plymouth player to be treated for injury! Sometimes football fans can have long and bitter memories.

Colchester were just edged out 1-0 by the Blades, but for once, were able to leave the oldest Cup competition in the world with their heads high. However, the result at Southend just 48 hours later was devastating. There would be no "day out". The season was petering out. Colchester had picked up only four points from the previous eight league outings, and had not won in the League since mid December. The cup exertions had clearly taken their toll on League form. When they exited the LDV Vans Trophy, Colchester had dropped to 14th in Division Two and the play offs were looking like a distant dream.

A worrying aspect for Phil Parkinson was the team`s disciplinary record. There had been yellow cards galore, but more worryingly, seven red cards by the end of February. There had been some rash challenges, and some dubious refereeing decisions, but some of it was pure indiscipline. Unfortunately Craig Fagan, still only 21, had shown that if there was a Referee in earshot his jaw work could be as nifty as his footwork. Peter Heard always had a sharp eye on the club`s disciplinary record. He was an ex referee, but more importantly he knew the club could not budget to bring in new squad members when players were unavailable due to suspension. He remembers,

*"Craig Fagan was a nightmare in relation to discipline, and Alan White wasn`t much better. He was a solid Darlington lad. When we played at Hartlepool his parents came to watch. They had a bigger than normal crowd, and Alan`s parents were a little delayed getting into the ground. By the time they got in he had been sent off!"*

Parkinson was also anxious to see this side of the team's performance improve,

*"As a team we were picking up far too many cards, which taught me how important good discipline is. Craig had plenty of brushes with authority and I spoke to him about it often. I was a passionate player myself and no stranger to the referee's notebook, and I get fired up on the touch line sometimes, so I couldn't preach too much. However, I think I got through to Craig and the other players, as our discipline did improve.*

*The cup runs we had in 03/04 certainly affected our league form. If you are successful in cups, it can be very difficult to maintain league form with a small squad."*

In February, Parkinson made another defensive signing who would be highly significant to the club's future. 26 year old Wayne Brown arrived on loan from Watford. Like Chilvers, Brown was on his second loan spell at the club. He had spent the first 7 years of his career at Ipswich Town, making fifty appearances. He had however been sent out on a number of loans, including one at Layer Road which had not been successful. The first job for anyone with an Ipswich background playing at Colchester is to win over the brooding resentment and suspicion of the U's faithful. This can only be done by playing well, and Wayne Brown failed to win anyone over during his 2 appearances, both as a substitute, in the autumn of 1997.

He had never established himself at Portman Road, and it seemed not before time when he finally decided to try his luck with a permanent move away from Suffolk. He went to Watford, but things did not go terribly well at Vicarage Road either. In fifteen months as a Watford player Brown made only twenty five appearances, mostly as a full back, despite believing centre back to be his best position. Shortly after his return to Layer Road he explained, "I am a centre half, I learned my trade as a centre half and that's where I want to play. That is the main reason I wanted to come here. "

Club captain Scott Fitzgerald was being eased out of the team. At thirty four, Parkinson may have felt his legs were going. No doubt this influenced the acquisition of Wayne Brown. The fans saw an Ipswich reject who had already had an unimpressive loan spell at the club. Hopes for Wayne Brown were not high, but Parkinson saw it differently,

*"We signed Wayne Brown in the second half of that season, and the crowd were quite negative towards him. He was dropping down a division because he wanted to play games, an attitude I always like. I'd seen him play a couple of times for Watford reserves, and I liked him when I met him. I thought he'd just lost his way a bit. There*

*was no doubt in my mind that he was a centre half and not a full back, and he turned out to be a real leader for us."*

Colchester went into March in fifteenth position, but still harbouring distant play off hopes. Realistic fans, however, knew the season had effectively finished with the cup exits in February, and the feeling of anti climax could be measured in the crowds which were dipping below 3,000.

The U`s were unlucky to lose 2-1 at Brighton when a certain Chris Iwelumo scored one and made the other in front of Phil Parkinson`s notebook. There was a three game winning run including a triumph over Sheffield Wednesday in front of over 20,000 at Hillsborough in late April. Otherwise form remained patchy as the U`s finished the season eleventh.

The Play offs were never seriously threatened after Christmas, but nevertheless another mid table finish was no disgrace, and at least there had been some cup excitement. In reality it was probably the cup runs and the sheer number of games played, especially in the two months after Christmas, which cost Colchester a top ten spot, maybe even a play off place. A squad the size of Colchester`s was never likely to be able to sustain a sixty one game season without some dips in form. That eleventh place had been achieved was testament to Phil Parkinson`s expert handling of the squad.

Another example of the manager`s modern techniques was the introduction of sports psychologist Sam Kotadia. Defender Alan White had been one of those contributing heavily to the yellow and red cards. He talked about Kotadia`s work, "You can`t control the decisions given by officials. You can control your reaction to them. We have used what we call environmental cues such as using a decision to re-focus. So if the referee gives a bad decision you give your team mates an encouraging call, rather than complain at the official."

The season had witnessed the emergence of Greg Halford under Parkinson`s careful handling. Following his debut on the final day of the previous season, he had established himself in the first team during 03/04 making twenty four appearances and scoring four goals, including a free kick at Chesterfield that was nothing short of world class. He had shown himself equally at home, whether at full back or in midfield where his classy control shone and his languid running style hid a steeley determination and some real pace once he got going. He also boasted a long throw, which went like an exocet missile- powerful, flat and extremely difficult to defend against. He would have a big part to play in the future of Colchester United, and Parky needed no persuasion as to his potential,

*"Greg was an exciting young player. He could defend or attack very effectively at*

*set plays. He was very good at near post flick ons and of course he had that great throw."*

Some feeling of "what might have been" was inevitable, but Club and fans could look back on a good season. One in which the club had become more professional, and the player investments made in the summer had borne fruit. What had generally been a steady upward curve, ever since relegation to the Conference in 1990, had been maintained.

The question was whether that curve could be plotted upwards into the future. If it could, the play offs could be achieved. Of course, in the extremely unlikely event of Colchester United ever qualifying for the Division Two play offs, the chances of them being the one club from the four qualifiers to go up seemed next to impossible. The prospect of the club achieving automatic promotion was quite simply the product of a deranged imagination.

The following conversation was overheard in a pub in High Street Colchester during the summer of 2004,

"another pint of Stellberg extra strong wife beater John?"

"don`t know Pete, already had 12 and I`ve got these pills to pop"

"oh go on, 3 more for the road won`t hurt and I`ll still be able to hit a vein with this needle "

"ok Pete but I`ve got to be up by midday tomorrow for my electroconvulsive therapy"

"U`s done well last season John "

"yeah, 2 or 3 good signings and I reckon they could go up next year Pete"

At this point a horrified bystander sat bolt upright. He could not believe his ears and realising that John and Pete constituted a grievous threat to themselves and the safety of the community he immediately invoked Section 2 of the Mental Health Act 1983. They were forcibly detained for mental assessment.

The Tribunal was given a litany of John and Pete`s escapades. How they would regularly run amok on alcohol and drug fuelled benders causing property damage, traffic chaos and terrorising anyone who crossed their path. The Tribunal chairman said "seems like a normal Saturday night in Colchester to me, let them go"

Our hero, the bystander then stood up. "Mr Chairman, I clearly heard these people having a serious conversation about the U`s playing in the second tier of English football"

"Oh my God" said the chairman, "they`re bonkers, take them down"

This topic of conversation had never been discussed in Colchester before.

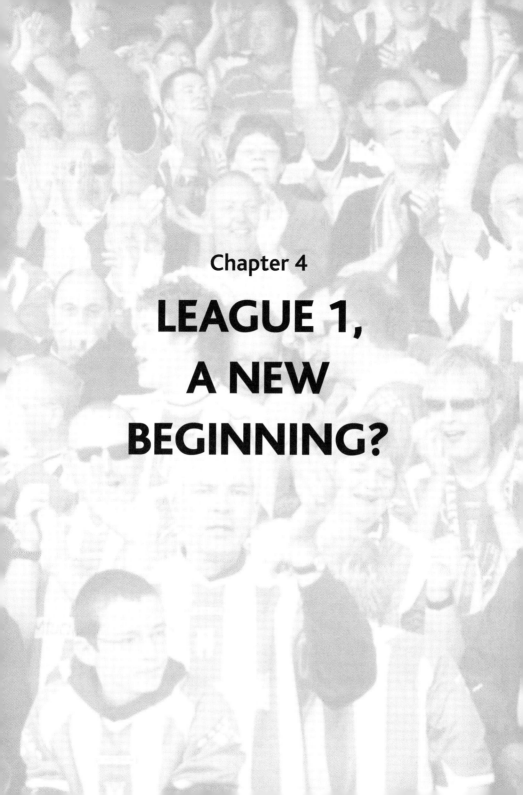

Chapter 4

# LEAGUE 1, A NEW BEGINNING?

# Chapter 4
## LEAGUE 1, A NEW BEGINNING?

The Football League was formed in 1888 by a goup of men with absurdly bushy beards. Only four years later, it was decided that more clubs (and presumably more beards) were required. The Second division was formed.

Although by 1920 men had discovered the razor, they still looked extremely silly in fedoras and knickerbockers. So attired, the group of men running the Football League at that time set up a Third Division which was quickly expanded and regionalised into North and South. In 1958 regionalisation was scrapped and so were born nationwide third and fourth divisions.

In 1992, the philanthropic owners of the elite clubs were desperate to improve the fortunes of the national team and comply with FIFA dictates to reduce the size of England`s top division. Thinking of nothing but the greater good of football, they unselfishly resigned from the Football League and, in an amazing stroke of unintended good fortune, were able to take sole advantage of new money coming into the game from multi channel satellite TV.

Instead of sharing £6.3 million around ninety two clubs, as in 1986, the owners of the country`s top twenty two clubs were able to share £304 million, with most of it going to the dominant few among them. Little more than twenty years later, that would become £5.14 billion. During this period, in which TV money increased by 80,000%, the owners generously only increased match ticket prices by 1,000%!

Reducing the competition to eighteen clubs slipped their minds, as they set about creating a whole new generation of arm chair jockeys and glory hunters, who could think of nothing better to do with their discretionary incomes than pour it into the pockets of needy foreign players, managers and agents.

In a welter of avarice the Premier League had been born. The Football League, which had run for one hundred and four years and survived two World Wars, had been broken up.

The overriding image was one of pigs and troughs, but there was a positive side effect for Colchester United. When they returned to the Football League in 1992 they expected to be returning to Football League Division 4. Instead they found themselves in Barclays League Dvision 3. Barclays League Division 1 was what had previously been called Football League Division 2 and in 2004 the clubs of that division had been speaking to the marketing world.

They had watched the Premier League turn into "feeding time at the Zoo", but had been denied a piece of the action. They wanted to differentiate themselves from dirty little places like Scunthorpe and Colchester, so it was time for the word "rebranding" to enter the football lexicon. It was decided that the young demographic, exclusively targeted by the marketing industry, did not recognise the word "division". So, in one flourish of blue sky thinking, out went 116 years of tradition and in came The Championship, Football League 1 and Football League 2.

Colchester United had ascended to the "1st Division" as it was referred to by an increasingly confused football public. The generation of Kenneth Wolstenholme and David Coleman had looked for a 1st division in the Premier League and the Championship but decided that League 1 looked most like it. Promotion celebrations at Layer Road were muted. The truth was the U`s had finished 03/04 in the third tier and would begin 04/05 at exactly the same level. They would still be looking up at the second tier as the impossible dream and down at the fourth tier as their natural home.

Compared with the previous summer, Phil Parkinson clearly thought some significant surgery was required on the U`s squad. Some contracts came to an end, and decisions were made not to renew, in some cases by the club, in some cases by the player, and in some cases a bit of both. Some popular and experienced players saw their time at Layer Road come to an end. Simon Brown, Scott Fitzgerald, Alan White, Scott McGleish and Thomas Pinault represented a lot of games in the blue and white stripes and all were highly rated by sections of the support. Also leaving was Rowan Vine whose season-long loan from Portsmouth had ended, and who had fallen out of favour with Parkinson in any event.

There was no outcry at the departure of so many popular players. This was perhaps testament to how much the Layer Road faithful had bought into Phil Parkinson`s vision of Colchester United`s future, and how well he sold it on a weekly basis. He had put the club on a more professional footing, and his first full season had been a good one.

In total eleven players left over the summer, which gave Parky the chance to raid his contacts book. This resulted in the arrival of a new goalkeeper and lynchpin midfielder.

Aidan Davison and Phil Parkinson were more or less the same age. They met when Davison joined Bury in 1989. They were together at Gigg Lane for two years, but never played together because Davison never got a game for Bury, being kept out by the consistency of club stalwart Gary Kelly.

Davison started to gather League experience during spells at Millwall and Bolton, where he also picked up 3 caps for Northern Ireland. When he arrived at Colchester, he was coming to the end of a twenty four year playing career which encompassed nineteen spells (some permanent and some on loan) at fourteen clubs. This included a short spell on loan at Ipswich Town in 1996, a crime mitigated by the fact that he made no appearances.

He made Premier League appearances at Bolton and during one of three spells at Bradford City.

In a classic example of Colchester United making their limited resources go a long way, Davison`s desire to move into coaching was exploited. As well as being first choice keeper, he would also be the club`s goalkeeping coach, helping to progress youngsters such as Dean Gerken and Mark Cousins.

Kevin Watson`s career started at his local club Tottenham Hotspur. He made only 5 appearances for Spurs, and after a number of loan spells in the lower divisions he joined Swindon Town and helped them survive in Division 1 (the second tier). He then moved on to Rotherham United who he helped achieve consecutive promotions from the fourth to the second tier.

In 2001, Watson was snapped up by ambitious Reading in the 3rd tier, where Phil Parkinson was in the twilight of his playing career. Manager Alan Pardew hoped Watson`s two promotions at Rotherham might rub off on Reading. Sure enough, Watson put another promotion on his CV, and then helped the Royals into the Division 1 play offs in the following season. In the Summer of 2004 Watson had just turned 30, and was exactly the sort of experienced head Parkinson was looking for in his engine room. He also had the happy knack of being around when clubs were promoted.

Four other players joined during the summer, all youngsters who were not expected to be immediate first team regulars. In addition, Gary Richards was promoted into the first team squad from the youth team.The promising Dean Gerken, who had made his debut at Brentford the previous April, would be the number two keeper following the departures of Simon Brown and Richard Mckinney. Liam Chilvers and Wayne Brown both made their loan moves permanent. The squad was smaller than the one which had finished the 03/04 season, but it was hoped that there had been no reduction in quality.

As the season went on, however, it became clear that new club captain Karl Duguid would miss all of it due to a serious knee injury sustained at home to Stockport in the previous March. In addition, Kem Izzet started the season injured, made three appearances in October during which he aggravated the same injury, and then missed the remainder of the season. Wayne Brown would wear the captain`s armband for most of the season.

One concern was a lack of height up front. Parkinson tried to persuade Chris Iwelumo to sign from Brighton, but he preferred a move into the German second division with Alemania Aachen. 6ft 1inch Millwall striker Ben May had already enjoyed one loan spell at Layer Road during Parkinson`s first weeks in charge. He was brought back in on a two month loan.

Parky looks back on the pivotal signings of Davison and Watson,

"Aidy was a friend and Kevin was a former team mate. I had kind of vowed not to bring in mates, but there's an exception to every rule!

The goalkeeper position needed to be addressed. I never thought that either Simon Brown or Richard Mckinney quite had what it took, and looking back I think I should have done something about this a year earlier. We thought very highly of Dean Gerken, and we wanted Aidy to help bring him on. Before Aidy we had no keeper coach, and again he was ideal for Colchester because he could fill two roles.

Aidy was at Grimsby. They had been relegated letting in eighty one goals. Only Wimbledon had conceded more in the whole League! This didn't worry me as I knew Aidy's qualities well. I knew he would be a great addition both on the pitch and the staff. He was married to an American lady, and he had promised her that they would move to the States when his career was over. With the sort of season Aidy had endured at Grimsby, they both thought that time might have come. I took them to the Alma at Copford and talked them into moving down south. He stayed for four years, and was one of the best signings I made.

It was good to have a friend on the staff, and he was a very good goalkeeper and an outstanding character. We used to talk a lot about goalkeeping. He had worked with some of the best, Neville Southall and Peter Shilton for example. He would say that good goalkeepers restrict the number of saves they have to make by things like coming for crosses, and being in good starting positions. Aidy managed the game in front of him very well. He commanded a good wage by Colchester's standards, but Dean was a kid and so on very little. We got Davison and Gerken for about the same as we'd been paying Brown and McKinney, and of course we also got Aidy's coaching.

Kevin was a very good footballer. Good passer. He'd always receive the ball no matter what state the game was in. He'd already been there three times when teams were promoted and I don't think that was coincidence. He could make a team tick, and with him and the other players we had in midfield I never thought we became predictable. When other clubs watched us, it would have been difficult to know where the main threat was going to come from.

There was no point in the more experienced signings like Aidy and Kevin demanding too much, because we had a budget which Mr Heard had made clear was not going to change. If they wanted to come, they had to fit within the budget."

At around this time, and in a move towards transparency, it was decided that all payments made by professional football clubs to agents would be published. Normally, agents acted for players in securing the best terms from clubs. Sometimes however they acted for clubs in helping to secure the services of players and managers. In some transactions they were acting on both sides, in what was a clear conflict of interests. They were unregulated, unqualified and in many cases looking out for no-one`s interests except their own. They contributed significantly to what was already spiralling inflation in wages and transfer fees, as many a deal broke down over how much the agent was to be paid and by whom.

Colchester United owner Peter Heard found all this distasteful. His fingers had been well and truly burned in 1999 by ex player turned agent Barry Silkman and his ties with Mick Wadsworth who was the U`s manager at the time. The club found itself in litigation against Silkman, who was demanding payment for his services in facilitating the transfers of various players which had used up the club`s very limited transfer budget in a short space of time.

Heard wanted no more to do with this murky world, and could see no legitimate role for agents outside the top levels of the game. The club`s attitude was, if a player wants to use an agent, that is a matter for him. Under no circumstances, however, would Colchester United be paying the agent`s fee. The player would have to do that.

This was a very unconventional approach in football at that time, and came as a great surprise to many players, managers and agents. When club payments to agents were published in July 2004, the U`s were among a handful of clubs revealed to have paid nothing whatsoever. This truly was occupation of the moral high ground. However, it also probably put some good players beyond the reach of Colchester United before negotiations even began.

Even now Mr Heard`s attitude towards agents is uncompromising,

*"I could never fathom why football clubs paid for player`s agents. There are more footballers looking for clubs than there are vacancies. Why should we pay the player`s agent? I had little time for them. I used to make them wait in the car park! I would tell the player that if he wanted to consult his agent he could do it in the car park. I think that must have put over the message that we were not going to be paying the agent as part of any deal!*

*Some agents would refuse to steer their players towards us because of our policy. I said "alright then, there are plenty of other players." We missed out on some players but overall I`m certain that our policy saved us substantial sums of money. Sometimes, we would get the player anyway because he wanted to join the club, and he would sideline the agent in order to do so.*

*For a short while I was chairman of the FA committee which dealt with the licensing of agents. I kept turning applicants down because they couldn't answer questions properly, or they were blatant liars. I was moved off that committee because someone had clearly been complaining about the FA being too tough on agents. Ironic since the FA are often accused of being weak willed!*

*We also never engaged agents to help us acquire players. I could see no point in it when there were so many players available."*

The realistic aim for the season had to be a top half finish. However it was clear that some astute signings during the season would be required to achieve this. The bookies once again had Colchester installed as one of the favourites for relegation, and there was no doubt that a run of injuries, or suspensions, or a loss of form, could see the club fighting for its third tier life once again.

The U's could not have been handed a tougher looking opening game than to be away to the Division's biggest club by some distance. A crowd of 24,138 was at Hillsborough for the match against Sheffield Wednesday including 547 from Essex on a sweltering August day. Davison and Watson both made their debuts, and the match seemed to be petering out into a scoreless draw. A point at Hillsborough would have represented a good start to the season for Colchester but in an amazing finale Fagan, Stockley and Joe Keith all scored in the last five minutes to send the travelling support into raptures.

It was a great result, but Phil Parkinson's feet were firmly attached to Terra Firma, "If we had got beaten here today, then we wouldn't have got carried away, just as we won't be getting carried away by this win".

After spending the previous season on loan at Layer Road, Craig Fagan had now made a permanent switch from Birmingham City, and Parkinson was excited about the Midlander's potential. With more maturity helping him to count to ten when confronted by a referee, hopes were high that he would be able to form a potent strike partnership with Wayne Andrews.

Those hopes were dashed when, much to the surprise of most fans, a Premier League club came calling for Andrews. Ian Dowie had just led Crystal Palace into the Premier League, and knew Andrews well from their time together at Oldham. He decided to bolster his squad by acquiring Colchester's main striker, just before the August transfer window closed.

Andrews had perhaps not scored the weight of goals which had been hoped for. However, fourteen in just over a year was respectable, and there was no doubt that he possessed the kind of pace which frightened most League 1 defences. He had proved particularly adept at winning free kicks around the opposition penalty area. His loss was a blow, and not one which Parky was going to accept without compensation. Initially this took a predictable form.

Gareth Williams was at Crystal Palace. He had enjoyed two successful loan spells at Layer Road scoring an impressive eight goals in fifteen appearances. Williams now joined Colchester on a permanent basis as part of the deal which took Wayne Andrews in the opposite direction.

Parky was not finished there. A few days later, he signed Richard Garcia from West Ham, who could play up front or on the wing. An Australian, he had made a handful of appearances for West Ham, and a few more on loan at Orient, but he had then been blighted by injury. At twenty three it was thought that he possessed considerable potential if his fitness allowed this to be realised.

With the door still swinging from Garcia`s arrival, it was opening again to admit Neil Danns. An attacking midfield player joining from Premier League Blackburn Rovers, Danns was only twenty one but had spent good loan spells at Blackpool and Hartlepool, so he knew what the lower divisions were all about. Initially he joined Colchester on loan, but this was soon made permanent. He soon became a popular figure at Layer Road due to his love of communicating with fans. If he was not in the squad for an away match, he would most likely be found standing on the terraces with the Colchester fans. However his high energy midfield performances, ability to find space where there was little and his knack for scoring goals from midfield, meant that he was always in the squad if fit, and it would not be long until he became a pivotal figure in making history. Back to Parkinson,

*"Losing Wayne Andrews was a blow, but with Palace being in the Premier League there was no point in trying to stand in his way although I was under no pressure to sell. I think his head had been turned as soon as Ian Dowie went to Palace the previous Christmas, as he was Wayne`s former manager.*

*We swapped him for Gareth Williams and got £100,000. I really liked Gareth as a lad and I think he could have done better in the game. He could be a good goal scorer but he lacked a bit of athleticism and it never quite happened for him."*

Peter Heard had many interests in the game outside Colchester United. He seemed to know most club owners, and just about every significant figure in the FA and the Football League. He was usually keen to keep these activities separate from his role at Layer Road, but there seems little doubt that there were times when his profile inside the game worked for the U`s. The appointment of Phil Parkinson was the most spectacular case in point.

There were other occasions when he would discourage the manager from signing a player because he knew something about the player's character. The signing of Richard Garcia was another example of Heard's contacts helping the U's. He tells the story,

*"That signing got me into trouble. I got a tip off that there had been some mix up and West Ham had failed to re-sign Garcia to his contract. He had become a free agent as a result. This meant we were able to sign him for nothing. The West Ham chairman at the time was Terry Brown who rang me up and gave me a right going over. He thought I had not behaved as I should have done. He told me I was not a gentleman! Actually I think he was just annoyed about the mix up as Garcia would have commanded a significant transfer fee."*

The U's encouraging start at Sheffield Wednesday was continued as six of the first eleven league games were won. At the quarter way point in the season Colchester were nicely established in a play off position in fourth place. They had also reached the 3rd round of the League Cup with a stirring extra time home win over Premier League West Brom. This would be the last time a top flight side visited Layer Road. During this spell young defender John White made his debut.

Things then started to slide with a run of seven games without a win including only one point from three home games. Teenage keeper Dean Gerken played in six of these games in place of the injured Davison. Despite the results, he showed encouraging form. A hat trick from substitute Dexter Blackstock saw the U's out of the League Cup, losing 3-2 at Southampton of the Premier League.

It was hoped that a 3-1 win at Torquay had turned the team's fortunes around but sadly no. Three consecutive defeats followed, two of which were at home. Despite an excellent 2-2 draw at top of the table Luton on 28th December the U's had slumped to eighteenth place by the end of 2004.

The first half of the season had been a stuttering affair. Injuries had taken their toll and Gareth Williams had not been able to make the hoped for impact up front. He had only managed three goals and was rarely making the starting eleven. The same was true of Ben May, who had returned to his parent club. So, in terms of strikers it had been Scott McGleish and Wayne Andrews out, Gareth Williams and Ben May in. That particular balance sheet was showing a loss. Craig Fagan had missed a month with injury and had also been suspended. After hitting thirteen goals in the first five games the U's had managed only nineteen in the next eighteen games.

Richard Garcia was taking time to find his feet in League 1, and, like Jamie Cade, was principally a wide player. Parkinson`s forward options were often very limited, and on occasions he was forced to play Greg Halford as a striker alongside Fagan. Neil Danns had been showing his goal scoring potential, but his loan had finished on 10th November and he was not permanently signed until 23rd December.

Home form had been a real problem, with United winning only four from eleven. The goal music record was certainly not being worn out! After nine goals in the first three games at Layer Road only five more had followed in the next eight games.

The ongoing progress of Greg Halford had been a plus. He had shown himself well capable of flourishing either at full back, in midfield or up front. Most fans had been delighted to see the somewhat belated emergence of Pat Baldwin. He had been signed by Steve Whitton as a 19 year old from Chelsea in 2002. Big things had been hoped for, but his progress was not rapid. When he was loaned to non-league St. Albans in 2004, many speculated that he was on his way out of the professional game. However he established himself as an important squad member in 2004/05, becoming a first team regular, whether deputising for Brown or Chilvers, or slotting in at full back in what was a steady back line. Despite the U`s being as low as eighteenth only three teams in League 1 had conceded fewer goals.

It was therefore obvious where the problems lay. The team had to score more goals, and it had to do better at Layer Road. In the hope of addressing this Parkinson brought in a new forward. The exotically named Guylain N`Dumbu N`Sungu joined on a short term contract after being released by Sheffield Wednesday. Quickly referred to by the fans as "Dave", the Congolese forward`s name would have scored prolifically on the scrabble board had it not broken every scrabble rule. Unfortunately Guylain found scoring on the football field equally elusive and he managed only one in eight appearances.

With the notable exceptions of a 3-0 win at Swindon and a 5-0 home win over Paul Merson`s Walsall (containing former Layer Road hero Mark Kinsella), the goal scoring problem continued. After a 2-0 loss at MK Dons, Wayne Brown said, "Make no mistake about it, we are in a relegation battle, whether we like it or not".

The club did have the nice distraction of another good FA Cup run. Fine wins over Mansfield, Rushden and Hull delivered a fourth round tie at Premier League Blackburn Rovers. Here the struggling League 1 side were always going to be fighting the odds. Phil Parkinson`s game plan would not have allowed for a mole to pop up in the Colchester penalty area to head Kevin Watson`s back pass over Aidan Davison`s foot for a 21st minute opener. The U`s never recovered, and lost 3-0. Terms could not be agreed with the mole, which frustrated Parkinson`s attempts to sign it for Colchester`s forward line. Any puzzled readers should at this point consult "FA Cup Bloopers"!

After 36 games Colchester were again eighteenth and only four points above the relegation zone. The side`s form had been at best ordinary, albeit that they had continued to win the occasional game, which had been enough to keep them out of the bottom four. The paucity of goals scored still held the team back. In January they managed to go four games without scoring. Between the New Year and mid March they played thirteen games and failed to score in eight. There had been many shut outs at Layer Road and some of the fans were getting restless.

Remarkably, only top of the table Luton Town could boast a better defensive record than Colchester. 46 goals had been scored in 36 games and in fact there were eight League 1 teams who had scored less than United. However this hid the facts that whilst 27 goals had been scored in eight of these games only 19 had come in the other 28 games. So whilst the U`s were very capable of adding unnecessary goals in games already won, they could not score when the pressure was really on and a goal was needed to secure a result.

When the U`s went to Hull City on 26th February, Craig Fagan was leading the way both in goals scored and in red and yellow cards received. One might think that in a team which is finding it so hard to score important goals, and which is in the midst of a relegation battle, the loss of its only regular scoring forward was something to be avoided. One would be correct! The 187 U`s fans who congregated on Humberside that afternoon were unanimous in this belief, when they discovered that Craig Fagan had just been transferred to Hull City! After watching their team fail to score for the twelfth time that season, their mood became no more optimistic.

This could be described as a defining moment in a lifetime of supporting a small unfashionable football club. You turn up to support your team on a freezing February afternoon, in the distant East Riding of Yorkshire, to find that just about the only player you have with much idea as to the location of the onion bag now plays for the opposition. Manchester United fans don`t have to put up with this!

Never mind. There was presumably some master plan at Layer Road, although this seemed very well disguised when the following games at home to Brentford and away at Port Vale yielded one point and, yes you guessed it, no goals at all! At least we could enjoy speculating as to what the transfer fee received for Fagan might be spent on, or more particularly which intriguing players it might buy? But no. Even that pleasure was denied us. Fagan was transferred for "an undisclosed fee".

Enquiries were made about a variety of strikers, with Jamie Cureton and Rochdale`s Grant Holt being two of the more interesting names looked into.The club did sign two strikers in March. Marino Keith on a free transfer from Plymouth and highly rated youngster Ryan Jarvis on loan from Norwich. The former made an impact with four goals in the final weeks of the season. Helped by these, and five goals from midfielder Neil Danns, the U`s went unbeaten over the last eleven games, to secure what for most of the season had looked an unlikely fifteenth place.

So, we had no need to worry. There had been a master plan!

Parky remembers,

*"The 04/05 season was disappointing. A lot of things were against us. Losing Andrews and Vine robbed us of a lot of attacking verve, and even Craig Fagan was probably only available for about half of the season. Equally damaging were the injuries to Duguid and Izzet. Dugy`s injury was very frustrating. He had a staple in his medial knee ligaments from a previous injury. Stuart Ayles thought this might be causing the problem. He thought it might have become dislodged and need removing, but the specialist didn`t agree. Then about a year and three operations later, it was decided he should have the operation to remove the staple, which was what we had originally sent him for! He was then fine.*

*Dugy was always a great player to have in your squad. To have someone who could come in at right back, left back, right midfield, left midfield or even up front is a great bonus.*

*We signed Richard Garcia and Neil Danns, who in time would prove to be great acquisitions, but Richard continued to be hampered by injuries during that season. He was known to be a good player, but he`d had some bad injuries during his time at West Ham. He was very brave, which was why he would get injured. He was a great character. A real tough Aussie. Good in the air, and could play in different positions.*

*It was said that we had signed Garcia for "an undisclosed fee", but we actually got him for nothing due to a loop hole in his contract at West Ham. Alan Pardew was at West Ham then and he was very displeased!*

*The Danns move from Blackburn was another of those slow burners. I`d first seen him late in the 02/03 season, and I`d tried to get him on loan a few times but it had always been blocked by Graeme Souness. Souness left early in the 04/05 season and Tony Parkes was caretaker. I started to harangue Tony saying "come on Tony help me out, I need a midfield player". I remember ringing him at about 9pm. He was clearly reluctant to loan us Dannsy. He kept saying Graeme didn`t really want to do it and perhaps he shouldn`t either.*

*Eventually he sort of half heartedly agreed perhaps just to get me off the phone. He asked if I wanted Dannsy to come down tomorrow. I said no. Tell him to drive down now and I`ll meet him. I didn`t want to give Tony any chance to change his* *mind. I was worried he might speak to someone else at the club in the morning and it would all be off. I`m not sure what Dannsy must have thought having to drive down in the early hours of the morning but sometimes you have to strike while the iron is hot. It meant all the paper work had been done early the next morning.*

*Dannsy was a very good player for us. The loan turned into a permanent move, and the club got a good fee when he moved on.*

*Pat Baldwin came through during that season. He was another good character. He was comfortable on the ball and he liked to show he was a ball playing centre back. I didn`t mind that, but I had to remind him that his first job was to defend. For a big lad he was very mobile.*

*When the Fagan sale came up, I remember arguing against it with Peter Heard. However, he was unhappy with Craig`s disciplinary record and, to be honest, it was probably the right decision to let him go. After he left, there was an upturn in spirit and in results. We stayed up comfortably after what had been a difficult season."*

In the end, relegation had been avoided by a fairly comfortable eight points, but were we not now supposed to have higher ambitions than just staying up? It felt as though the foundations which had been laid during the previous season had not been built upon. The club had finished four places lower and with five fewer points. It was a bottom half finish.

There had been a real flirtation with relegation fears in the second half of the season, and home form had for the most part been dreadful. Colchester had failed to score in a staggering ten out of twenty three home games. In only eight home games had they managed to score more than once. The midfield players seemed to be restricted by a lack of space at Layer Road while the attacking pace which had been so prevalent during the 03/04 season had only been supplied by Fagan, and he had not always been available, and by March had left.

It would be going too far to suggest that Phil Parkinson had been welcomed to Layer Road as a Messiah in February 2003, but there was no doubt that his modern methods and commitment had penetrated the consciousness of the fan base, and there was real hope that something significant could be achieved at Layer Road. Merely surviving in the third tier, and having a few exciting cup matches was no longer enough. In some home games a very defensive looking 4-5-1 formation had been deployed by Parkinson, to the growing frustration of a sizeable minority of the support.

Unmet expectations, and a lack of entertainment on home soil, is a toxic mix for any football manager. Many U`s fans would probably now be ashamed to admit that in the late winter, and early spring of 2005, they participated in conversations about whether this new young manager should be jettisoned. More positive voices pointed to the injuries he had to cope with, and how much the squad would be bolstered next season by the return of Duguid and Izett. Furthermore, there was something to be encouraged about in the team`s fine defensive record, which owed much to the experience, leadership and organisational abilities of Davison, Brown and Watson. They, along with Baldwin and Chilvers, were developing a powerful spine through the team and all were contracted for the 05/06 season. Meanwhile, young flair players like Halford, Garcia and Danns were only going to get better.

Peter Heard looks back,

*"Although we finished 15th in 2004/05 there was never any feeling of discontent from the board towards Phil. We thought he was doing a good job and he and I always had a good relationship. Inevitably you get some bad runs in football but we were philosophical about it."*

Whether the glass was half full or half empty depended upon your outlook. Either way, 2005/06 looked like being a pivotal season in Phil Parkinson`s stay in North Essex.

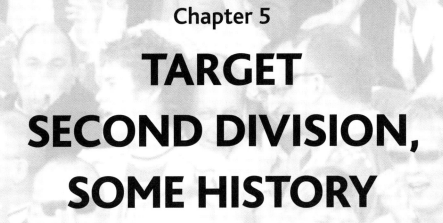

Chapter 5

# TARGET
# SECOND DIVISION,
# SOME HISTORY

# Chapter 5
## TARGET SECOND DIVISION, SOME HISTORY

It really is a little unfair when the thing you are targeting in life keeps disappearing. Especially when it has never been made clear that you only have a limited time in which to attain that target. All those hours spent in front of a flip chart, sky blue thinking in brain storming sessions, must seem wasted, if long before your mission statement looks tired the thing it is aiming for is taken away.

Colchester United could have no complaints though. By the time the Second Division or Football League Division 2 ceased to exist due to the advent of the Premier League, Colchester United had been unsuccessfully targeting it for at least forty two years. For a further twelve years the club`s mission statement carried a smudge of tippex as the Holy Grail became Barclays League Division 1, then Endsleigh League Division 1, then Nationwide League Division 1.

When the 2004 rebranding took place, the job had become too big for tippex. The target was now the Coca-Cola Championship. A word processer was seen at Layer Road!

For some years, Colchester United had been the club which refused to be born. It had been carried in the womb of the amateur club Colchester Town amidst many doubts as to whether Colchester could sustain a professional football club. When it at last came into being, it was delivered into the Southern League for the 1937/38 season. This followed a public meeting in March 1937 presided over by the Mayor, Councillor Gerald C Benham. The meeting was advertised under the question, "Shall Colchester have professional Association Football?"

Colchester Town had been struggling in recent years and Layer Road gates were falling. A common term being used at the time was "sham amateurism" as players at competing clubs were being paid "under the table". Councillor Maurice Pye, who would later become the United`s first Chairman said, "If we want a successful football team in Colchester there is no alternative to a professional team." The cost of running a professional club was estimated at £80pw and the decision was made to go ahead.

One can only speculate as to the ambitions of Councillor Pye and his inaugural Board of directors. The provision of "brighter and better soccer" seemed to be the main reason to establish a professional club. Not the attainment of any particular position in the football pyramid. The club had endured a difficult birth and no automatic promotion existed between the Southern League and the Football League. It is therefore hard to imagine that the founders of professional football in Colchester spent very long dreaming about life in the top league, let alone in its second tier.

Nevertheless, the U`s had been born and were in a League which fed directly into the Football League. Promotion to the Third Division South of the Football League could only be achieved through being elected by all Football League clubs. It was a system which owed as much to back scratching as football prowess, but it had been successfully negotiated by close neighbours Ipswich Town. They had won the Southern League title in 1936/37 and finished third in 1937/38 following which they were elected to the Football League. Colchester finished a respectable 6th in the first season of their life, and then won the title themselves in the next season.

The first manager was Edwin "Ted" Davis who had played at the top level for Huddersfield and Blackburn. He had also managed Bath City in the Southern League. He was the first of, so far, four ex goalkeepers to manage the U`s.

United had made a very encouraging start, which had brought national attention. In January 1938 the News of the World heaped praise upon Ted Davis. It said, "We raise our hats to Mr Ted Davis, the best manager in the game, who during the close season was given a day off by his directors, and a £10 note and told to go out and get a team, and to be sure and bring back some change as a supply of oil would be required for the turnstiles". Even then it was clear that financial backing at United was very limited and way behind that available at Ipswich.

Nevertheless elevation into the Football League was already on the minds of some, and in February 1938 a local paper felt a dose of reality was required. A columnist in the Colchester Telegraph wrote, "I can definitely say that a mere 300-odd-share-holders and £1500 or so in capital is not nearly enough for League status".

Just over a year later, and buoyed up by the Southern League title win, an application for membership was made to the Football League. Sadly the U`s only managed to secure one vote. The Football League clubs voted to re-elect Walsall and Bristol Rovers, and potential newcomers were kept out. Colchester`s cause was not helped by having taken on to their books a number of players who were registered with Football League clubs, without consulting the clubs concerned.

The 38/39 title win in only the second season of the club`s existence had made people think. There was no sign of discouragement at the electorial failure. After the club`s first two seasons, who knows how high Mr Pye and his colleagues were aiming. In fact it didn`t really matter. An Austrian rabble rouser had ambitions of his own and the 1939/40 season only lasted three games.

When football returned in 1945 the Southern League was a pretty chaotic affair. Only eleven clubs had considered themselves ready to enter, and even then some fixtures were never fulfilled. As reigning champions eighth place out of eleven was a disappointment for

Colchester, but everything was in short supply, including players, and for Colchester United and football in general, 1945/46 was just a case of getting going again. The board had been split as to whether the club was ready for competitive football, but decided to go ahead without a full time, or indeed a salaried manager. This situation was addressed in April 1946 with the appointment of ex West Ham player, Ted Fenton.

In January 1947 Colchester United were represented at a Football League meeting called to consider the formation of a Fourth Division. Any Fourth Division at that time would have been split into regions. However it might have meant there being one nationwide Third Division. With petrol rationed, and all sorts of post war austerity still in place, the increased travelling such ventures would have required probably put them out of the question. No changes were made and it would be another eleven years before the League added a 4th tier.

There must have been disappointment at Layer Road, as it meant the vagaries of election would continue to represent the only avenue of progress into English football`s third tier. To have any hope of achieving that, it would be necessary to remain successful in the Southern League, to be noticed as a well run, well supported and solvent club, and to make friends in the right places.

The U`s continued to be a force in the Southern League although they were never able to replicate the 1938/39 title win. Ted Fenton`s two seasons in charge saw the club finish eighth and fourth. It was the second of those seasons which really put Colchester on the football map, courtesy of the FA Cup.

Being a non-league team, they had to start in the Fourth qualifying round, where local rivals Chelmsford City were dispatched. Fellow non-leaguers Banbury Spencer were the next victims in the First round proper. The U`s then really got underway, beating Wrexham of the Football League Third Division North and then sensationally Huddersfield Town. The Yorkshire club were then in the First Division or what would now be called the Premier League, and in Peter Doherty boasted one of the truly great footballers of the day. They had won three consecutive Football League titles and an FA Cup in the 20`s and whilst glory on that scale was behind them, they were still a force to be reckoned with in the First Division. Now they were to run out at little Layer Road.

A crowd of 16,005 was packed in on 10th January 1948 and amazingly non-league U`s ran out 1-0 winners. It was the first time in the modern history of the FA Cup that a First Division side had been beaten by a non-league team, and suddenly Colchester United were the talk of football nationwide. The press had a field day amidst talk of lucky champagne corks down shorts, Fenton`s F plan tactics and players trained on oysters!

In the Fourth round, Colchester faced Bradford Park Avenue captained by future

England manager Ron Greenwood. They should not be confused with the completely separate club Bradford City. Unfortunately, a magnificent photograph of Ted Fenton addressing the crowd in the immediate aftermath of the match, which currently hangs in the West Stand concourse of United`s current home, does exactly that!

Compared with Huddersfield, Bradford PA were minnows but they were in the Second Division of the Football League, and so should have been too strong for Colchester. This was not to be, as United ran out 3-2 winners and became the first ever non-league club in the modern era to reach the FA Cup Fifth round. All dreams come to an end though, and Colchester`s dream ended in a 5-0 defeat on the Lancashire coast against First Division Blackpool. At this time, Blackpool were one of England`s greatest teams possessing world stars like Stanley Mathews and Stan Mortenson.

It had been an amazing adventure which had captured the imagination of the football world. Ted Fenton had become a celebrity, column inches galore had been dominated in the national press and the U`s had even made their debut on British Pathe News. About as close as it was then possible to get to an appearance on "Match of the Day"!

Despite the distractions of the FA Cup run, Colchester finished the 47/48 season a creditable fourth in the Southern League. Manager Ted Fenton had already tasted the big time as a player at West Ham, and when the opportunity came to return to Upton Park as assistant manager at the end of the season, it was too good to turn down. Within two years, Fenton had become the Hammers manager. He held the post for eleven years, and delivered the 1957/58 Division Two championship which secured top flight football at West Ham for the first time since 1932.

Fenton was known for being mean with money, a trait which must have served him well operating on a limited budget at Colchester. He used to say he had taken a pay cut to join West Ham from Colchester, but maybe that was a negotiating ploy. After joining West Ham, he continued to live in Colchester, and would often travel by train to East London with the Colchester based West Ham player Derek Parker. Parker recalled how Fenton would omit to purchase a ticket "Ted knew that the ticket collector would always start from the back. Halfway through the journey Ted would get out and go to the back".

Colchester were seen as a highly ambitious non-league club. Well set up for, and desperate to attain, Football League status. It was always going to take a good opportunity to tempt Fenton away from Layer Road.

The next man in the hot seat was the former Portsmouth, Aston Villa and England centre half Jimmy Allen. Under his leadership fourth place was achieved for the second season running, while the club were beaten finalists in the Southern League Cup for the third consecutive season.

After the FA Cup glories of 1947/48, hopes were high for another good cup run in 48/49. As a reward for the success of the previous season the U`s were put straight through to the First round proper where they were drawn at home to Reading of the Third Division South, managed by Ted Drake. This is always said to be the occasion of the biggest crowd ever to attend Layer Road. The match was abandoned after 35 minutes due to fog, with the score 1-1. The attendance was given as 19,072 but in fact this was only the number of tickets sold. The number in the ground was much less as many were unable to reach Layer Road because of the fog.

When the game was re-staged Reading won 4-2, in front of the relatively disappointing crowd of only 13,371! In fact, even if all the ticket holders had made it for the first match the ground would not have been full. At that time Layer Road had a capacity of 20,000!

In the wake of the Reading matches one fan felt compelled to write to the Essex County Standard about the lack of sportsmanship amongst the home support. He pointed out that when a Reading player had been hit in the face by the ball, someone had shouted, "serves him right"! Later, when a Colchester player had been injured in a tackle, a cry had gone out, "dirty swine" and "chuck him out"! "Should we have heard the same comments had the positions been reversed?" asked the appalled spectator! He took no comfort in the increasing number of females attending matches, "Their enthusiasm is equalled only by their ignorance of the play". It may have been nearly seventy years ago but perhaps we should still draw a veil over the identity of the correspondent!

The late 40`s and early 50`s were of course the golden age of football. Admission was cheap, and there were few competing activities for the working class man. A shilling could get you into the match, and as long as he had a thick coat, a hat to throw in the air and a woodbine in the corner of his mouth the British male was never seen happier than when supporting his local team. Women were attending in greater numbers as well. This can clearly be seen in the British Pathe footage of the Cup match against Bradford PA.

Crowds of more than 10,000 were common place at Layer Road in the days when the Health and Safety Executive did not exist, and there was no such thing as a Football Stadium safety certificate. But as the 1940`s approached their end, concern was being expressed about falling attendances. Anything below 9,000 was thought to be worrying. Perhaps the excitement created by the 1947/48 Cup run was waning? Or perhaps there was a reduction of interest in non-league achievement? Despite all this, the fact remained that Colchester were one of the nation`s best supported non-league clubs. They were without question the best known, due to that fantastic Cup run. They were ready for the Football League, but did the Football League agree?

After the failure of 1939, there had been two more failed applications for membership.

Due to the war the next opportunity did not come until 1947. No fewer than twenty seven non-league clubs applied for membership, so Colchester were most likely lost in the crowd. The other great problem was that the two clubs relegated from the second division were Newport County and Swansea Town, who would both go into the Third Division South. So there was no real chance of a southern club like Colchester being elevated into that division.

The bottom two clubs in each of Third division North and South were required to retire from the League and seek re-election. Due to the geographical imbalance which would otherwise be created, the Football League Secretary suggested that all four clubs be re-elected en bloc and this was carried with no dissenting voice. More disappointment for Colchester.

Undeterred they tried again in 1948. This time they had the great Cup run to back them and they had been assured of support by Huddersfield, Bradford Park Avenue and Blackpool. Halifax had been struggling in Third Division North on gates sometimes dropping below 3,000. The hope was that Port Vale would be moved from the Southern to the Northern section, in Halifax`s place, thereby opening up a position for Colchester in Third Division South.

One of Ted Fenton`s final acts as Colchester United manager was to prepare the club`s submissions to the Football League. He said the facilities at Layer Road were "well worthy of the high standards set by clubs in the Football League", and that, "we have the largest supporters club in the country with 10,560 members and only three clubs in Essex, Suffolk and Norfolk, an area of 4,500 square miles and a population close to one million".

He went on, "I can assure you that you can place your vote for Colchester United with the firm knowledge that in the event of their election they would uphold the high and sporting traditions of the League".

Again it was a crowd scene as seventeen other clubs applied, about half of whom would most likely have been considered southern. Even Lovell`s Athletic had a go, and they did not even represent a town or city. They were a works team for the Lovells sweet factory of Newport Monmouthshire. It is hard to believe today that such a team could exist in the pro ranks but at that time they were competing in the Southern League and had reached the FA Cup Third round in 1946. Now they wanted League status! They ceased to exist in 1969.

Doncaster Rovers and Millwall had been relegated from the Second Division and clearly that would be one club for each of the northern and southern sections of the Third Division. The only hope for any of the southern clubs seeking entry was that one of Norwich City, or Brighton and Hove Albion, (the bottom two in the Third Division South ) would be consigned to non-league football. It was in fact the second season in a row that Norwich needed to apply for re-election. Despite this there was never much chance of their Football League colleagues voting well supported city clubs like Norwich or Brighton out of the League. All eighteen applying clubs were rebuffed. It did at least get to a vote this time but the four re-applying clubs were overwhelmingly re-elected. Colchester received two votes, Gillingham and Worcester one and the rest none. Brighton and Norwich received forty seven each! U`s Chairman Bill Allen said, "it`s very disappointing but it proves that it`s a cut and dried affair". The whereabouts of Sepp Blatter during this vote is unknown!

Strangely the U`s did not apply in 1949 although eleven non-league clubs did. Aldershot must have been in some peril as they had been struggling in the lower reaches of the Third Division South for a number of years. However they were re-elected as were the other three clubs.

Two things can therefore be seen. Firstly, it was extremely difficult to persuade the existing League clubs to banish one of their brethren. Secondly, there was huge pressure building up below the Football League, where there existed a clutch of clubs as well equipped to compete at Football League level as the clubs already there, and in some cases better equipped.

Furthermore, a club`s chances could be adversely effected by the geographical position of clubs being relegated from above the third tier. Depending upon where the geographical line was drawn, some clubs might have two chances, as they could go into either the northern or southern section. This is illustrated by Mansfield Town, who had to apply for re-election in 1947 after finishing bottom of Third Division South. Their application was successful, but in the following season they found themselves in Third Division North! Clearly they found the northern air more to their liking as they finished eighth in 1947/48.

Under Jimmy Allen, the U`s finished their final season as a Southern League club in the runners up position, pipped to the title on goal average by Merthyr Tydfil. In June 1950 it was time to go "cap in hand" to the annual Football League meeting once again.

By this time no club had been elected to the Football League since Ipswich Town in 1938. The Football League had comprised 88 clubs since 1923. The decision was taken to expand the League by adding two clubs to each of the Third Divisions North and South. Clearly this was a huge opportunity for Colchester United. Regardless of the expansion, the club`s case was starting to look irresistible due to its consistent performance in the Southern League, its level of support and the fact that its Cup exploits had made it known around the world.

Plymouth Argyle, and our old friends Bradford Park Avenue, had been relegated from the Second Division so again that would be one club each for the Southern and Northern sections of the Third Division. All four re-applying clubs were re-elected including the bottom two in the Southern section, Newport County and Millwall, who Colchester would have been targeting. This left ten clubs seeking the two expansion places in the Third Division South.

Clearly Merthyr Tydfil had strong claims having just won the Southern League. In fact in the four seasons since 1946 they had twice been champions, and twice finished third. The two seasons not won by Merthyr had been won by Gillingham. They had dropped out of the Football League in 1938 and had been applying to go back in every year since. In June 1950 their application was into the Football League as usual.

Two other applying clubs had powerful claims for League membership. Peterborough United of the Midland League were a well supported, centrally located club with a good stadium. Yeovil Town had been strong in the Southern League since the war, and like Colchester could boast a recent and spectacular Cup run. In 1949 they matched the U`s achievement in reaching the Fifth round as a non-league club, accounting for First Division Sunderland along the way.

The voting structure was complicated, but in all there were ninety eight votes up for grabs. Llanelly, Cradley Heath, Nuneaton Borough, Worcester City and Chelmsford City were the other southern based clubs applying, the first three of whom garnered no votes at all. Surprisingly Yeovil and Merthyr only managed one vote each. The existing Football League clubs clearly did not fancy a trek west! Peterborough`s performances, in what was a weaker league than the Southern League, were not seen as strong enough for Football League membership at that time as they won only 5 votes. Worcester and Chelmsford had both been strong in the Southern League, and had regularly been applying for Football League membership since the war. However their claims were not seen as strong enough. Chelmsford polled eight votes and Worcester eleven.

The other 72 votes were shared between Gillingham and Colchester with the Kent club coming out on top with 44 of them. There would have been no disappointment at Layer Road about coming second with 28 votes. The dream had become reality. Football League membership had been achieved. It was a dream which probably began in the early 20th century as Football League membership gradually spread south, prior to the birth of Colchester`s professional club in 1937.

As Colchester Town, "The Oysters", ran out to play at their various early homes, and later at Layer Road, membership of the top league must have been dreamt of. However it took professionalism to bring it about, and if the second tier of English football was the ultimate aim, meaning Division Two of the Football League, another massive stride had been taken in that direction.

The formation of a professional club had been the first step. Membership of the Football League had been the second. Now Colchester had to show that, as a town, it could compete with the big boys of the beautiful game. And not just in the occasional Cup match, but over the course of a gruelling season.

Nothing of any worldwide, or even national significance occurred on 19th August 1950. That is unless you count ABC's commencement of Saturday morning children's television, the birth of future royal correspondent and "I'm a celebrity get me out of here" contestant Jennie Bond or the death of Italian Physicist Giovanni Giorgi. The way was therefore left clear for Colchester United's Football League odyssey to begin on that day.

History does not record whether Signore Giorgi hung on long enough to see the U's safely into their Football League world. Nor do we know whether Ms Bond's journalistic enquiring mind had her asking for the football results immediately she appeared. However, it can safely be said that the Giorgi International System of Measurement would not have been required to calculate the score in United's first match. Some of Colchester United's performances over the years have been sufficiently anarchic to form part of children's TV. The defence has certainly been in a tiswas on many occasions, and has had spectators expecting the imminent arrival of the phantom flan flinger and the four bucketeers! Such was not the case on 19th August 1950 when a huge and expectant crowd gathered at Gillingham's Priestfield Stadium to witness a 0-0 draw.

Somehow, whatever passed for a fixture computer in 1950 paired the two new entrants on opening day. United had spent nearly £10,000 on player transfers in preparation for life in the Football League and it was a fairly experienced side which took to the field in Kent that afternoon. The first ever Football League match at Layer Road attracted a crowd of 13,687, and was another tentative affair with no goals against Bristol Rovers. United started with three draws and then went on a run of four consecutive victories which must have had some people already thinking about promotion to the Second Division.

Membership of the supporter's club was now up to 12,000. This included future Prime Minister Anthony Eden, he paid a shilling to join the supporter's club while attending a fete in Castle Park. He was, at the time, trying to take the Conservative Party leadership from Winston Churchill which might explain why he never rose to take office within the Colchester United supporter's club! A standing season ticket for the U's inaugural League season would have set you back £2 and 5 shillings, about £70 in today's money. This was clearly too rich for Mr Eden who was never seen at a match.

Amongst Colchester United's backroom staff as they entered the Football League was one, Mr L.St.Leonard.A.Haug. A Norwegian physiotherapist from Black Notley Hospital.

According to manager Jimmy Allen, this made United the first football club to have a physiotherapist on their staff.

On 15th September 1950, we find a rare early statement about the ambitions of Colchester United. One of the Directors was Alderman C.Harper and he said, "Our ambition must be to get to the Second Division and even eventually the First Division". However, Jimmy Allen had been more circumspect, "I would be very foolish to say we are going to win the Third Division, but I am confident we will worthily uphold the name of Colchester United".

After seven games the U`s were in second place but it did not take long for reality to come crashing in as United could not maintain the consistency required to threaten in the top half. They finished sixteenth which was respectable for a first season, and better than Gillingham who were twenty second. It would have been necessary for them to finish top in order to be promoted. Only two clubs were promoted, and the other would be the Third Division North champions. There were no play offs, and second place got you absolutely nothing except a few extra pounds in prize money and a weight of expectation for the following season. The southern champions were Nottingham Forest, and the thought of Colchester even challenging seriously for promotion was the stuff of fantasy. In 1951/52 they finished tenth. A top half finish which represented very encouraging progress, which was sadly not to be sustained.

1952/53 was the start of three consecutive seasons of struggle for the U`s. Crowds reduced, player`s financial demands increased and the income position of the club worried the cautious directors. Often finding it difficult to match wage expectations, the Board set about a policy of buying up properties which could house players and their families, thereby making it easier for the manager to attract players to the club. The capital value acquired no doubt improved the club`s balance sheet, but ready cash was still at a premium.

A good deal of the optimism of the Southern League years and the first two seasons in the Football League must have been ebbing away during this period. As one looks back over the decades, one can hear the ghosts of 1950`s football fans imploring the club to "speculate to accumulate", or whatever the popular expression of the day was. This is always easier to say than to do, if your own money is invested or if you feel a weight of responsibility not to drive an organisation to a financial wall.

Things got steadily worse as United finished twenty second in 52/53, then twenty third and then ignominiously bottom. At the end of the 52/53 season the Directors wanted a reduction in the playing budget. Supporters, unused to finishing third from bottom of any league were criticising the manager. These things led to the departure of Jimmy Allen the manager who had steered Colchester United into the Football League and through their first three seasons at that level. He never held another management position and died in 1995 at the age of 85. He should, perhaps, hold a more prominent position in the history of Colchester United than he does.

So who would the club turn to in its quest for the holy grail of Second Division football. Or more realistically in its battle for survival in the Third Division South.

We move on to the lovely episode of Ron Meades. One can imagine this cheeky Welshman whistling his optimistic way up Layer Road for his interview to fill the job vacated by Jimmy Allen. Allen had played for many years in the First Division, commanded a huge transfer fee when moving from Portsmouth to Aston Villa, captained his team in the FA Cup final and played for England.

That day Meades was carrying two CV`s in his brief case. The correct one said he had made a handful of first team appearances for Cardiff City during the war years, when League games were suspended and many clubs had difficulty fielding competitive teams for obvious reasons. Subsequently his coaching career, such as it was, had taken him to the football hotbed of Treharris, nestling in a Welsh valley or teetering at the top of a deep mine shaft, depending upon whether you are feeling positive!

Meades then swapped Treharris and the Western League, for Wadebridge Athletic and the South Western League. This sounds like a demotion but, frankly, it`s impossible to know! It seems quite likely that he was chased out of the valleys, and with helmet lamp shining and a face black with South Welsh coal dust, the Wadebridge Athletic committee probably had no idea who they were interviewing. As they would have had no way of paying him, they were probably anxious that he have some means of self support, and seeing him appropriately equipped one imagines him being shoved down a North Cornwall mine and told to emerge only on match day!

It surely must have been a chance to spend some time in daylight which motivated dear Ron to travel to Essex for his interview, rather than any serious belief that he would get the job. One can only wonder what must have been going through the collective minds of the Colchester United Board, when they responded to Meades application by inviting him for interview. It all happened in Coronation week, so perhaps the Board were too eager to have a coronation of their own. Money saving would certainly have been high up the agenda, as 32 year old Meades was offering himself as a player/manager and backed by that vast experience at Cardiff saw no difficulty in making the step up from the South Western League. A level of football which currently resides at the same position in the football pyramid as the Essex and Suffolk Border League!

He must have had something about him though. Having Colchester United`s Board of successful local businessman ranged in front of him must have presented a different challenge from that posed by the Treharris or Wadebridge committees. He must have left his helmet and shovel in Cornwall and dazzled the Layer Road chiefs with the breadth and depth of his experience, and the luminosity of his imagined and exaggerated career.

To the astonishment of all, he was duly presented as the new manager of Colchester United a tenure that lasted precisely four days, during which the Press did some mining of their own. Some uncomfortable facts were dug up, including that Meades had barely ever made the Cardiff first team even in war conditions, and that his coaching career from Treharris and Wadebridge needed some stepping stones before it should land in the Football League.

It must have been more difficult to research a person`s past in 1953 than it is today. A World War is going to make it easier for a person`s antecedents to be shrouded, but even taking these things into account, the Meades episode was not one which did Colchester United any credit.

So Meades was sacked without having taken a match, or even a training session. He was an RAF veteran of the Burma campaign, and took it as calmly as you would expect of such a person. He did not give up. He applied unsuccessfully for a number of Football League management and coaching roles. He eventually landed a job at Ross County (then of the Highland League) where the local press mysteriously announced him as a former England international! He was gone within a week and subsequently worked as a coach for the FA all over the world.

The 1953 Board could not have known it, but a future resident of Wadebridge would be one Andrew Ridgeley who perhaps made as profound a contribution to Wham as Ron Meades did to Colchester United!

Amazingly Meades`s four day tenure at the U`s is not a Football League record. Bill Lambton lasted three days at Scunthorpe in 1959 but did at least take charge of a match. Dave Bassett did the job at Crystal Palace for four days in 1984, before deciding to go back to Wimbledon. The unwanted record, though, is held by Leroy Rosenior, whose second spell at Torquay lasted ten minutes, the time it took for some ownership take-over papers to be completed!

The Layer Road hot seat eventually went to Jack Butler, who, unlike his predecessor, was well qualified, having played at Arsenal for 16 years and being recommended to the club by the famous Arsenal secretary/manager Tom Whitaker. He had previously held two Football League management positions, and had even coached the Belgian national team.

There was to be no immediate improvement in fortunes though. The Meades fiasco had made Colchester seem like a club in crisis, rather than one harbouring realistic ambitions of Second Division football. The 1953/54 and the 54/55 seasons were little short of disastrous. At least the Directors knew where to find the Football League`s annual meeting, as they were forced to apply for re-election after both these seasons.

Being a Colchester United goalkeeper during these dark days must have been challenging, but it could prepare you for higher things. Seventy eight goals were conceded in 53/54, and in an effort to shore up the defence Butler signed a new keeper that summer, one James Kirk from Bury. He played most of the games in 54/55 in which ninety one goals were conceded. He refused to re-sign for 55/56, having presumably been made a better offer by Star Fleet Command!

The U`s had now been in the League for five seasons, during which they twice had to apply for re-election, and in another season avoided that fate by only two points. Hardly a proud record. Second tier football was a million miles away. A return to the Southern League looked far more likely as Peterborough, Yeovil and even Merthyr Tydfil were still pluckily applying every year for Football League membership. There was no question of the League being expanded again, so the only way to accommodate any of these ambitious clubs was to jettison an existing club.

Colchester now became the beneficiaries of the same system which had kept them out of the Football League pre 1950. In both 1954 and 1955 all four clubs seeking re-election were overwhelmingly successful with Colchester garnering 45 and 44 votes respectively. In fact no change in membership was made until 1960 when Peterborough finally got in at the expense of Gateshead.

The club`s struggles had become too much for Jack Butler. He suffered a nervous breakdown and left the club in January 1955. The new manager was Ted Fenton`s 36 year old younger brother Benny, who was coming to the end of a playing career spent mostly in the First Division. He still had a little in the tank though and would be player/manager. He quickly set about re-building the failing squad and twelfth place was achieved in the 1955/56 season.

55/56 had been a vast improvement, but few went into the following season believing that the Second Division was anything other than a distant mirage. In fact, 1956/57 proved to be the U`s best season so far, and one of the few when the dream looked as though it could be realised.

Benny Fenton was a wonderful fit for Colchester United. Bearing a striking resemblance to his elder brother Ted, he was young, energetic and ambitious. After a short amateur spell with Colchester Town, he had played his early career in the Second Division with West Ham and Millwall, before getting his big break in the top flight with Charlton at the age of 29. This was one of Charlton`s most successful periods, and Fenton was a first team regular for nearly eight years and eventually captain.

Bernard Webber`s excellent book "The Way U`s Were" carries many personal recollections of this time, and he says "Benny and Ted were direct opposites. Ted was tall and debonair, while Benny was stocky, excitable, quick witted and streetwise. As a player he was hard as nails, a dynamic wing half who never spared himself. Invariably, he angered rival fans, who barracked him non-stop. He often fell foul of officials. He was a cross between Vinnie Jones and Dennis Wise". It is interesting that this might also be a description of Phil Parkinson!

Despite having no obvious connection with anything north of Watford Gap, he had a scouting network across the Scottish non-league scene which seemed to be able to turn up players suitable for the English Third Division at the drop of a hat. John Fowler, Sammy McLeod, Bobby Hill and Chic Milligan were all sourced in this way, and were all major influences on the successful 56/57 campaign.

He made other excellent signings. Full back George Fisher had been very successful at Millwall and arrived rather portly from a short unsuccessful spell at Fulham. Fenton`s fitness campaign soon sorted him out, and he went on to make 164 appearances for the U`s including 46 during 56/57. Eddie Smith stayed at Layer Road for less than a year but scored 13 vital goals in this campaign. In November Fenton boosted the squad with winger Tommy Williams from non-league Carshalton. He went on to make 150 appearances for the U`s over five years before tragically dying at the age of 32.

Fenton spent next to nothing in assembling the squad, but very few of his signings disappointed.He showed how well he could work with young players, developing home grown talent such as Russell Blake, Brian Dobson,Trevor Harris and Ron Hunt into useful squad members while Peter Wright blossomed under him to such an extent that he was coveted by much bigger clubs.In Ken Plant, Reg Stewart, Kevin McCurley, Bert Hill and Bob Dale he inherited some experienced players who flourished under him.

His last line of defence was Percy Ames who had been a fringe goalkeeper at Tottenham. He found a home at Colchester, where what he lacked in height he made up for with agility and speed of thought. Fenton signed Ames for the start of the 55/56 season and he went on to make over 400 appearances for the club missing only a handful of games until his departure in 1965. At the heart of it all was the midfield driving force that was Benny Fenton.

The first half dozen games were steady if unspectacular but they heralded four consecutive wins during which twelve goals were scored. This included a 3-1 win over Southampton who had come to Layer Road top of Third Division South. Results continued to be encouraging despite a 3-1 reverse at Alf Ramsey`s Ipswich Town in front of over

20,000 on 6th October. The U`s took three points out of four from struggling Norwich City on Christmas and Boxing day and by the turn of the year were handily positioned in the top half.

In fact the 5-1 home win over Northampton on 22nd December was the start of a remarkable and record breaking twenty game unbeaten run which took the U`s, unbelievably, to the top of the table. This sequence included a home match with third placed Ipswich on 16th February in front of 18,559. Layer Road`s highest ever attendance, taking account of the ticket holders who failed to negotiate the fog for that Reading match in 1948.

It is likely that significantly more were in the ground for the Ipswich match. There were people on the stand roofs and up trees. It is estimated that about 4,000 were locked outside and turned away and many were thought to have got in without passing through the turnstiles. It finished 0-0 but only because Benny Fenton had a penalty saved. Colchester fans were convinced it should have been re-taken because Ipswich keeper Roy Bailey moved before the ball was kicked.

This match has gone down in folklore for a number of reasons. The myth goes that Fenton missed the penalty deliberately, because Colchester could not afford the financial demands of Second Division football. It goes on that Ipswich took the one and only promotion place from Colchester, due to the point dropped in this match. A fork in the road which took Ipswich into the higher reaches of European football, and left Colchester in the doldrums.

This is all rubbish. Whether or not he moved early, Bailey made a magnificent save, diving to his left to finger tip the ball onto the post. Hardly something Fenton could have manufactured. It occurred as early as the twenty first minute, so there was plenty of time for other things to alter the course of the match.

It is true that the season ended in heart break for United, who finished third with 58 points, one point behind both Torquay and the champions Ipswich who were promoted through having the superior goal average. A win in that match would have leapfrogged Colchester over Ipswich, and taken them to the top, and Second Division football, because their goal average was better than Torquay. However, there were thirteen more matches to play after the Ipswich game and some vital points were dropped.

In the next home match, promotion rivals Torquay were beaten 2-1 to send the U`s into raptures. It was then only two points for a win and they were now four points clear at the top. Four points clear in March! How likely would that have seemed during those black days of 1952 to 1955! Only seven years earlier Colchester were playing non-league football. Now they had Division Two in touching distance.

The twenty match unbeaten run, which started in mid December, went on until 20th

April when a visit to Millwall brought defeat. However, nine of those matches had been drawn, and this, along with the fact that three of the last four games were lost, meant United could not stay at the top. Those three defeats had all been against sides in the bottom half, and this is ultimately what cost fulfilment of the dream. A draw in one of those games, and Colchester would have missed out on goal average behind Ipswich. Two draws or one win from those three games would have brought the Second Division to Layer Road.

Twenty years earlier, the former Councillior, now Major Gerald.C.Benham had presided over the meeting called to decide whether Colchester should have a professional club. He was now club President and was forced to deny rumours that Colchester United had not wanted promotion, "I would take this opportunity to contradict the rumour as emphatically as possible. There is not a word of truth in it. If you go in a League you try to win and that is what we will be trying to do next season".

Although one cannot blame the outcome of one match, it is difficult not to compare the fortunes of Ipswich Town and Colchester United in the aftermath of this eventful season. Four years later, Ipswich were being promoted to the First Division, while Colchester were being relegated to the Fourth. Another year on and Ipswich were the Football League champions.

Was this because Benny Fenton missed a penalty? Or was it because Ipswich had a larger population, and a larger and fantastically well appointed stadium capable of immediate development, which was set up for top flight football? A package which allured not only Suffolk folk but also people from Cambridgeshire, Essex, Hertfordshire and beyond, in an age when the football fan was more mobile and perhaps lacking in local pride. He was much less likely to be chaining his bicycle to the nearest railing.

Against this, Colchester could only fight back with Third and Fourth Division football from a stadium some way out of town and which was looking tired even in the late 50`s.

Whatever the reasons, the healthy rivalry which Colchester fans felt towards Ipswich Town grew into complete contempt, born of jealousy. While planning their next trip around England`s and Europe`s premier football venues, Ipswich fans looked back with disdain, unable to notice Colchester United enough to dislike them. Ipswich fans refusal to hate Colchester only made Colchester fans hate Ipswich even more, and they had a very long time to wait before they could exact revenge.

After the excitement of the previous season 1957/58 was always likely to seem like an anti climax. After coming so close to Second Division football the U`s now knew it was possible. Ipswich had gone, and the new club in the division was Port Vale. The Division therefore looked no stronger than it had been in 56/57 but some key players moved on or retired, and it quickly became clear that promotion was not going to be a realistic aim. However it was vitally important to achieve a top half finish because change was in the air in the Football League.

In 1956 there had been a number of proposals for re-organisation. Colchester United were in favour of maintaining regionalisation at Third Division level and backed a plan for there to be a Midland section added, which would have admitted a raft of the ambitious clubs still knocking at the Football League door every year. It would also have kept down travelling costs, an important consideration for small clubs like Colchester.

The alternative was the scrapping of regionalisation in favour of one nationwide Third Division and a nationwide Fourth Division. Apart from the travelling costs point, it is not difficult to see why this was not a popular proposal at Layer Road. The club were aiming at the Second Division and this proposal carried too great a risk of being dragged further away from that promised land.

No other country in the world had nationwide football below its second tier, but the post war boom was under way. We had "never had it so good". Post war austerity had been relaxed, and people were travelling. Britain's first motorways were being planned. We saw ourselves as world leaders in football, so why should we not have the world's first nationwide Third and Fourth tiers. The nationwide proposal carried the day, and regionalisation in the Football League was gone for good.

The new Third Division would comprise those clubs finishing 1957/58 in the top half of the Third Division North and Third Division South. The bottom half clubs would form the new Fourth Division. Undiluted by regionalisation, the new Third Division would be stronger than the old northern and southern sections but there would be two promotion places.

All this meant that a bottom half finish in 1957/58 would seem like relegation. The Second Division, which had just been at Colchester's fingertips, would seem as far away psychologically as some of the U's new opponents would be geographically.

It came down to the last game. The U's had been around mid table all season and went into their final match twelfth out of twenty four, one point ahead of Northampton. Both sides faced tough final matches. Colchester were at home to sixth placed Southampton, while the Cobblers would visit eighth placed Southend on the following day. United could not afford to lose and, perhaps, with more to play for than the Saints ran out 4-2 winners. They could once again aim at the Second Division in 1958/59.

Things started to look rosy in early 1959. It was the new Third Division, and a top two finish would deliver Second Division football. By the end of February the U's had eased into third place. However, they were seven points from second place, which was going to be difficult to make up under two points for a win. Unfortunately, United never threatened to do it. Their season was ended by losing five consecutive games in March, although they still managed to finish in a very respectable fifth place. It would be twenty one years before there was another serious flirtation with promotion to the Second Division.

There were disastrous relegations to the Fourth Division in 1960/61, 1964/65, 1967/68 and 1975/76. Each time they were relegated the U`s managed to get back to the Third Division fairly quickly, thereby earning the tag of a Yo-Yo club. It was often exciting stuff, but it did not look like delivering Second Division football.

Managers came and went. Benny Fenton gave way to ex England international Neil Franklin. The 1968 relegation did for him, and the former Crystal Palace, Orient and Walsall manager Dick Graham became the club`s second ex goalkeeper manager. There were some fantastic cup days under him, but his brief was a return to the Third Division and he was never quite able to fulfil it.

There were severe financial restrictions for the 1972/73 season, and Graham was forced to field many untried youngsters. After four seasons of being marooned in the Fourth Division, but at least looking like candidates for promotion, Colchester were now in unfamiliar territory near the bottom of the fourth. Finishing third from bottom, it was back to the Football League annual meeting to seek re-election.

Could all the hard work of the previous twenty five years be undone? Were Colchester to find themselves in the fifth tier of English football, when they were supposed to be aiming for the second? Ten non-league clubs were applying to get in. These included Wimbledon, Wigan Athletic and dear old Yeovil. Still there. Still friendless. Applying almost every year, and usually achieving no votes. They would have had a better chance if they had acquired Norwegian nationality and entered the Eurovision song contest!

In fact, Yeovil were a successful non-league club who would finally achieve Football League status in 2003, after the discredited election system had been consigned to history. One might have thought that 1980 would have sounded the death knell for that system. That year Altrincham thought they were in at the expense of Rochdale, as they were sure they had won the votes of Grimsby Town and Luton Town. However the final result was 26 votes to Rochdale and only 25 to Altrincham. It transpired that the Grimsby delegate had forgotten to vote while the Luton representative had returned from lunch too late to vote!

Automatic promotion and relegation between the bottom of the Football League and the top of non-league was finally introduced in 1987. In 1973 Colchester had nothing to fear, winning forty eight votes they easily maintained League status.

Next in the hot seat was "the bald eagle" Jim Smith. Something seemed to be building under him. He achieved promotion to the Third Division in his first full season. No mean achievement after the pitiful 72/73 season. 74/75 was about consolidation and eleventh place in the Third Division was quite satisfactory and seen as a launching pad for a real assault on the Second Division in the following season especially as the top three were now promoted.

In October 1974 Smith replied to a letter of encouragement from the author of this book, saying "we can go forward to the Second Division together". Eight months later he became the manager of Blackburn Rovers. It can be difficult to be a Colchester United fan!

Assistant Manager Bobby Roberts was elevated to the top job, but he presided over a slump as United returned to Division Four in 1976. It is now unusual for a relegated manager to avoid the sack, but the U`s remained loyal to Roberts, and this was rewarded with an immediate return to the Third Division followed by two decent top half finishes. Any serious hope of getting to the Second Division in either of those two seasons failed to outlast the Christmas decorations. Injuries and a lack of goal power saw to that, as the economic realities of the U`s existence bit.

Attendances had been steadily declining since the late 50s, and, in an age where financial clout was increasingly dictating league success, United never seemed to have much wealth on the Board. The club`s record transfer fee paid had been set in 1957 and stood until Paul Aimson arrived from Bournemouth in 1973. He cost £8,000, gargantuan by Colchester United`s standards but small change to almost every other club in the League.

This led to accusations of the club lacking ambition, and in response United were becoming more open as to what their plans were. How far United could go had always been discussed by fans. Assuming an absence of unprescribed drugs and a blood alcohol content under 30% (neither of which can be assumed of U`s fans especially after defeat by Southend) most would have described a glass ceiling around mid-table in the Second Division.

For the club, it seemed obvious that ambition was linked to the stadium. In the early 70s serious discussion about re-developing Layer Road or moving to a new stadium began. These discussions got as far as realising they would cost money. At this point, the Board would turn to the Finance Director. He would shake the club`s porcelain pig, and would have to report no audible sound beyond the rustle of unpaid bills and County Court summonses. The club did have the advantage of owning its own stadium, but as this came with a covenant preventing the building of houses, there wasn`t much that could be done with it except play football.

Nevertheless, the club gamely published an ambition to reach the Second Division. "Layer Road Larry" was seen in the official programme, striding purposely at the head of "U`s drive to Division Two". It was notable that this cartoon character lacked a route map and a wallet, but at the end of 1977 Chairman Jack Rippingdale was saying "our plan for the future is geared to the Second Division". A year later he was more strident," The Board and I really want Second Division football, make no mistake about that. It's always been our objective".

These were laudable statements, as there is little doubt that a perceived lack of ambition had been keeping people away from Layer Road for years. And they were not just words. Real efforts were being made to increase the club's commercial income, and that transfer fee paid record had been almost doubled. In December 1977 £15,000 was paid for Eddie Rowles from Darlington and within twelve months this had been matched twice with the acquisitions of Bobby Hodge and Trevor Lee. Admittedly, similar sums had been received for the sale of players, but at least incoming money was going on player acquisition instead of the funding of debt.

Let us not get the wrong idea though. Colchester United had been "spending big". But only by the standards of Colchester United. Going into the 1979/80 season it had been common for Third Division clubs to be spending six figure sums on players such as Blackpool who acquired striker Tony Kellow for £125,000. The U's could not even be in the market for such players. However, they were now going into their fourth consecutive Third Division season and were aiming to go up.

The squad going into the 1979/80 season had an experienced look about it. A healthy percentage had developed through the club's youth ranks. Some of these were still untried but in Steve Leslie, Steve Foley, Steve Dowman and Ian Allinson the club could boast proven Third Division performers who were home grown. The latter two were being tracked by top clubs. In addition, defender Steve Wright came through the youth ranks to make thirty three appearances during that season.

Micky Cook had been with the club for almost his entire career, and was undoubtedly one of the best full backs at Third Division level. The remainder of the defence was made up by Steve Wignall, Mick Packer and goalkeeper Mike Walker, all of whom had "been round the block". Leslie and Foley were in midfield, and width was provided by Allinson and Hodge. Rowles, Lee and Bobby Gough usually carried out striking duties.

At this time Colchester were in the middle of a truly amazing appearance record from their goalkeepers. Walker was the Percy Ames of his day. Signed from Watford for the 1973/74 promotion season he went on to miss only nine matches in ten seasons before retiring with 522 Colchester United appearances to his name. Alec Chamberlain took over from Walker and he played in every League and Cup match for four seasons before being transferred to Everton.

So in fourteen seasons of League and Cup matches the Colchester United goalkeeper was either Walker or Chamberlain in all but five matches! Being the number two goalkeeper at Colchester United during this time, you were about as likely to be seen as a white rhino!

Bobby Roberts was never one of the more popular or charismatic Colchester United managers. He came over as a dour Scotsman and he believed in building a team from the back. The highlight of his playing career had been representing Leicester City in the 1969 FA Cup final. By 1979 he had, like most of the squad, been at Layer Road for a while, joining as number two to Jim Smith in 1973. Although he had started his time as manager with a relegation, he had been given and had taken the opportunity to quickly turn this round. He had followed this with two consolidatory seasons in the Third Division and with a small amount of financial backing and that other precious resource, time, had assembled a squad which looked capable challenging near the top. It was, however, a small squad. Such depth as existed was provided by youngsters, so minimal injuries and suspensions would be vital to success.

After a steady start, things slowly picked up. A 2-1 win at promotion rivals Sheffield United on 9th October was the start of four consecutive wins, which propelled the U`s to second place. Although results then dropped off a little, the U`s were proving difficult to beat. It was two points for a win and one for a draw, so draws were more valuable than they are today. At the turn of the year nineteen of their twenty five games had produced points, and they were in the promotion zone at third place.

Proving to be the masters of tight one goal wins, United hit the top with a 2-1 Friday night home win over struggling local rivals Southend. After the following day`s games the U`s dropped back to second, but it was 23rd February, and they were still four points into the promotion zone. A quarter of the season to go, and a strong finish would bring the Second Division to Colchester. Sadly this is not what happened.

The next seven matches produced only one win, and United had dropped to fifth after the 2-2 draw at Gillingham on 5th April. They were now six points outside the promotion zone. A season of great promise effectively finished on 19th April when, following defeat at Chester, United were unable to muster a goal at home to twelfth placed Millwall. There were still three games left, but no permutation of results could produce a top three finish. Colchester finished fifth, six points from promotion.

It had been an excellent season, but when a grandstand finish was needed the U`s spluttered. The Second Division continued to shimmer over a horizon that United just could not reach.

Perhaps the most notable feature of the season had not been the results, but the attendances. Colchester had been in the promotion mix all through the season, but the only time when Layer Road had seen respectable gates was when the opposition brought a big following. The average was a pitiful (considering the league position) 3,818. On 2nd

April, with the promotion race raging only 2,780 turned up for a Wednesday night clash with Exeter.

This was a time when Ipswich Town were permanent features in the top five of the First Division, as well as enjoying Cup success. Home matches rarely clashed, but Third Division fare clearly did not appeal when one of the best teams in Europe were so close. Members of Colchester`s footballing public who did not fancy Portman Road would often choose a trip to London over Layer Road`s tumbledown terraces.

So it was against this background that Colchester United entered the 80s trying to plot a course to the Second Division. Sadly the course could not be found, and the rocks of relegation were soon hit, before the ship completely foundered at the end of the decade.

Some say the 1980s was a bad decade for music. It was even worse for Colchester United.

Personnel changes were minimal for the 1980/81 season, with the only significant loss being Steve Dowman who was transferred to Wrexham. Trevor Lee departed half way through the season, quickly followed by Bobby Hodge and Bobby Gough, but some good player acquisitions were made and it was therefore difficult to understand why it was such a season of struggle. A repeat of the promotion challenge was never on the agenda, but some poor early season form appeared to have been rectified.

When Colchester beat top of the table Charlton at the end of February, they rose to twelfth position. Boring compared with the previous season, but no need for alarms. Disastrously, the next ten games produced one win and seven defeats. They also produced Fourth Division football, which was confirmed with a 1-0 defeat at Newport in the penultimate game.

For the next seven seasons Colchester tried to re-gain Third Division status, and looked likely candidates to do so. They usually fell victim to a slump in form after Christmas. Never finishing outside the top ten, sixth place seemed to be their preferred position of near miss failure. By 1982/83 it was 3 points for a win and the U`s finished sixth only two points from the promotion zone.

Changes of manager increased in frequency. The failure to get back to the Third accounted for Bobby Roberts in 1982. He was replaced by the former Ipswich and Northern Ireland centre half Allan Hunter, but he only lasted nine months. Deeply effected by the suicide of striker John Lyons, he decided management was not for him and resigned. In came Cyril Lea, another ex-Ipswich man. He struggled manfully against financial restrictions to maintain the U`s in the upper reaches of the Fourth Division, but could not deliver promotion.

Lea lasted until 1986, when he was sacked by the club`s new owner Jonathan Crisp.

Crisp had bought a controlling interest in the club ten months before. He was described as a "millionaire businessman". His background was in marketing. His stated aim was to get Colchester United to the Second Division within 5 years, and it appeared as though his regime would bring financial backing never previously seen at Layer Road.

Sadly, the early promise was not fulfilled. His links with the locality seemed tenuous, and his interest in the club appeared opportunistic. He did not court popularity and did not receive it. It transpired that part of his investment was in the form of a loan, which seemed to threaten rather than improve the club`s solvency.

While there was no doubt that Crisp meant well, it seemed that the harder he tried, the more he failed. There were a series of bizarre initiatives, such as the sacking of Lea`s replacement and club legend Mike Walker. He had just presided over a run of six wins and a draw from seven games, which had seen the team rise from twenty second to sixth and Walker named as manager of the month. In the previous season under Walker, United had finished fifth and qualified for the Play Offs which had been introduced that season, where they lost to Wolves.

Then there was the membership scheme, by which anyone attending a game had to be a club member. This was intended to combat hooliganism and reduce Police costs by banning away fans. It alienated an already small fan base, and reduced crowds to unheard of levels which still look embarrassing in the club`s statistics now.

In his defence, Crisp said that financially he had rescued the club from oblivion and that if he walked away it would die. There may have been some truth in this. Crisp eventually left a disillusioned, and much poorer man, having honoured his pledge to get the club out of the Fourth Division, unfortunately at the wrong end. He has since emigrated and become involved in professional golf. He was a Director of the Australian PGA, and perhaps surprisingly his "linkedin" CV continues to quote his time at Colchester United. It was reported that he tried to get involved in a bid to save the Australian club Gold Coast United. That club was dissolved in 2012.

During all this time a number of plans to build a new stadium, or rebuild the Layer Road stadium, were developed and scrapped in the absence of finance, planning permission or both.

Crisp felt that Roger Brown was the man to address what he perceived as Walker`s unsatisfactory performance. Plucked from the manager`s chair at non-league Poole Town, Brown had enjoyed a decent playing career at Bournemouth, Norwich and Fulham. He made a promising start at Layer Road, but things quickly slid into a decline, and he resigned after an 8-0 defeat at Orient. Arguably the worst single result in the club`s history.

There have been a number of low points during the writer`s time as a Colchester

United fan. However, nothing can beat the tragicomedy of seeing Mark Walton and Steve Cartwright on their posteriors in the back of Colchester's net, accompanied by the ball on that bleak October day in East London. I think it was the sixth goal, but few U's fans were counting by that time.

We watched in disbelief as the ball seemed to develop a magnetic attraction for the back of our net! Believe it or not it was eleven v eleven for the whole match. It may be a cliché, but we were actually lucky to get nil!

With the U's staring at relegation out of the League, Jock Wallace rode into town as the club's fourth ex goalkeeper manager in January 1989. He was a big name, and a charismatic figure. He had done National Service in the jungles of Malaya, and so was not to be trifled with. A journey man pro, he had hit the headlines as the player-manager of the Berwick Rangers side which had knocked Glasgow Rangers out of the Scottish Cup.

He would later become the manager at Ibrox Park, where he won hero status to the blue half of Glasgow by ending Celtic's nine consecutive years as champions. Under him, Rangers were champions in 1975, 1976 and 1978, winning the treble in the latter two seasons.

After a spell managing the big Spanish club Sevilla, Wallace was living in contented retirement under the Spanish sun. Somehow, Jonathan Crisp persuaded him to swap this for a Fourth Division relegation fight in Essex. As a proud Scot, he was less than happy to find the team captained by Tony English! He arrived with the U's rock bottom, and immediately set about galvanising the team and the public. Gates increased by more than 50%, and results went with them.

The effect was not immediate, however, and when United took on Wrexham on 25th April they were four points adrift at the bottom. The last five matches were all won, and Colchester escaped relegation comfortably. It seemed that Mr Crisp had finally done something right. We were now four years into his five year plan to achieve the Second Division, and had just escaped dropping into the fifth tier, but it seemed a revival was happening.

Alas this was not sustained. The awful 80s had not yet finished with Colchester United. Wallace's health was failing, and he left in December 1989 to be replaced by the ex Ipswich and England full back Mick Mills. The club's finances were dire, and it was clear that Crisp was fed up with being sniped at by fans, former directors and just about anyone with an opinion. He was unable, or unwilling, to sink any further funds into the bottomless hole that was Colchester United. The team lacked experience, spark and organisation.

The 1988/89 season had been the worst ever. Worse than those three seasons in the early 50s. Worse than the 1972/73 season. There was no longer any comical re-election process to provide redemption. Bottom now meant automatic relegation out of the

Football League. The 1989/90 season turned out to be worse still. This time there would be no Rob Roy character riding to the rescue.

The decline, which had started with the worsening financial situation in the early 80s heralding the jinxed regime of Jonathan Crisp, finally reached its nadir on 29th April 1990 with a 4-0 defeat at Cambridge. Colchester United were a non-league club again. They finished bottom, six points from Halifax Town and another unlikely escape. To be honest, there had been an inevitability about it all season.

Target Second Division? The question now was, would the U`s survive at all? To his credit, Crisp announced that the club would continue to use full time professional players. Less helpfully, he informed the football world that this would make the club`s immediate return to the League little more than a formality. Something that was taken as a challenge by every other club in the U`s new home, the GM Vauxhall Conference.

It did not happen. United, now managed by another former Ipswich defender Ian Atkins, were pipped to the Conference title by Barnet, and Crisp finally found a way out of what must have become a personal nightmare, claiming that it had cost him a million pounds. Atkins also departed.

Without a receptacle into which to relieve itself, and no longer even owing its own stadium, the club cast around for a new manager. It must have been an attractive prospect! Fourteen players, a transfer fee war chest of £640, and a weight of expectation that would be satisfied by nothing except the Vauxhall Conference championship.

One of those players had some grey hairs and seemed to have been around the game for quite a while. Since the club could not afford to bring in a proper manager, this experienced head was the obvious choice.

Roy McDonough had indeed "been around a bit". He had been a disappointed man ever since not quite making it at the top level with either Birmingham City or Chelsea. Now nearing 33, he had spent the ensuing years taking out his disappointment on the ankles and chins of Third and Fourth Division defenders, including a previous spell at Layer Road in the early 80s. His chief qualifications for the job, were that he was already here and was prepared to work with, and for, next to nothing. For these qualities the new Layer Road board were prepared to overlook the reputation McDonough had forged as a drinker, womaniser, red card collector and general abuser of almost anyone he came into contact with. Not always on the right side of the law, he had once emerged from a particularly long drinking session in Colchester town centre to find that a market stall had been built around his car!

When asked for his tactical masterplan he said it was "to win the league in style by getting more goals than any other f****r". His assessment of the GM Vauxhall Conference was that it was a "Mickey Mouse league packed full of posties, washing machine repair men and pub players". So there was never any chance of the U`s being overawed in their second Conference season. He would need a number Two. Former U`s player Ian Phillips was prepared to put a few hours in when his proper job with the Gas Board allowed!

So it was with this level of professionalism that United joined battle in a mini league with the far better resourced Wycombe Wanderers, one of the few Conference clubs aside from Colchester with serious Football League ambitions. Much to the surprise of the football world, McDonough`s brand of management proved to be very effective as the non-league double of Vauxhall Conference title and FA Trophy were won.

In the unlikely hands of Roy McDonough, a revival was taking place at Layer Road. Those hands more normally seen clasping a pint of lager, or in the shape of a fist, had nurtured and manipulated a rag tag bag of free transfer misfits into champions. The forehead that was typically posed in the face of an opponent, had taunted and outthought all that the Conference could put in front of him, including the "great" Martin O`Neil.

The team was winning again. The club was back in the hands of local businessmen. The fans once more felt part of the club and they were coming in good numbers, over 25,000 travelling to Wembley for the Trophy final. We felt good about ourselves. Now, where were we with that Second Division plan?

Colchester were back in the Football League. They were in Division Three, but let us not forget that by now the Murdoch dollar had spoken and the Premier League had been born. Division Three was therefore the Fourth tier of English football. The dream was two promotions away.

Peter Heard was now becoming the major influence in the running of the club, and under his calm and methodical stewardship the U`s firmly established themselves back in the League with five out of six top half finishes, and no more flirtations with relegation. In 1995/96 they finished seventh and qualified for the Play Offs being edged out by Neil Warnock`s Plymouth Argyle. The only slight blip was 1993/94 when they finished seventeenth and McDonough`s reign ended. This was followed by the short lived tenure of George Burley, after which former U`s centre half Steve Wignall returned as manager.

In 1997/98 a big step was taken towards the second tier, when promotion was achieved through the Play Offs. United emerged victorious from exciting Play Off semi finals against Barnet, before beating Torquay 1-0 at Wembley. The club were back at third tier level for the first time since 1981. In the intervening years there had been big changes in football, none of which benefitted the smaller clubs.

Match day proceeds were no longer shared. Since 1919, it had been the rule that 20% of gate money went to the visiting club. This recognised that the better supported clubs needed opposition in order to put a match on. The away team were therefore part of the attraction and should receive something from the gate. It also promoted good competition by spreading football`s profits around. This was scrapped in 1983.

The advent of satellite TV in the early 90s introduced huge and growing sums into the game, which were concentrated at the top level. This also attracted all kinds of commercial income to the bigger clubs.

Then there was the Bosman case. This began life in the Belgian courts, but finished as a ruling of the EU Tribunal in 1995. It allowed players greater freedom of movement. Players aged over 24 could now move to another club when their contract had finished without a transfer fee being payable.

Transfer fee income had long been a staple of many smaller clubs. A fee could be demanded for an in demand player who wanted to leave. This could help to keep clubs afloat and/or be invested in a replacement player. Not anymore. Much of the money which had circulated as transfer fees now ended in the pockets of players and agents.

Colchester had always looked like a small fish when at third tier level, but these developments had transformed a gap into a gulf and then a chasm. In the 1998/99 season they had to find a way to compete with clubs the size of Preston, Stoke and Reading. In addition, Manchester City were in Division Two that season, one of the biggest clubs ever to compete at this level. Finally, there was the little matter of Fulham funded by Mohammed Al Fayed!

Promotion to the second tier was out of the question. Survival was the only realistic ambition.

It was a daunting prospect, and Wignall walked half way through the season, worried about a relegation appearing on his CV and frustrated by the financial demands of Bosman liberated players. Mick Wadsworth came in and made some good short term signings which got the U`s out of the relegation zone to finish eighteenth. He left early the next season, following disagreements over budgets.

Steve Whitton was promoted to the hot seat, and managed the not inconsiderable feat of keeping Colchester United at third tier level despite the financial restrictions. In 1999/00 the U`s repeated 18th position and this was followed by seventeenth and fifteenth in the next two seasons. Small improvements, but at no time did promotion look possible, nor was it ever mentioned as a serious aim.

When Whitton was replaced by Phil Parkinson, the new man was not told that his job was to get the club promoted to the second tier. If such a notion was ever discussed at Layer Road, it was never made public. Some things are just too outrageous to be the subject of conversation between serious people!

Chapter 6

# NO SIGN
# OF THINGS
# TO COME

# Chapter 6
## NO SIGN OF THINGS TO COME

In the summer of 2005, Phil Parkinson was looking forward to his third full season in charge at Layer Road. For the fans, the previous season had been a slight disappointment. The progress of Parkinson's early days had not been sustained. At least that was how it appeared. The U's had finished 04/05 four places lower than the previous season. For nine consecutive seasons before that, starting with 1996/97, the U's finishing position had been better than the year before.

There were expectations among fans, but they were not out of control. Most would have been satisfied with being just above half way and having another cup run. The fear was that the four places dropped would herald a slide back into the familiar territory of a relegation fight. Most fans recognised that Layer Road attendances were such that the club was punching above its weight, just being in Football League 1. Accordingly, most bookies saw Colchester as likely relegation fodder.

In view of the downward trajectory the club seemed to be on, one might have expected a flurry of inward transfer activity during that summer. The ship appeared to have leaks which needed to be plugged. However, almost all movement that summer was outward.

It was farewell to old favourites Gavin Johnson, Joe Keith and Bobby Bowry, all of whom had been instrumental in helping to keep the U's at third tier level for a number of seasons. Ryan Jarvis had returned to his parent club, and Jamie Cade was released.

The case of Ramon Calliste illustrated the recruitment problem the U's were often up against. A youngster being released by Manchester United, he arrived as a trialist and quickly stirred interest with some impressive performances in pre season. He saw Colchester as a good place to kick start his career, and he seemed capable of providing some much needed flair to the U's front line. It looked a perfect fit. Then his agent learned of United's reluctance to deal with agents and their outright refusal to pay them. The club was informed by the agent that, if it did not pay the agent's fee, the player (who appeared to have no say in the matter) would be going elsewhere. There was no budging Peter Heard, and it was farewell Ramon.

His is a sad story. A Welsh Under 21 international, he had been labelled the best thing to come out of Cardiff since Ryan Giggs. A measure of how highly he was rated is that he signed for Liverpool after the Colchester move broke down, but however tempting a move back to a big club must have been what he actually needed was to get his career started with some first team football. Predictably he got nowhere at Anfield and had brief spells at Brentford, Cambridge City, Farnborough, Newport, Swansea, Staines, Wycombe and Lincoln, before a trial spell at Scunthorpe ended with a serious ankle injury in a pre season friendly. He was last heard of playing for West London Saracens in the Middlesex County League! His agent no doubt lost interest in him a long time ago, and we will never know whether he might have become one of the many players who have been able to get a foothold in the game at Colchester.

The one piece of inward business which the press had to write about that summer, was the acquisition of old fashioned centre forward Chris Iwelumo. The son of a Nigerian father and Scots mother, twenty seven year old Iwelumo had come through the youth ranks at St.Mirren. From there he moved into the Danish Super League with Aarhus, before making his first foray into England with Stoke City.

Iwelumo never fully established himself at Stoke but was always in or around the first team and making sufficient appearances to attract regular interest from other clubs. Stoke liked him enough to give him a second two year contract, and he had loan spells at York, Cheltenham and Brighton, helping the latter achieve promotion from League Two. In the summer of 2004, he turned down the advances of Phil Parkinson to make a second excursion abroad. This time it was the German second division with Alemania Aachen. The move did not work out, and after one year he wanted to return to the UK. Having kept close tabs on him, Parky pounced.

Iwelumo arrived saying, "This is such an important season for me. I`ve been given a big opportunity by the club and I`m determined to take full advantage"

Parkinson refused to be drawn on the club`s prospects for the season, he said "the only thing I`m focussed on is the first game. I`m not looking beyond that at the moment."

Of the twenty four clubs starting the 2005/06 season in League One, only Colchester United and two others had never played above that level. Yeovil Town had only been a League club for two seasons, so in real terms it was only Colchester and Hartlepool United who had never been as high as the second tier.

Where could the main competition be expected to come from? Amongst the favourites to do well in League One that season were **Huddersfield Town**. Financial troubles had held them back for years, but they had emerged from administration in 2003, and under highly rated manager Peter Jackson had gained promotion from League Two a year later. With a big and noisy following they looked like a Championship club in waiting.

**Swansea City** looked much the same. This would be their first season in the new £27M Liberty Stadium. They almost dropped out of the League in 2003, but finished their time at the Vetch Field with promotion. Now, after many years on the edge of financial extinction as one ownership consortium squabbled with another, they finally looked like a club destined for big things.

**Bristol City** had just missed the play offs in 2004/05 and would be throwing a good budget at 05/06. This much was apparent from their capture of Marcus Stewart and Michael Bridges, both replete with top flight experience. Stewart was expected to be a prolific striker in League One, having just helped Sunderland into the Premier League with seventeen goals.

Clubs just relegated from the higher division are often strong contenders to bounce back. **Rotherham United** was one of these, but no-one expected much from them as they had all kinds of financial woes and even occupation of their stadium was under threat. **Gillingham** had been badly effected by the ITV digital collapse and needed to spend substantial sums on the refurbishment of their stadium. Perhaps their ability to mount a strong promotion challenge is best put in perspective by the fact that their electricity supply was cut off during the season due to the fact that they owed EDF Energy £100,000!

Perhaps the biggest club in League One for the 2005/06 season was **Nottingham Forest**, the other relegated club. With a glorious heritage provided by Brian Clough and Peter Taylor, they had for many years been trying to re-capture those times. Becoming the first European Cup winners to drop into their country`s third tier would not have been part of their plan, and they were desperate to get back at the first attempt.

Promoted from League Two alongside Swansea were **Yeovil Town**, **Scunthorpe United** and **Southend United**. None looked equipped to sail straight through League One. Consolidation was the name of the game for them.

Another League One club with a famous past was **Blackpool**. Their glory days were a very long way behind them, since which they had been down through all four divisions. They were now trying to get back. In Colin Hendry they had an untried manager, and the previous manager, Steve McMahon, had left due to unhappiness with the budget. They did not look quite ready for further progress yet.

In Paul Merson, **Walsall** had a big name manager who had steadied them with a mid table finish following their relegation from the Championship in 2003/04. They also had a prolific marksman in Matty Fryatt. However, all was not well behind the scenes at the Bescott Stadium, and Merson`s "health" left something to be desired. Few were backing them.

**Port Vale** were hoping to attract investment from famous fan Robbie Williams, but this would not avert the need to take out a £2.25 million loan from the local council in order to dig them out of the hole which the ITV Digital collapse had put them in. They had managed to avoid being seduced into a take over by a consortium who intended to install Paul Gascoigne as manager, but they were hardly a stable club ready for a promotion push.

**Oldham Athletic** were starting their ninth consecutive season at this level, and had new owners. Unfortunately the new owners` only real aim could be stability, as they fought to recover the club from a fire sale imposed by the outgoing owner. The predictions of most commentators would see Oldham hitting ten consecutive third tier seasons.

The three clubs who had missed out in the play offs in the previous season were **Tranmere Rovers**, **Brentford** and **Hartlepool United**. Tranmere were desperate to get back to the second tier where they had spent the whole of the 90s, sometimes knocking on the door of the Premier League. They had won an impressive seventy nine points in 2004/05 finishing third, and looked like being dangerous League One opponents in 05/06 under experienced manager Brian Little.

Like Tranmere, Brentford had been founder members of the Third Division in 1920. They had been promoted to the third tier in 1999, and after a couple of seasons of consolidation finished third with eighty three points in 2001/02. They had finished fourth in 2004/05, and both these excursions into the play offs had ended in tearful frustration. In 2002 they had been minutes away from automatic promotion. Martin Allen took them into the 05/06 season with one aim, promotion.

Hartlepool had been the butt of music hall jokes for generations. For many years they had been perennial strugglers in the League`s basement division. They had been forced to apply for re-election to the League on no fewer than fourteen occasions, a record. Brian Clough`s stellar management career had started there, but even he, when offered the job, had said "I don`t fancy the place". He also said, "to call Hartlepool a tip would make a tip ashamed to be called a tip". In 2005 they had been enjoying their most successful period ever. Not only were they having a rare sojourn above the bottom division, they had very nearly made it to the second tier. They had qualified for the play offs in sixth place, and then beaten Tranmere in the semi final. They then lost the final to Sheffield Wednesday after being 2-1 up with eight minutes left. Would they now continue this form, or would they return to more familiar struggles?

**Swindon Town** had spent the 1993/94 season in the Premier League, financially overstretching themselves in the process. They had been trying to recover ever since. They had been in League One for the previous five seasons, reaching the play off semi final in 2003/04. They had been mid table in 04/05, but with precarious finances and a difficult relationship with the tax man, they did not look well placed to challenge near the top.

Another club with a Premier League past and basket case finances were **Bradford City**. They found themselves in League One for the 04/05 season after two relegations and two administrations in five years. Still beset with the consequences of "chasing the dream", and with a business plan taken from the pages of "Alice in Wonderland", they had finished eleventh and their ambitions for 05/06 went no higher, despite possessing free scoring Dean Windass.

**Bournemouth** had narrowly missed out on the play offs in each of the previous two seasons, and under the relatively long serving Sean O`Driscoll they looked well placed to challenge again.

After many years of struggle, and the torching of their stadium to claim insurance money, **Doncaster Rovers** dropped out of the League in 1998. They did not return until 2003 as their former owner languished in jail ruing his decision to employ the least competent former member of the SAS as his fire starter. The man and the whole plot were easily uncovered after he left his mobile phone at the scene! Rovers immediately achieved promotion to the third tier. In 04/05 they had finished a very creditable tenth. They were on their way to a new stadium, and under ambitious ownership devoid of pyromania were in the course of implementing a ten year plan set in 1998 to achieve second tier football. They could well be dark horses for promotion.

As well as being the club of Michael Parkinson, **Barnsley** have another claim to fame. They have spent more seasons in the second tier of English football than any other club. In 2005 that number was at sixty five, but they were facing a fourth consecutive season at third tier level, and they had shown little sign of getting back to their natural habitat. They had spent the 1996/97 season in the Premier League, one of five clubs to have had one solitary season in that league.They had been badly effected by the ITV Digital crisis, but now seemed to be moving from under those dark clouds. There were signs of a revival at Oakwell with the appointment of ambitious young manager Andy Ritchie and with future Colchester United player Paul Reid as captain.

**Chesterfield** had been promoted to the third tier in 2001. In each of the four seasons since then they had been fighting a desperate battle to stay up. They were hopeful of better times in 05/06, but even the play offs looked a step too far.

Sadly it is not possible to complete an analysis of the clubs making up the 2005/06 League One without looking at **MK Dons**. Opportunistically creating themselves out of the ashes of Wimbledon they engineered their way into League One. The final season of the old Wimbledon had been 2003/04, when they finished bottom of Division One (the second tier). MK Dons took their League place, part of their name and their history, until they were shamed into returning the latter. All were driven up the M1 to Milton Keynes in a bag marked "swag". League One football found itself at the National Hockey Stadium. Winkleman and his motley crew did not intend to be detained for long either. They were targeting Premier League football in a new stadium before you could say franchise. However, in their first season they had been lucky to retain League One status, goal difference saving them. It seemed that advancement through the playing of football was proving difficult, and a big turnaround would be required for them to be a factor in 05/06.

How would **Colchester United** have seemed to the outside pundit? One who did his homework might say, defensively solid, they would probably stay up and with minimal injuries and suspensions even a mid table finish was possible. How did they seem to most lazy journalists and bookmakers? Small crowds, poor stadium, no money. Relegation fodder!

If you happened to be over 65 and a Colchester United fan, the start of the historic 2005/06 season had a familiar look about it. The first game on Saturday 6th August was a repeat of the fixture which started the U`s Football League history in August 1950. We were off to the garden of England to play Gillingham. Seven hundred and twenty five Essex girls and boys took occupation of the temporary seating (which seems to have become permanent) at the Priestfield Stadium`s open end.

New signing Chris Iwelumo was in the team, and there was another new face on the bench. On the day before the game, Mark Yeates had joined from Tottenham on a season long loan. A 20 year old Irish winger he had made three appearances at White Hart Lane, and gained further experience during loan spells with Brighton and Swindon. He had good skill and pace and a fearsome shot, but his temperament could be challenging. His loan at Swindon was cut short early after a row with manager Andy King. Sometimes he seemed to threaten team harmony with shows of frustration at team mates, but there was never any doubting his will to win.

Another "new face" at Gillingham was Karl Duguid, who was returning after 17 months out with injury. Parkinson marked his return by making him club captain. As he had not played for so long this was a tremendous show of faith in the ex U`s trainee. Over to Parky,

*"I knew that Chris Iwelumo hadn`t settled in Germany, so I tried again to sign him. I met him at the Holiday Inn near Halstead. I said "Chris, look at your career, you`ve drifted from club to club. You`ve been a loan player and a sub. At this stage you need to be playing games or you`ll be seen as a perennial squad player. We can`t afford to pay what you might get elsewhere, but I`m telling you now, at this stage you need to be somebody`s number nine." He agreed, and signed straight away although other clubs were interested. He didn`t miss a game for two years. He then got a good move to Charlton and international recognition.*

*Just before the season started, we got Mark Yeates on loan from Spurs. I really liked Mark both as a lad and as a player. He was a cheeky chappy. We could have lost patience with that deal and ended up with a lesser player. I thought we should*

*persevere with it and I`m glad we did. He was a fiery character but he worked hard and he could open up a tight defence.*

*It was a great boost to have Karl Duguid and Kem Izzet back. Kem gave you different options, whereas Dugy was a leader.*

*I knew we had a decent squad at the start of the 05/06 season and that we had every chance of doing well. I don`t remember thinking we would be promoted, but you don`t think like that. You just want to do as well as you can and see what happens. I do however remember telling the squad before that season that they should be going for promotion. I think that surprised them as they had never heard that from a Colchester manager before. We were talking about expectancy levels and I was telling them that they could not hide behind the fact that they were playing for a small club. I told them that it was no good following two good performances with two bad ones and thinking that`s ok because we are a small club. I made it clear that I was not going to accept that sort of attitude."*

Playing with Iwelumo on his own up front, Colchester had looked like a good unit for seventy minutes at Gillingham. Parkinson had felt that a lot of the attacking threat would come from Neil Danns, and sure enough he struck to give the U`s a fiftieth minute lead. United were now dominant, and had the chances to put the game beyond doubt, but somehow they lost their way. The Gills mounted a late revival. They equalised through Andrew Crofts, before Darren Byfield (boyfriend of pop star Jamelia) scored the winner in the eighty ninth minute.

The first home game of the season brought the much fancied Swansea City to Layer Road on the following Tuesday. Mark Yeates came in for his debut, with Karl Duguid moving into the back four in place of Pat Baldwin. The Welshmen completed their second consecutive win, to give Colchester a pretty miserable opening to the season. Again the score was 2-1 as the U`s looked tentative going forward and prone to error at the back. Greg Halford scored, but it was looking like a long season ahead at Layer Road.

For the visit of Barnsley, Parkinson decided to give Iwelumo an attacking partner. However, he had few options, with Richard Garcia and Marino Keith injured, and Jamie Guy thought to be too green. He did have Gareth Williams, who had appeared off the bench in the first two games, but despite this, he decided to move the versatile Halford up front. Iwelumo scored his first goal for the club right after half time following a great burst by Yeates and an excellent Duguid cross. This proved enough to beat the Tykes, and the U`s were off and running.

Although they had recorded their first win, the old problem of scoring goals continued to hold United back over the next few games. There was no doubting the character in the side though. They battled back from one down at MK Dons to grab a valuable point, despite being reduced to ten men when goalkeeper Davison saw first red mist, and then a red card. His protégé Dean Gerken had to take his place between the sticks and perhaps later lecture his coach on self controll Useful experience for Gerken though, as he deputised for the next three games while Davison served his ban.

Young George Elokobi made his debut at home to Oldham, and he and his defensive colleagues did a fine job to keep out the Latics who had scored nine in their first four games. Unfortunately the U`s fired blanks up front, and it was another draw. So the first five games had seen one win, two draws and two defeats. United had also succumbed at home to Cardiff in the Carling Cup.

Duguid said, "It`s fair to say the start to our season has been somewhat bitty, because as a team we haven`t settled yet. I have so far played in four different positions, so I`m sure things are going to take a little time to settle. We can`t take too long however, as the last thing we want is to find ourselves on the bottom of the table." Boss Phil Parkinson said, "a vital spark is missing", but he could not put his finger on what.

Over a thousand Colchester fans travelled to Southend on a warm Bank Holiday Monday for the big Essex derby. Left sided Dean Howell, who had signed from non-league Halifax Town earlier in the month, made his debut in place of the injured Danns.

The U`s fell behind after only three minutes, when Southend`s Manchester City legend Shaun Goater scored. A rare goal from full back Sam Stockley levelled things in the nineteenth minute. This was followed by one of the great Colchester United goal celebrations, as Stockley sprinted the length of the pitch with arms aloft towards the ecstatic travelling fans. Maybe a steward left a door open and Stockley ran straight out of the stadium, as he was nowhere to be seen when Mitchell Cole exploited cavernous gaps in Colchester`s rearguard to restore Southend`s lead ten minutes later. A second from Goater settled the matter in the seventy eighth minute as Colchester pushed forward in search of an equaliser.

The next match, at Bristol City, was covered live on Sky, and although it was goalless Rupert Murdoch had his money`s worth from an entertaining encounter. Colchester arrived without Keith, Garcia, Danns, Chilvers and Duguid all injured. Stockley was then injured in the warm up, and Baldwin during the game. Teenagers Robbie King, John White, George Elokobi and Garry Richards all had to be pressed into service. And as if that did not make the task difficult enough against one of the more expensive and fancied teams in the division, the U`s had to play the last half hour with ten men, following Wayne Brown`s decision to copy Davison`s pugilism in Milton Keynes. It was a magnificent point and hailed as such by Parkinson, who was quick to see the opportunity to use this adversity to spark the entire season, "I`ve never seen a more heroic performance in my life" he said. If Kem Izzet had not somehow contrived to hit the cross bar when alone six yards out, it might have been even better.

There was no doubt that some encouraging words were needed after what had been a disappointing start to the season. Just six points from seven games had the U`s fifth from bottom. Parkinson had criticised the team after the Swansea home defeat for not being strong enough. He dropped the slick passing Kevin Watson, moved Duguid back into midfield and played a more direct style using Iwelumo`s height and ability to hold the ball up front. However injuries, rather than the manager, were soon dictating team selection, and the unsettled line up had not been helping United`s cause.

Only 2,721 bothered to turn up at Layer Road for the Doncaster match on 10th September but they were rewarded with an entertaining game. Colchester recorded a much needed win by the odd goal in five, helped by the visitors generosity in notching two own goals. Parkinson freshened up the forward line by giving Gareth Williams his first start of the season alongside Iwelumo, and there was an explosive start, with both sides scoring in the opening five minutes. The first of the own goals came in the twenty third minute and the second four minutes later. Rovers pulled a goal back in the second half but it was not enough.

The U`s then stretched their unbeaten run to five matches, with a win and a draw at Port Vale and Bradford respectively, and a home point against Huddersfield which saw young defender George Elokobi score his first Football League goal. He had come in during the injury crisis and done well enough to keep his place. Port Vale and Huddersfield had both made good starts to the season, so these were encouraging results.

The U`s were starting to show what strength in depth they had defensively. Baldwin was still injured, but Stockley and Wayne Brown couldn`t get back in the side due to the form of youngsters White, Elokobi and Richards. At Bradford, Richards found himself marking Steve Claridge, a man more than twice his age!

To establish themselves in the upper reaches of League One, United needed to turn some of the draws into wins by finding a goal scoring touch. This was still eluding Gareth Williams, but Neil Danns was coming back from injury which had sidelined him for over a month.

Inconsistent form continued with only a win and a draw from the next four matches. The highlight was a win at Blackpool. The U`s looked to have snatched another draw from the jaws of victory when, after Halford had put them ahead in the sixteenth minute, they conceded an equaliser in the ninety second minute! Fortunately the referee`s watch must have been running slow as there was still time for the three points to be secured. With Blackpool still celebrating their equaliser, Halford scored again from inside the box.

After the goaless draw at Tranmere on 22nd October, Colchester stood sixteenth in the table with four wins, six draws and five defeats from their fifteen matches. Southend, still utilising the momentum built up during their promotion season, were top closely followed by two fancied sides in Huddersfield and Swansea. Only twenty third placed Gillingham had scored fewer than Colchester's fourteen goals, so it was obvious where the improvement needed to be made.

Swindon were five points adrift at the bottom. Amongst their ranks was a Bristolian who had scored goals throughout his career and was a former team mate of Phil Parkinson. They appeared to have no idea what they possessed.

| 1 | Southend United | 15 | 9 | 3 | 3 | 28 | 17 | +11 | 30 |
|---|---|---|---|---|---|---|---|---|---|
| 2 | Huddersfield Town | 15 | 9 | 3 | 3 | 29 | 21 | +8 | 30 |
| 3 | Swansea City | 15 | 8 | 4 | 3 | 32 | 19 | +13 | 28 |
| 4 | Brentford | 15 | 7 | 5 | 3 | 19 | 12 | +7 | 26 |
| 5 | Port Vale | 15 | 7 | 3 | 5 | 18 | 16 | +2 | 24 |
| 6 | Bradford City | 15 | 6 | 5 | 4 | 20 | 16 | +4 | 23 |
| 7 | Scunthorpe United | 15 | 6 | 4 | 5 | 24 | 22 | +2 | 22 |
| 8 | Chesterfield | 14 | 7 | 1 | 6 | 23 | 22 | +1 | 22 |
| 9 | Yeovil Town | 15 | 6 | 4 | 5 | 18 | 20 | -2 | 22 |
| 10 | Oldham Athletic | 15 | 6 | 3 | 6 | 18 | 23 | -5 | 21 |
| 11 | Nottingham Forest | 15 | 6 | 2 | 7 | 19 | 19 | 0 | 20 |
| 12 | AFC Bournemouth | 15 | 5 | 5 | 5 | 15 | 16 | -1 | 20 |
| 13 | Walsall | 15 | 5 | 5 | 5 | 22 | 24 | -2 | 20 |
| 14 | Barnsley | 14 | 5 | 4 | 5 | 18 | 15 | +3 | 19 |
| 15 | Doncaster Rovers | 15 | 5 | 3 | 7 | 17 | 17 | 0 | 18 |
| 16 | Colchester United | 15 | 4 | 6 | 5 | 14 | 16 | -2 | 18 |
| 17 | Rotherham United | 14 | 4 | 5 | 5 | 18 | 17 | +1 | 17 |
| 18 | Hartlepool United | 14 | 4 | 5 | 5 | 15 | 19 | -4 | 17 |
| 19 | Bristol City | 14 | 4 | 4 | 6 | 19 | 25 | -6 | 16 |
| 20 | Blackpool | 15 | 3 | 7 | 5 | 17 | 23 | -6 | 16 |
| 21 | Tranmere Rovers | 15 | 3 | 5 | 7 | 14 | 17 | -3 | 14 |
| 22 | Milton Keynes Dons | 15 | 2 | 8 | 5 | 15 | 19 | -4 | 14 |
| 23 | Gillingham | 14 | 3 | 5 | 6 | 10 | 18 | -8 | 14 |
| 24 | Swindon Town | 15 | 2 | 3 | 10 | 15 | 24 | -9 | 9 |

☐ Automatic promotion area     ☐ Play off area     ▨ Relegation area

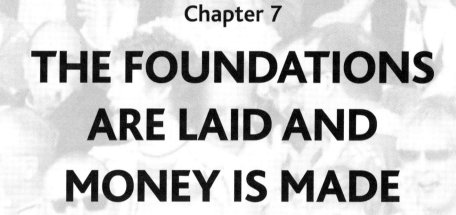

Chapter 7

# THE FOUNDATIONS ARE LAID AND MONEY IS MADE

# Chapter 7
## THE FOUNDATIONS ARE LAID AND MONEY IS MADE

Jamie Cureton made his League debut for Norwich as an 18 year old. Three years later, and finding his progress blocked at Carrow Road, he had a successful loan spell in his home city with Bristol Rovers. This led to a permanent deal in October 1996. In his second season he helped Rovers into the Division Two (third tier) play offs.

After scoring seventy two goals in one hundred and seventy six appearances he was sold to Reading for £250,000 in August 2000. He immediately helped them to the Division Two play offs, and then to automatic promotion in his second season. In the 02/03 season he helped them make the Division One play offs. When his contract ended, and in the wake of the ITV Digital collapse, he found it difficult to find a club in England which could match his wage demands. He moved out to South Korea to play for Busan IPark, but he was unable to settle and quickly returned to these shores with QPR, where his former Bristol Rovers boss Ian Holloway was in charge.

Cureton had always thrived in a strike partnership. At Bristol Rovers he had Jason Roberts. At Reading he had Martin Butler and then Nicky Forster. He was now finding it difficult to recreate those partnerships, and his sixteen months at Loftus Road were largely frustrating and punctuated by injury. For the 2005/06 season Andy King signed him for Swindon Town as a replacement for Sam Parkin, but King was promptly sacked.

Cureton did not seem to fit into the plans of the new manager Iffy Onuora, spending most of his time as an unused substitute, if in the squad at all. Swindon had an embarrassment of riches so far as strikers were concerned. They had Rory Fallon, Christian Roberts and Tony Thorpe on their books, none of whom seemed able to gel with Cureton. At this point Cureton had one hundred and forty six goals to his name at a rate of more than a goal every three games and Swindon were bottom of League One. Despite this Cureton was deemed surplus to requirements, at least for the time being.

Jamie Cureton was exactly the sort of player that Colchester United badly needed. He was also the sort of player they could never afford. Phil Parkinson had been keeping close tabs on Cureton, probably more in hope than expectation. In Chris Iwelumo he knew he had the kind of player who would bring the best out of Cureton, and vice versa. An enquiry was made, and a one month loan deal was done.

At the time Parkinson said, "Curo is a player I know well from my time at Reading. He is a proven goalscorer. We`ve been creating chances but not converting them so I thought it was time to act. He`s one of those players who operates well in the danger area and I`m pleased to have him on board." Now looking back,

*"I had no hesitation in going for Jamie Cureton when the opportunity came up. He had been playing with Tony Thorpe at Swindon and that was not a good combination. I had always rated him highly. I knew Curo would put away the chances we were creating but not taking. In fact he did more than that because he sparked everyone off."*

Cureton made his debut coming on as a sub in the goaless draw at Tranmere. It is often amazing how good strikers get goal scoring chances which do not seem to fall to other players. Cureton was only on the field for ten minutes at Prenton Park, but he had two great chances to win the game. Unfortunately he missed them both, perhaps rusty from lack of game time in recent weeks.

On 29th October, United were at home to Yeovil. Many people look back on this game as a turning point in the season. Cureton made his first start, and scored his first goal, in Colchester's colours. Parkinson showed that he had no favourites as neither Duguid nor Danns was able to get in the starting eleven. Chris Iwelumo secured the win with a ninetieth minute goal after Yeovil had twice taken the lead. It finished 3-2, with Iwelumo also scoring in the first half. This sparked the U's first good run of results in that season with five consecutive victories.

It was in this game that the beginnings of the good attacking unit that the U's would become could be seen. Yeates wreaked havoc down the left side, being instrumental in the creation of all three goals. Yeovil could not handle Iwelumo's physicality up front, and Cureton's goal was a classic example of the penalty area poaching which marked his career. It might have been Cureton who scored the winner, but the ball rolled agonisingly just beyond his reach before being put in by Iwelumo. As the crowd went wild, and most of the team celebrated by the corner flag, Cureton sat forlornly in the six yard box, mourning the goal he thought he should have scored. It is often said that strikers have to be selfish, and it would certainly be hard to find a better example of the mindset of the single minded goal poacher.

Not for the first, or last time, in 05/06 the U's had shown their character. Assistant Manager Geraint Williams said, "The important thing for me was the way the lads kept believing. We went behind twice, but they kept faith with what we had been instilling in them all week on the training ground."

So it would seem that a real belief in the ability and potential of the team was developing from inside it. It is difficult to remember quite the same belief being present amongst the fans. Unlike most of the football world we knew we were not relegation material. Far from it. But the idea that any sustained promotion push could be mounted still seemed fanciful.

With hindsight, it is possible to see that something happened with the acquisition of Cureton. It was much more than the arrival of an experienced player on a one month loan. It was a jigsaw becoming complete, albeit temporarily. There was experience all the way through the side. There were good characters. There was a togetherness. And, there was much more than a good starting eleven. If a good team can be judged by the quality on its bench, it is worth noting that the bench against Yeovil was Gerken, Danns, Duguid, Baldwin and Garcia. Crucially there were also two good men at the helm in Parkinson and Williams.

The Yeovil result moved the U`s up to thirteenth. It was a false position. In those early weeks, United had suffered with injuries and new players had to bed in. Rotherham, Blackpool, Gillingham and Hartlepool were now to feel the strength coming out of Layer Road. All were beaten in a whirlwind of eleven goals. There were three more for Iwelumo and two more for Cureton. The team was settled. The only changes in those games being Danns coming in for the injured Cureton against Rotherham, and then Cureton coming back at the expense of Izzet.

With the visit to Hartlepool on 6th December came another milestone in the season. There is little glamour to be had on a cold, windy Tuesday night in Hartlepool. The Champions League is on the TV and the A1 never seems to end. Even Peter Mandelson hardly ever went there and he was the MP!

The locals find a sense of humour to be an essential ingredient of surviving by the North Sea. They are called "the monkey hangers", because during the Napoleonic wars a French ship sunk just off the coast and the only survivor was a monkey wearing a French uniform. The good people of Hartlepool hanged it, believing it to be a French spy because it wouldn`t answer their questions.The Mayor at the time of Colchester`s visit was one Stuart Drummond aka H`angus. He had campaigned in a monkey suit on a platform of free bananas for school children, and had been elected twice! These were not people to be trifled with, and It is on this sort of night that you discover whether you have winners in the team.

Premiership scouts are seen much less frequently than suspended monkeys at Victoria Park, especially on a Tuesday night in December, and Greg Halford was feeling an injury. Phil Parkinson employed his man management skills to convince the young utility player that he was fit enough, and that this was the sort of night when the character of a young starlet could be judged from afar by the managers of big clubs.

The only goal came in the sixtieth minute from that man Cureton. He hooked in from the tightest of angles from a deflected cross that many players would have given up. The U`s then showed their mettle by surviving a battery of long throws and corners with Aidan Davison dominant in goal. It was the sort of night when promotion credentials are established, and Parkinson commented about how the rest of the Division would now be noticing Colchester.

This seemed something of an understatement. The period from 29th October to 6th December saw five consecutive league wins, two wins in the FA Cup and one in the LDV Vans Trophy! In one of the FA Cup wins, the club`s biggest ever winning margin had been equalled, 9-1 against AFC Leamington. In the other, two goals had been put past a goalkeeper called Joe Hart playing for League Two Shrewsbury. Another good result for Colchester during this time was the extension of Cureton`s loan from Swindon. However, it seemed that the only way the U`s might be able to afford to make his switch permanent would be by selling the increasingly sought-after Greg Halford

United had now moved into the Play Off positions in sixth place. However, there were some potential distractions. They were in the third round of the FA Cup and the LDV Vans Trophy area semi final.

Next up were Swansea City, and this would be a real test in front of over 13,000 at the Liberty Stadium. Swansea were two points clear at the top, but United had won a club record equalling eight in a row in all competitions, and went into the game with the same starting eleven for the fourth consecutive league match.

So United were looking to set a new record of consecutive wins, and were brimming with confidence. Swansea opened brightly but the big crowd were silenced in the thirteenth minute when Cureton showed that he could supply, as well as score, by slipping in Iwelumo for his tenth league goal of the season. A free kick controversially awarded against Wayne Brown on the edge of the box led to Swansea`s equaliser in the thirtieth minute. Davison again showed his qualities in goal to keep the league leaders at bay in the second half. Colchester were finishing the game the stronger side and seemed to have the new record in the bag when Iwelumo was brought down in the eighty fifth minute for a penalty.

Iwelumo was himself the team`s penalty taker, and had already scored from the spot in confident style against Blackpool. For some reason this penalty was given to Neil Danns. Perhaps Iwelumo had been shaken up in the tackle which earned the penalty. Whatever the reason Danns took it, the keeper guessed correctly and made the save. A distraught Danns offered apologies to everyone afterwards, but the truth was United would have been delighted before the match if they had known they would draw. Nine wins in a row would have had a nice ring to it though, especially in the league leader`s back yard.

The winning run had ended, but the U`s were still unbeaten in ten games in all competitions and this soon became twelve with victories over MK Dons, first in the LDV Vans Trophy and then in the league. They won the league match 2-0 at Layer Road. Danns made amends for his penalty miss by scoring the first goal and allowing Iwelumo to score the second from the penalty spot.

This result saw United leapfrog Southend into fourth place. Belief was building that perhaps, at least, the Play Offs could be achieved. However, Chris Iwelumo only had eyes for promotion. "There`s a strong belief in the squad that we can do it this season. Now we`ve got to play out of our skins and make that dream come true. We`ve gone twelve games unbeaten and everyone`s showing confidence and a great competitive spirit."

Sadly, Boxing Day brought the first defeat since 15th October when United went down to a ninetieth minute Rory Fallon goal at Swindon`s County Ground. Parkinson had at last been forced to make a change, bringing in Garcia for Cureton who was not allowed to play against his parent club. This was a disappointing result, as Swindon were three points adrift at the bottom with the second worst goal scoring record in the Division. U`s fans could only wonder at their generosity in allowing a striker of Jamie Cureton`s calibre out on loan.

New Year`s Eve brought another big fixture. Sixth placed Colchester had to go to Griffin Park to face Brentford, who had eased into first place with a fine win over Swansea. Another big test of Colchester`s promotion credentials.

Parkinson brought the axe down on Sam Stockley. Perhaps holding him responsible for not stopping the cross which led to Swindon`s winner. John White switched sides to go to right back, and George Elokobi came in at left back.

This was the match which signalled the arrival of Mark Yeates as a top League One player. He was on fire throughout. In fact, he was laying down fire at one point. A simulated gunning down of about a thousand Brentford fans, following his thirtieth minute goal, earned him a yellow card. He then tortured U`s fans by missing a number of fine chances to put the game beyond doubt. Some might have been ready to put him in front of a firing squad, as a Brentford equaliser began to look likely and was only prevented by the agility of Aidan Davison and the width of a post. But all was forgiven when the little bundle of Irish energy popped up in the eighty ninth minute to secure the win.

Brentford had been knocked off their perch in their own home. Although there had been some scares along the way, it was no more than Colchester`s fine performance deserved, and it was another result to make people sit up and take notice. There was however a cloud on the horizon. Jamie Cureton`s second loan month had ended, and Swindon thought they had better have him back! Parkinson must have been disappointed but he was not surprised,

*"There was never any question of Curo staying after his second month either as a loan continuation or a permanent signing. Swindon made clear that they would be taking him back. It was in his contract that he could leave on a free if they were*

*relegated and that was how we were able to sign him permanently the following May."*

Cureton's seven League starts had brought him four goals. Perhaps just as significantly, those games had seen Iwelumo score seven. This was a prolific partnership and it was such a shame to see it broken up. They had also scored five in two FA Cup matches.

For Cureton, it was back to the bottom of League One. As if that was not bad enough, his first game back at Swindon was Hartlepool away, but at least his Colchester form had earned him a return to Swindon's starting eleven and the goals began to flow. He started most of Swindon's remaining games and scored seven times, but it wasn't enough to keep them up.

Colchester had bounced back from disappointment on Boxing Day with a magnificent result and performance at Brentford. Another of the hallmarks of a successful football team had been displayed. All teams have set backs. What counts is how you respond. Colchester responded to the defeat at Swindon with seven consecutive victories. Just for good measure they also threw in another LDV Vans Trophy win and two FA Cup wins, both against Championship opposition. Another amazing run of results, and the club's post war record had been beaten. Pre war had, of course, been non-league, so this was without question the best run of results ever achieved by the U's.

Phil Parkinson and Geraint Williams excelled themselves through this spell. They had seen their potent forward line broken up and they had to re-marshal their forces. Cureton's goals had been lost but this was when the scoring prowess of Neil Danns came into it's own.

The next game would see Nottingham Forest make their first visit to Layer Road since 1950. After the Brentford match, Parkinson must have been desperate to keep an unchanged team, but this was not possible. Cureton had returned to Wiltshire, and Halford was suspended. Duguid came into the midfield, and Richard Garcia replaced Cureton, just as he had at Swindon where the U's had looked toothless.

People being turned away from a full Layer Road underlined the need for a new stadium, and what a match the late comers missed. It was goalless with twenty minutes left, but then the fireworks started. A tremendous twenty yard strike by Neil Danns looked to have been enough to secure the points, but the emotional rollercoaster really started as the match entered stoppage time.

As only three of United's back four tried to play offside, Forest's £700,000 striker Nathan Tyson raced through to equalise and break U's hearts. But this was a Colchester United team that did not clock off until the final whistle. Yeates scored straight from the restart, before Garcia ensured there would be no more Forest recovery with a fine drive into the bottom corner. Danns was confident that the U`s form could be maintained through to promotion at the end of the season, "I definitely think it`s possible. If we can go on another run, then I`m sure we can do it this year." And he had nothing but praise for the fans, "The crowd always help us. The atmosphere at Layer Road was brilliant and they cheered us on to two late goals."

Goals from Danns and Iwelumo gave Colchester victory at mid table Walsall, and started a slump for Paul Merson`s men which finished with relegation in last place. The U`s were now fourth, four points behind top of the table Southend with two games in hand.

A quirk of fixtures now presented the U`s with four consecutive home games, starting with underachieving and relegation haunted Bristol City. This was followed by mid table Port Vale and Bradford City and then seventeenth placed Scunthorpe United. Each game looked winnable and each game was won, though not without difficulty. It was becoming clear that the U`s knew how to force wins out of games when they had not played particularly well. Another hallmark of a successful football team.

The goals were still flowing, with nine scored in these four games. Gareth Williams made a rare start against Bristol City and scored. Danns scored twice, as did the ever reliable Chris Iwelumo. Garcia scored two in each of the Port Vale and Bradford matches. The win over Vale on 21st January sent United to the top of the table.

Just before the Walsall match, Swindon loaned Colchester another from their battery of misfiring strikers. This time it was Tony Thorpe. He looked like Cureton mark two. He was now thirty one and had enjoyed a good career scoring prolifically at Luton and Bristol City amongst others. He signed a short term contract at Layer Road with one hundred and thirty seven league goals to his name but Parkinson only needed him as back up. Danns and Garcia were flowering and providing Iwelumo with all the support he needed.

There was simply no holding the U`s in January 2006. Perhaps the best month in the club`s history. Seven games played in all competitions and all won. A virtual reserve team was sent to Cheltenham for the LDV Vans area semi final, but they came back with a victory, such was the surge of confidence running through the entire squad. FA Cup ties against Sheffied United and Derby County, both from the Championship, looked like formidable challenges especially as the former was away from home and the Blades were second in the table. Both were confidently brushed aside.

It is worth noting that five of the team which dispatched Derby were products of the club`s youth system. They were complemented by Baldwin and Izzet, who were both as good as Colchester products, having spent their entire senior careers at the club.

As January came to an end Colchester were second, with games in hand on the teams around them and they were in the FA Cup fifth round and the LDV Vans Trophy area final. The worry for some U`s fans was fixture congestion. We had a decent squad in terms of talent and experience, but it wasn`t huge. Could we really sustain a war on three fronts? At least we had got out of the transfer window without losing the much scouted Greg Halford. We could now look towards the end of the season knowing that the squad was settled. A huge relief as Danns, Iwelumo, Chilvers and Yeates had all been linked to bigger clubs along with Halford. There were even some worrying rumours about Phil Parkinson which we can now learn the truth of from the man himself,

*"Mr Heard had always told me that he would let me know of any approaches made for me. In late January he told me that Leicester wanted to speak to me about becoming their manager. They were in the Championship at the time and had just sacked Craig Levein. We had been getting lots of enquiries about our players, especially Greg Halford and Neil Danns but the club were brilliant. There was no pressure to sell. On the contrary Mr Heard said he preferred to keep the squad together to the end of the season.*

*I still had about eighteen months to go on my contract at Colchester, although it was pretty flimsy. I told Mr Heard that on this occasion I would decline the chance to speak to Leicester. I wanted to see the job at Colchester through. None of the players were agitating to get away. We were all on a mission to get the club promoted. I thought it would be wrong for me to upset that by speaking to another club. However, I did say that I mght want to talk to other clubs at the end of the season".*

Any pressure on the finances which might have prompted the sale of Halford was relieved when the draw was made for the fifth round of the Cup. The Sky Sports cameras focused in on the squad and mascot Eddie the Eagle shoehorned into one of the bars at cosy Layer Road. The marble balls rattled, before kindly arranging themselves in such a way that the aristocrats of West London would be playing host to the country bumpkins of North Essex. "Chelsea will play Colchester United" set the cash tills ringing, the calculators clicking and the spreadsheets doing whatever spreadsheets do. In fact Chelsea still had to beat Everton in a replay to earn the right to take on the U`s, but this was a formality. After many years in the FA Cup wilderness the U`s had hit the financial jackpot.

At Layer Road backs were slapped, hands were shaken and agents were rung as a squad of journeyman pro`s contemplated their moment in the sun. Even Eddie the Eagle got on the phone to order a new sofa for his eyrie, before assaulting the impassive and "seen it all before" Aidan Davison with flailing talons.

Some of us found it difficult to know how to react to this. An FA Cup tie at Stamford Bridge had the capacity to take over the entire season. If we were reconciled to mid table obscurity, this would be a lovely distraction. However, we were on the cusp of making history in the League and some were worried this might be sacrificed for one glamour game in a competition we could never win. As it was, the number of games played in January had taken a toll with Davison, Brown, Chilvers, Watson, Izzet and Iwelumo all carrying injuries.

Phil Parkinson had no such reservations, "I`ve had to wait three years for a draw like this." he said "The club really deserve it. All the lads in the squad have been working hard this year. The people behind the scenes have been working tirelessly for many years to keep this club going on limited resources and the fans have really earned it".

There was no doubting that the team had earned it having won eighteen of their previous twenty games in all competitions. The club would receive £265,000 from Sky TV coverage alone. Predictably, Parkinson received the League One manager of the month award for January. "It must have been the easiest decision the awards panel have ever had to make", said Chief Executive Marie Partner.

Davison returned in goal against Bradford, having missed the Derby cup tie, but Brown and Chilvers were still out. The centre of United`s defence therefore had an unfamiliar look about it with Pat Baldwin teaming up with Gary Richards. Although Watson was able to return, despite having been carried off against Port Vale, it was clear that the club`s resources were being stretched when youngster Robbie King had to come on for Neil Danns. There was a hiccup when Dean Windass gave Bradford the lead, but once again Colchester`s self belief shone through as a Garcia brace and another from Iwelumo brought victory.

So the club record for consecutive wins, which had been equalled earlier in the season, had now been broken. On the following Tuesday night nine consecutive wins became ten when Scunthorpe came to Layer Road and left with a 1-0 defeat. However the excitement of the forthcoming cup tie was now being cranked up, and it looked as though it may be affecting the team. Nothing flowed against Scunthorpe, and in truth Colchester were very lucky to get the three points courtesy of Iwelumo heading in a Halford long throw just before half time.

| 1 | Colchester United | 30 | 17 | 7 | 6 | 47 | 28 | +19 | 58 |
|---|---|---|---|---|---|---|---|---|---|
| 2 | Southend United | 31 | 16 | 9 | 6 | 48 | 28 | +20 | 57 |
| 3 | Swansea City | 31 | 14 | 10 | 7 | 55 | 34 | +21 | 52 |
| 4 | Barnsley | 30 | 14 | 9 | 7 | 45 | 28 | +17 | 51 |
| 5 | Brentford | 29 | 14 | 9 | 6 | 49 | 34 | +15 | 51 |
| 6 | Huddersfield Town | 31 | 13 | 11 | 7 | 47 | 42 | +5 | 50 |
| 7 | Chesterfield | 31 | 12 | 12 | 7 | 46 | 40 | +6 | 48 |
| 8 | Oldham Athletic | 31 | 12 | 7 | 12 | 39 | 45 | -6 | 43 |
| 9 | Nottingham Forest | 31 | 11 | 8 | 12 | 39 | 36 | +3 | 41 |

This made it twelve consecutive home wins and returned the U`s to the top of the table. However fans were becoming more demanding, and there was a feeling that the Scunthorpe performance indicated that the team were stuttering a little. By now Chelsea had been confirmed as the fifth round opponents, and Parkinson and Williams were going to have their work cut out to keep the eyes of their troops on the main prize. There were two vital games before the Chelsea match, and the first was going to be an especially tough test against sixth placed Huddersfield at their impressive Galpharm Stadium.

Wayne Brown returned in place of the unlucky Baldwin, but it simply wasn`t Colchester`s day on a bumpy windswept pitch. They hit the post three times, had two goals disallowed and Gary Richards was controversially sent off. To add insult to injury, Huddersfield`s first came from a lucky deflection. The U`s went down 2-0. Walsall at home on the following Tuesday looked like easy pickings as they were on a terrible run and were without a manager, having sacked Paul Merson after a 5-0 drubbing at Brentford. With 6,000 tickets for Chelsea snapped up the crowd was 3,810 which showed where the misplaced priorities of the casual supporter lay.

With the Chelsea match five days away the town was now bedecked in blue and white, weddings were being delayed and even the Town Hall was flying the Colchester United flag. Not only were fans crawling out of the woodwork, some were flying in from distant lands. Sadly, none of this was for the visit of Walsall even though it was the far more important match. The national media was crawling all over Layer Road, and the players would not have been human if their focus had not been a little distracted by all this. Although they dominated Walsall, a goal would not come, and two more points were dropped.

The big day arrived on Sunday 19th February. With 6,000 people to get to London,

National Express East Anglia entered into the spirit of the occasion by carrying out engineering works between Witham and Shenfield, thereby consigning fans to queue in the pouring rain for the "special" bus services. Goodness knows there were many fair-weather supporters amongst the travelling army, but there was precious little fair weather as the heavens opened and stayed open.

Failure to score against struggling Walsall was not the ideal preparation to face the reigning Premier League champions on their own patch. They had won the previous season`s Premier League by the little matter of twelve points, and on 19th February stood clear at the top by, yes you guessed it, twelve points. They had a stadium capacity around 42,000, seven times that of Layer Road. They had an average attendance around 42,000, eleven times greater than Colchester United.

They had just posted losses of £140 million. Chelsea that is. Not Colchester United! They were so inconvenienced by this, that they spent a mere £56 million on players at the start of the 2005/06 season. Chelsea that is. Not Colchester United! They had a squad which had cost just over £202 million. Chelsea that is. Not Colchester United! It was said that only two players in the U`s squad had cost a fee, in both cases "undisclosed". One was Garcia, and of course we now know he had actually cost nothing. The other was Danns, who probably cost around £50,000. The Chelsea squad therefore cost around four thousand times that of Colchester!

The Chelsea owner, Roman Abramovich, was said to be worth over 12 billion US dollars. We will not speculate as to the wealth of Peter Heard, but it may have been less than this!

Two years before, Chelsea had met Scarborough in the FA Cup. It seemed certain that if you wanted to find the two matches in the world history of association football with the greatest gulf in financial resources between the participants, you need look no further than Scarborough v Chelsea in January 2004, and Chelsea v Colchester in February 2006.

As the Colchester players inspected the Stamford Bridge pitch before the game they would have been struck by the gulf in quality, compared with what they were used to at Layer Road. But it was not as you would expect. Layer Road boasted a fine playing surface. Stamford Bridge resembled a "potato field", to quote Chelsea`s own manager.

One of the great things about English football, which is almost never celebrated, is its strength in depth. There is probably no other country in the world where a third tier club can go to one of the top clubs, take 6,000 fans, play to a full stadium and actually believe that they can win!

The quality of League One was evident in Colchester`s performance and was remarked upon by Joe Cole and, more significantly (given the breath of his experience) by Jose Mourinho. In his own inimitable style, "I am in love with the FA Cup. Last season

– Scunthorpe at home, League Two opponents, full house. This season - Huddersfield at home, League One opponents, full house. Now we have Colchester at home – League One opponents, full house. It is fantastic. What is more, the games have been close and good."

There is no need to detain ourselves with a close analysis of what took place at Stamford Bridge. It is well known, and this book is not about FA Cup achievement in any event. Suffice to say that the outcome was in doubt until stoppage time, to the eternal credit of all those associated with the club. Everyone had a great day out despite the weather and National Express East Anglia, and the U`s made a packet. Chelsea`s next match was against Barcelona. Colchester`s next match was against Barnsley.

Chapter 8

# THE RUN IN
# BEGINS

# Chapter 8
## THE RUN IN BEGINS

The Chelsea match was a massive and richly deserved occasion. It did, however, have the potential to derail an historic season. No-one knew this better than Phil Parkinson, but that did not necessarily mean he could prevent it.

At least the players were saying the right things. Karl Duguid, "The FA Cup is done now. It is over. Tomorrow we have Barnsley and that has become the most important game of the season". Neil Danns, "The League is our main priority. If we can perform like we did against Chelsea week in week out, then I don`t see any reason why we can`t get promoted this year".

The performance against one of Europe`s top clubs must have given tremendous self belief for the league run in. The club probably made around £1 million. With the loan market still open, this meant Parkinson could bolster the squad if he wished.However, both Southend and Huddersfield had picked up impressive wins while the U`s were preparing for Stamford Bridge.

The first test of whether the team could re-focus would come at Barnsley`s Oakwell stadium. The Tykes had got four wins and a draw from their previous six games which had moved them up to sixth in the table and they had a good home record. Colchester could not spark especially up front. A solitary goal from Brian Howard sent the U`s home pointless. They had now picked up only one point from the last nine available.

If it was a case of the post FA Cup blues, what better way of shaking from it than an Essex derby against the crab molesters. It had been twenty years since Southend had been beaten at Layer Road, and it was a fine chance for the U`s to avenge their defeat at Roots Hall back in August.

There was some money in the coffers courtesy of the cup run, and knowing a blip when he saw one, Parkinson took his squad away for some warm weather training in Portugal. Not something many Colchester managers have been in a position to do!

Would it be beneficial? Greg Halford said, "It was good to get away, relax and recharge the batteries. We had a couple of training sessions but the rest of the time was putting our feet up. Everyone is up for the challenge against Southend". Neil Danns said,"it has definitely given us a bit of a rejuvenation". Karl Duguid said, "Everyone has recharged their batteries ahead of a final push for promotion".

With all this talk of batteries one might have thought they had been away on a car maintenance course. It sounded like a rebirth. We looked from the Barside and tried to detect signs of renewed vitality and vigour but the Portuguese reincarnation seemed remarkably well disguised as Che Wilson prodded in Southend's third goal in the thirty second minute! Never mind recharged batteries. They looked in need of a complete rebore. They were still sitting by the pool, and looked more interested in studying the Tibetan yogas of dream and sleep than tracking runners or blocking shots. Another three points had gone west. Or, to be more accurate, south.

United had now dropped to fifth, eight points behind Southend, but they still had games in hand on all the teams around them except Brentford. The problem was that, on current form, it was difficult to see those games yielding many points. "I feel we have gone away from being a team and look like individuals", was Phil Parkinson's verdict.

Never mind. The next match was Oldham away. Always a lovely place to visit, and such fertile ground for Colchester teams down the years! Good old Boundary Park. With a pitch rutted from recent Rugby matches, a training goal stacked in one corner of an empty terrace, and one side of the ground a demolition site, this was not Stamford Bridge. It was also not the performance Colchester put in at Stamford Bridge. It was, however, a fairly typical Boundary Park performance and result. Despite the apparent activities in Portugal, there was no internal combustion. The engine did not start at all. Oldham 1 Colchester 0 meant one goal scored in the previous seven games, and that an own goal by a Portuguese international worth £20 million! To make matters worse Izett was sent off.

That was four defeats and a draw from the five league matches around the Chelsea cup tie. This was not promotion form. It was a serious hiccup. Parkinson tried to get the winning formula back by reshuffling his pack. His tried the midfield bite of Kem Izzet, and briefly dropped Kevin Watson. He rested Richard Garcia, and started to use Tony Thorpe. He recalled experienced full back Sam Stockley, and rested John White.

Either side of the Oldham match came the two legs of the LDV Vans Trophy Area Final. League One promotion rivals Swansea City provided the opposition, and fringe players Gerken, Stockley, Elokobi and Williams got run outs in the first leg which was lost 1-0 at the Liberty Stadium. Parkinson tried Duguid up front in the second leg but Swansea also won this, 2-1 at Layer Road in front of only 3,236 suggesting that a trip to the Millenium Stadium in Cardiff for the final was not uppermost in the minds of supporters. At least Neil Danns goal brought an end to an agonising twelve hours of football without a Colchester player scoring. It was disappointing, but we now had to get back to the serious business of rediscovering league form.

With the goals not coming, Parkinson took the opportunity to bring Blackpool striker Scott Vernon in on loan. This was a swap loan deal, with Sam Stockley and Gareth Williams going in the opposite direction in search of more regular games.

Even having played two extra games, Southend were now looking uncatchable. They were top with eleven points separating them from Colchester in sixth. With less than a quarter of the season to go, top spot looked out of Colchester`s reach, but the other automatic promotion spot seemed attainable. It was currently occupied by Brentford, who were five points ahead of Colchester, having played a game more. However, unless current form could be reversed, Colchester would be dropping down towards mid table.

Phil Parkinson recalls the effect of the FA Cup and how he tried to turn round the slump in form,

*"The cup run had a massive draining effect on everyone at the club. I had been advised that I might have trouble getting the team going again after the Chelsea game, and I think doing that was the biggest challenge I had.*

*I had decided to take the players away to Portugal but this did not have the desired effect. We had been awful at Barnsley and when we returned from Portugal we were no better against Southend, losing 3-0 at home. That night I remember going to the Lemon Tree restaurant with Aidy and another friend. We spent most of the evening talking about what was going wrong and arranged to go over some videos at my house the next day which was a Sunday.*

*Aidy came round with his wife and kids and a big piece of beef, and the two of us locked ourselves away. We were trying to identify examples of what we had been doing right during our good runs, and what we were doing wrong now. It was many hours later when we emerged to eat our Sunday roast. When that was finished I went into Layer Road and worked until gone 10pm, on editing two 25 minute "before and after" videos.*

*I showed these to the players the next day and I remember the room going very quiet. It was all there in front of them and there was nothing they could say to argue about it. The attacking players had stopped making runs in behind, and no-one was closing down. I remember them shuffling out deep in thought. I think it had a big effect. The improvement was not immediate, but I was able to keep banging on about those videos.*

*I sat down with a number of the players like Greg and Big Chris. I told them what they weren`t doing and asked if they could do it. Of course they knew they could because they had seen it in the videos. I told them they were cheating on their team mates and I think this got through. Slowly performances picked up. Greg was very close to his Mum, and there were times when I would coach him through her! I`d tell her what I needed him to be doing and what he wasn`t doing. She`d tell him and he came on very strong towards the end of the season. He was such a good player and*

*I`m surprised he hasn`t quite gone on to establish himself at the top level."*

When you are looking for your first win in eight games, it may be no bad thing that your next game is home to the team second from bottom. Swindon still occupied twenty third place, just as they had when Jamie Cureton went back there at the beginning of January. Cureton played the whole ninety minutes but made little impact. Sentimental Colchester fans may have thought he was playing on automatic pilot against the team he would rather be playing for. Fans were certainly surprised to see such a good goal scorer taking corners!

The top of the table going into the Swindon game,

| 1 | Southend United | 37 | 20 | 10 | 7 | 60 | 33 | +27 | 70 |
|---|---|---|---|---|---|---|---|---|---|
| 2 | Brentford | 36 | 18 | 10 | 8 | 58 | 39 | +19 | 64 |
| 3 | Swansea City | 38 | 16 | 15 | 7 | 67 | 44 | +23 | 63 |
| 4 | Huddersfield Town | 37 | 16 | 13 | 8 | 60 | 49 | +11 | 61 |
| 5 | Barnsley | 37 | 16 | 12 | 9 | 52 | 37 | +15 | 60 |
| 6 | Colchester United | 35 | 17 | 8 | 10 | 47 | 35 | +12 | 59 |
| 7 | Oldham Athletic | 37 | 16 | 8 | 13 | 46 | 47 | -1 | 56 |
| 8 | Chesterfield | 37 | 13 | 12 | 12 | 54 | 53 | +1 | 51 |
| 9 | Doncaster Rovers | 36 | 14 | 8 | 14 | 44 | 43 | +1 | 50 |

Tony Thorpe got his first start, but it was by no means a vintage performance from United. It did however bring a desperately needed win, and with it the belief that Colchester could get their season back on track. Thorpe played with the energy of a man looking to keep his place in the side, and it was one of his incisive runs which earned United a fifteenth minute penalty, which was converted by Iwelumo. This was the only goal, although Colchester looked much more like extending their lead than Swindon ever did equalising.

On the following Tuesday, Colchester made their last ever visit to Belle Vue, Doncaster. A Tuesday night trek up the A1 for another of those "are you really up for this?" games. Colchester were up for it, withstanding a battering in Yorkshire with Davison and Brown dominant in defence to earn a valuable point.

Even more valuable, shortly afterwards was the announcement that planning permission had been granted for the building of a new stadium at Cuckoo Farm. Could it be that the realistic prospect of Championship football had finally galvanised Colchester`s movers and shakers to end the near forty year wait for a decent stadium? Council leader John Jowers said it was "95%-plus likely" that the stadium would be ready for the start of the 2007/08 season, a prediction which proved to be twelve months out.

Four points from two games. The U`s were slowly coming back to some form, but the goal scoring touch was still eluding them. Garcia was injured, while Iwelumo and Danns were having barren spells. Thorpe was starting to look dangerous, but he had played little first team football and hadn`t yet found the target.

Parkinson decided to make two more loan signings. In came Ipswich`s highly rated 18 year old striker Billy Clarke, and winger Jamal Campbell-Ryce from Rotherham. Brentford and Huddersfield had suffered hiccups while Colchester had been picking up those four points, and the play off positions had contracted.

Liam Chilvers had picked up another injury for the trip to Scunthorpe and was replaced by Gary Richards. The match was nothing to write home about, as once again the U`s failed to find the net. Typical of their recent luck in front of goal, an eighty ninth minute strike from substitute Billy Clarke was controversially disallowed.

The now customary defensive solidity was there. Another clean sheet and another vital point. Also, great news from elsewhere. Brentford lost their third game in a row and everyone else chasing second spot dropped points. Only three points now separated second from seventh with Colchester fourth. However, on the following Tuesday Brentford got back to winning ways at MK Dons, which set them up nicely for a visit to Layer Road.

It was April Fools Day and 5,635 turned up for the vital League One promotion clash, fourth v second. Confident that his goal scoring touch would return, Parkinson gave Tony Thorpe his fourth consecutive start and persisted with a four four two formation. He had both the recently loaned strikers, and Campbell-Ryce on the bench.

There was no doubting that something had to change if anything was going to be achieved in this season. The cause had not been helped by having four "goals" disallowed in recent games, but even taking this into account the stats made for stark reading. United had scored twice in the previous nine league games! From a long throw and a penalty. They had been stuttering ever since the FA Cup fifth round draw had been made. Before that, goals from open play had been flowing freely for over three months. The days when Iwelumo, Cureton, Danns and Garcia were on fire now seemed distant, and it was only the defensive side of their game which was keeping United in the hunt. This was a triumph of organisation, given that injuries and suspensions had forced many changes of personnel in the back line.

Colchester fell behind after six minutes against Brentford, but dominated the rest of the match. Iwelumo headed in a Duguid cross for a thirty first minute equaliser and after that it was Mexico v Davy Crockett as the Londoners` goal led a charmed life. The breakthrough would not come and it was now one win in nine. Phil Parkinson was concentrating on the positives though, "The hardest thing in football is putting the ball in the back of the net. But I can`t praise the lads enough. That`s four games unbeaten and we played as good as we have all season".

With an average gate around 20,000, Nottingham Forest had flexed their financial muscle in the January transfer window. They had also sacked manager Gary Megson and brought in Colin Calderwood. Automatic promotion had been the minimum expectation for them, but this now looked unrealistic. However, the play offs were very much in their sights going into their home match with Colchester United on 8th April.

Seven points above them, one might have expected the comparatively tiny Essex club to be favourites but recent form suggested otherwise. Forest had five wins and two draws from their previous seven games and had risen to the edge of the play off zone.

It was the kind of fixture that highlighted what Colchester could be up against as they fought for promotion from League One. The January transfer window is an opportunity for clubs to boost their squads for the second half of the season. Forest used it to bring in strikers Grant Holt and Nathan Tyson for a cool £1M. The only personnel change at Layer Road was the departure of Jamie Cureton when he was recalled by Swindon. Forest had other big money players in their squad, and even the idea that Colchester could be favourites bordered on the preposterous, whatever the league positions.

It must therefore have been a strange feeling to be a Colchester player running out in front of 22,680 at the City Ground. You were accustomed to playing in front of less than 1/6th of this attendance and were quite possibly up against some players earning more than six times your wages. Nevertheless you were under the pressure of expectation to get a favourable result.

The U`s put in a spirited performance in Nottingham, but fell to a James Perch goal in the seventy second minute. Vernon made his first start, while Clarke and Campbell-Ryce both came off the bench. Ironically, Forest`s winning goal was scored by a defender who had cost nothing. Brown made a fine tackle on Holt, only to see the ball cannon off Perch into the net. An Iwelumo volley almost brought a deserved equaliser, but once again it was simply not Colchester`s day.

The Gods seemed to be against us but there was better news from elsewhere. Brentford had been held at home as had Barnsley. Huddersfield, Swansea and Oldham had all lost and United remained fourth.

| 1 | Southend United | 41 | 22 | 11 | 8 | 67 | 37 | +30 | 77 |
|---|---|---|---|---|---|---|---|---|---|
| 2 | Brentford | 41 | 19 | 12 | 10 | 63 | 45 | +18 | 69 |
| 3 | Huddersfield Town | 41 | 18 | 14 | 9 | 66 | 53 | +13 | 68 |
| 4 | Colchester United | 40 | 18 | 11 | 11 | 49 | 37 | +12 | 65 |
| 5 | Swansea City | 40 | 16 | 15 | 9 | 69 | 48 | +21 | 63 |
| 6 | Barnsley | 41 | 16 | 15 | 10 | 54 | 40 | +14 | 63 |
| 7 | Oldham Athletic | 41 | 18 | 9 | 14 | 55 | 52 | +3 | 63 |
| 8 | Nottingham Forest | 41 | 17 | 10 | 14 | 60 | 46 | +14 | 61 |

Phil Parkinson was now talking about a six game season and we only had to wait until Tuesday for it to start. The Monkey Hangers were coming to town.

Chapter 9

# SQUEAKY BUM TIME!

# Chapter 9
## SQUEAKY BUM TIME!

On 8th April Southend were eight points clear at the top, and barring a massive collapse, had promotion in the bag. The remaining promotion place and the four play off places were between the following seven clubs, who were separated by eight points. All had five games to play, except Colchester and Swansea who had six. Their game in hand would respectively be Hartlepool and Swindon at home on that Tuesday evening. It was essential that both took advantage of their extra game.

The 04/05 season had been one of Hartlepool`s best. They came very close to going up through the play offs, with Adam Boyd and Joel Porter scoring forty goals between them. Both had missed most of 05/06, through injury and it had been a season of struggle. A change of manager had brought about a small improvement, but they were still twenty first when they came to Layer Road, and staring relegation in the face.

Parkinson continued his efforts to kick start the forward line by giving Billy Clarke his first start. A feature of the League One season had been surprising results, and there was no reason to suppose that fourth from top would beat fourth from bottom. Sure enough, Hartlepool lacked nothing in motivation or belief, and were unlucky not to take the lead at least twice. However, the U`s were also creating plenty of chances, but just could not find the net. The bar was hit, and there were good saves and dramatic goaline clearances.

Thorpe and Vernon were brought on to try to make the breakthrough, but it looked like yet another draw and another blank in front of goal. Hartlepool had been reduced to ten men, and both nerves and frustration were bubbling over at Layer Road. This would be a good time for a Liverpudlian to score his first league goal for nearly three months.

It is the eighty third minute. There is a ball into a crowded box, and up pops a dreadlocked head belonging to Neil Danns. He is shorter than most of the players around him, but he has timed his jump better. He nods into the bottom corner for 1-0. Danns has been waiting for that bus a long time, and a few minutes later another comes around the corner. He fires home from close range to send the primate executioners spiralling towards the basement division.

There is joy and relief in equal measure at Layer Road. Not such good news is that Swansea have beaten Swindon.

Everyone now has five to play. Colchester are third, one point behind Brentford, and ahead of Huddersfield due to having a goal difference which is one goal better. Swansea are two points behind in fifth. Then there are Barnsley, Oldham and Nottingham Forest, each with a small outside chance of automatic promotion and every chance of the play offs.

Brentford`s remaining games were all against teams in the bottom eight. Huddersfield and Colchester only had bottom half teams to play. Swansea and Barnsley both had tough looking games against Oldham and Southend amongst their last five. So Oldham`s run in looked difficult, while Forest`s toughest match looked like being at mid table Bradford on the final day.

Easter would bring two games in three days. First it was a trip to Chesterfield`s charming Saltergate. Home of the open air toilets. Where the call of nature meant no interruption of one`s enjoyment of the action. Provided you could stand on tip toe while doing the necessary. Where, in January 1993, we lost 4-0 while playing into the teeth of a wind so strong it looked like the roof of the main stand would come off and the floodlights would come down. Where Carl Emberson`s goal kick reached the halfway line only to blow back and go off for a throw ten yards from the goal line. Where in the first half a wayward and wind-assisted Martin Grainger shot flew over the open end, and was last tracked by air traffic control heading towards Dublin.

Parkinson preferred Thorpe to Clarke for this match, but otherwise it was an unchanged starting eleven. Izzet had returned from an ankle injury, but could not even make the bench.

Chesterfield had been perennial League One strugglers in recent seasons. Always doing just enough to stay up. This season they had secured their future much earlier than normal, and against Colchester played with the freedom of a job done. United could not come to terms with the bumpy pitch and were dominated in the first half. After eighteen minutes, Chesterfield were two up and Phil Parkinson was squabbling with Spireites manager Roy McFarland.

This was a time for big characters and somehow the match was pulled out of the fire. Mark Yeates, in particular, took the game by the scruff of the neck. On the stroke of half time he scored a brilliant individual goal from a fine angle after a mazy run. In the second half he ran the Chesterfield defenders ragged as an equaliser looked more and more likely. It came in the seventy third minute when Iwelumo volleyed in following great work by Yeates and Duguid.

It was only a point, and Colchester must have travelled hoping for three. However, after being two down it felt like a win. Swansea lost, while Brentford and Huddersfield only drew. Barnsley won at Oldham, while Forest picked up another good win.

United now had to host an improving Tranmere side. What an opportunity this was. On this day, Swansea and Oldham would lose while Brentford and Barnsley would both be held to home draws. Then Huddersfield would lose on the following day.

Tranmere had been well fancied at the start of the season, but had spent the first half of it in or around the bottom four. They had been steadily improving however and now looked safe in seventeenth place.

Parkinson recalled Billy Clarke in Thorpe's place, while John White came in at full back as Baldwin dropped to the bench. The U's found it hard going against a resilient Tranmere team and chances were at a premium in the first half. For the second home game in a row, the opposition went down to ten men when O'Leary saw red. Now the Merseysiders had clearly come for a point, and at half time Parkinson made a bold substitution. Winger Jamal Campbell-Ryce came on for White. The Rotherham loanee impressed with some jinky runs on the left, but the breakthrough would not come. Yeates had been released into a roving role and was starting to attack the Tranmere defence through the middle.

In recent weeks the fans had been surprised to see Wayne Brown taking an interest in free kicks around the opposition's penalty area. In the first half of this match he actually took one. Let's just say it did not make the club's end of season DVD! The budget for this venture would not stretch to the time lapse photography necessary to detect movement in the ball. The defensive wall was beaten but sadly not the keeper, who not only had time to throw his cap on it, he could have clad it in full ceremonial dress, taken it out for a five course meal and returned it in time to be picked up three yards from the line as it ran out of all energy.

In the sixty first minute Clarke was replaced by Thorpe and two minutes later Yeates in full flight was brought down by Jason McAteer twenty five yards out. This looked like Halford territory, but to everyone's horror Wayne Brown was once again loitering with intent. With everyone expecting the big centre half to be ushered gently away to more normal duties, Halford dummied it and Brown ran in to curl a perfect kick past the keeper and over the defender on the line. Joy and delirious astonishment unconfined!

The U's knew how to close out a game, and Tranmere never looked like equalising. With seven points from three games Colchester had now eased into second place, helped also by the slip ups of their rivals. They were a point above Brentford and three above Huddersfield. The second automatic promotion place would almost certainly now be between these three clubs.

Colchester's visits to Bournemouth's Dean Court had always been tricky down the years. They had frequently left with nothing. On 23rd April 664 U's fans made their nervous way to the south coast knowing that winning the final three games would deliver second tier football to Colchester for the first time, no matter what other clubs did. What better place for the club to spend its seventieth year than in the Coca Cola Championship?

The well worn cliché of each game being a cup final had started to apply several games ago. The phrase no longer did justice. Now every game was the World Cup final, England v Germany!

Most fans were going to bed exhausted from having spent the day working through all the permutations in their heads. If we drew with Bournemouth, beat Rotherham and drew with Yeovil would this be enough? No! Huddersfield would surely win at Walsall and Brentford at Swindon. We'd then drop to third, the pressure would tell and we'd get, at most, one point from the last two games. We would go into the play offs a disappointed team and collapse. The manager and all the players would leave and we would be relegated next year. Then straight through League Two back to the Conference. Oh God. Better get some sleep! But wait. Walsall and Swindon will be fighting for their lives and at home. They might take something from those games. Salvation! If we all draw tomorrow we'll still be second............zzzzzzzz.

It's morning. The birds are singing. I know. I heard the first expulsion of intestinal gas from a stirring sparrow. Who cares about them! Did the team have a restful night? Good solid eight hours should have helped Big Chris's knee. With the money from the Chelsea game, they should have been able to stay in a hotel with decent blackout curtains and proper sound proofing. What if the carpets are lumpy? A player could trip. Sprained ligaments. That's it. A season in tatters and all for the want of an £18.95 carpet stretcher! I'll sue that hotel! Sue it for every Corby Trouser Press that it's got. Every minute's sleep that I've lost. Oh no, but another day of this!

It's likely that one nightmare which would have disturbed the slumbers of increasingly frantic fans would have been food poisoning suffered by a key player. But that could not happen. Not to us. Not at this time.

Going into the Bournemouth match Phil Parkinson must have felt like Sir Alf Ramsey. But not in a good way. Both were facing the three most crucial games of their career when they were told that their goalkeeper would be taking no part, unless it was possible and legal to set up a toilet cubicle in the six yard box! For Sir Alf this meant calling up Peter Bonetti who, lacking match practice, made the game changing error which lost the 1970 World Cup quarter final against West Germany, and with it the World Cup itself. Parkinson did not have as experienced a deputy to call upon.

When we arrived at Dean Court, all talk concerned the whereabouts of Aidan Davison. That unflappable pillar in front of our goal. Maker of good decisions. If it was a keeper's ball he came. If it wasn't he stayed. The back four knew where they were with him. Unspectacular but steady. Dominant when he needed to be. Made few mistakes and a good talker. He'd been there and got most of the T shirts. Exactly what you need when facing three momentous games.

It later emerged that he was suffering from food poisoning, so young Dean Gerken would be between the sticks. The other change was Scott Vernon starting up front in place of Clarke.

Bournemouth had not enjoyed a great season but they were nothing if not obdurate. They were sixteenth. Only Bradford had drawn as many games. This was surprising, as in Steve Fletcher and James Hayter they possessed two top quality strikers at League One level. They were unbeaten in seven. The opinion of most fans was that we could not afford to drop out of the top two at this stage of the season. Brentford and Huddersfield were both playing relegation haunted teams, so we needed to win.

Colchester made a great start when Liam Chilvers rose above everyone in the fifth minute to head in a free kick. The lead only lasted three minutes. Stephen Cooke attacked the U`s defence and Wayne Brown slipped leaving Cooke with a free run on goal. Gerken narrowed the angle, but Cooke finished superbly into the corner. That`s how it stayed at half time, thanks to an excellent Gerken save low to his right.

Early in the second half, the U`s were back in front. Karl Duguid made a magnificent run down the left flank and crossed. Vernon cooly controlled and volleyed into the top corner. Parkinson`s difficult selection headache between Vernon, Thorpe and Clarke had been justified.

United now had something to hang on to, and the introduction of Izzet and Baldwin helped to make sure they did. They had to survive a few scares, but with Gerken playing without fear in goal, and in particular standing up to the physical challenge of Steve Fletcher, the result never seemed in too much doubt. The backing of the travelling support was tremendous. There was no let up from the first minute to the last, and there were wild celebrations at the end.

A very difficult fixture had been successfully negotiated. In theory it should get easier from here! The news came through that Brentford and Huddersfield had both won making the result at Bournemouth all the more vital.

On the following day Greg Halford and Neil Danns were voted into the PFA divisional team for League One. Voted for by their fellow League One players, this was an accolade which had not come to Colchester United since Mark Kinsella was honoured ten years before. A great achievement, but how the likes of Aidan Davison and Wayne Brown missed out, given the team`s defensive record, was a mystery.

The weekend`s results meant no change in second, third and fourth. However, Southend needing one more win to secure promotion, had fallen at home to Doncaster. Only three points now separated them from Colchester in second. Colchester had to hope that it would not come down to goal difference between them and Brentford, as the Bees were superior by four goals in this department.

| 1 | Southend United | 44 | 22 | 12 | 10 | 69 | 41 | +28 | 78 |
|---|---|---|---|---|---|---|---|---|---|
| 2 | Colchester United | 44 | 21 | 12 | 11 | 56 | 40 | +16 | 75 |
| 3 | Brentford | 44 | 20 | 14 | 10 | 69 | 49 | +20 | 74 |
| 4 | Huddersfield Town | 44 | 19 | 15 | 10 | 71 | 57 | +14 | 72 |

United would now host struggling Rotherham at a sold out Layer Road. Brentford and Huddersfield also had what appeared to be straight forward home fixtures against Hartlepool and Yeovil respectively.

Phil Parkinson wanted all forms of communications media banned from the hearing of himself and his players, "I don`t want to know, and I don`t want my players to know what is going on at other matches important to us around the country. I don`t want a radio anywhere near our dugout. All I am interested in is making sure my lads are totally focused on what it takes to beat Rotherham".

The mood was caught by the Essex County Standard, "Colchester United Football Club are on the brink of something wonderful". Despite this, it was business as usual at Layer Road, "We`ve had our normal training sessions", said Neil Danns, "We have got this far doing the same things, so there is no need to change things and get panicky. Just doing the basic things has worked so well for us so why would we stop now?".

Despite Parkinson`s words, many fans were glued to radio sets throughout the Rotherham match. It was one of those occasions when it took little more than a half smile or a flinched muscle to send outrageous rumours raging around the ground like a wild fire. As there was little reliable information around, it was best to follow the manager`s lead and simply concentrate on the match in front of us.

Unsurprisingly, Parkinson stuck by the same eleven which had won at Bournemouth. Davison`s food poisoning had developed into something more long lasting and Dean Gerken would again deputise. Although he had only just turned twenty one, Gerken had shown at Bournemouth what a good temperament he had. He had made his debut in the final game of the 03/04 season. He then made sixteen first team appearances in the following season, and had made eleven in the current season before the Bournemouth match. All vital experience for the challenges now in front of him, as it looked unlikely that Davison would return for the final match either.

The U`s went into the match with the best home record in the division. Furthermore, the result at Bournemouth meant that the lowest they could finish was fourth. In turn this meant that the club was guaranteed its best finishing position since the league adopted its nationwide structure in 1958. At worst, a place in the Play Offs was assured and if we`d been offered that........... Lets not trot that cliché out. A place in the Play Offs would now be desperately disappointing.

It was possible that we could finish the Rotherham game a Championship club! If we won, Brentford lost and Huddersfield failed to win, promotion was secured. The 1600 who had already bought up Colchester`s ticket allocation at Yeovil would just be going for a party.

Rotherham were twentieth, two points above the relegation zone, but they arrived at Layer Road in good form. Two wins and two draws from their previous four games had lifted them out of the bottom four. These games had included a good draw against Brentford, and an impressive win at Swansea`s Liberty Stadium. So it was clear that playing top five teams held no fears for them, and there was no doubting that they had everything to play for.

The atmosphere was electric, and Colchester`s unity of purpose was never in doubt from the moment Vernon netted in the second minute only for this to be correctly ruled out for handball. Gerken saved from James Coutts, and Mark Yeates then rattled the bar with Vernon firing the rebound wide.

United were on top, but the goal wasn`t coming. In the twenty ninth minute Rotherham`s Shaun Barker decided to help out. Not content with the goal he had scored for the U`s when the teams met at Millmoor in November, he dealt with a long pass from Danns by heading over his own keeper into the net. Twelve players had scored for Colchester so far in 05/06, not counting poor old Shaun who must have been sick of the sight of the blue and white stripes!

Parky wasn`t interested, but at half time there had been no goals at Brentford`s Griffin Park, but David Graham`s goal put Huddersfield`s noses in front at the Galpharm Stadium where over 14,000 were roaring them on.

The U`s had to keep going. If they allowed an equaliser, and the other two games remained the same, it would be a right bun fight on final day, with one point separating the three clubs.

Even the destination of the title had been brought back into doubt with Southend`s defeat the previous week. Today they had by far the toughest task, facing Swansea, who were desperately trying to scramble into the Play Offs, in front of over 19,000 at the Liberty Stadium. They were 2-1 down at half time. At this rate, all three outcomes would be possible for Colchester at Yeovil on the final day. They could be crowned champions. They could be promoted in second place or they could be consigned to the Play Offs.

In the fifty third minute Iwelumo flicked on to Yeates who, given a yard of space just outside the box, drilled into the bottom corner. The U`s had torn into Rotherham, intent on making sure their job was done, regardless of events elsewhere. Although they could not add to the second goal, the result was never in much doubt to any neutral observer. Despite this, fatalistic U`s fans were grateful to hear the final whistle, which was followed by Wayne Brown carrying off a clutch of Player of the Year awards.

News came through that Southend had equalised and taken a point from Swansea. They were now one point above Colchester with a better goal difference. If they drew or lost their final game at home against the much improved Bristol City, and Colchester beat Yeovil, the U`s would go up as champions.

There had been a complete turnaround in Yorkshire, where Yeovil had secured their League One future by scoring twice without reply. That knocked Huddersfield out of the race for automatic promotion. Brentford`s stuttering and draw-ridden form had continued. They had gone ahead with six minutes left but then allowed Hartlepool an injury time equaliser. They had drawn five of their last six games.

Four points now separated top of the table Southend from third placed Brentford. So with one game left, Southend had secured promotion. They were now only playing to go up as champions.

The only sour note for Colchester concerned Mark Yeates. We still needed a result at Yeovil, and Yeates had come into sparkling form just at the right time. Sometimes his decision making on the field could be infuriating. Why did he take that man on, when a colleague was so well positioned? Why did he pass then when the shot was on? But he was only twenty one and improving all the time.

After his goal against Rotherham, most fans were in seventh heaven and beyond any rational thought. Yeates somehow had the presence of mind to wave away ecstatic team mates so as to give him room to run to the corner flag where the pitch had probably not been watered and was hardened from the recent dry weather. Here he made the decision to execute a kind of swallow dive of celebration in a move unlikely to deflect stereotypical opinions about the intelligence levels of many of his compatriots.

Like many things, goal celebrations have developed over the years. Long before 2006 they had become highly choreographed affairs honed over many hours on the training field, often with more than half an eye on the likely position of TV cameras. We no longer expected a Cholmondley-Warner handshake or a Stanley Mathews rustle of the hair, followed by a gentle jog back to the half way line. Even if a team mate wanted to give Yeates a good English pat on the back, it was no longer advisable. He emerged from his "Tom Daly" with 0 out of 10 for approach, flight and entry, a dislocated shoulder and having played his last football of the 05/06 season! Parky could have been forgiven if he had rearranged other parts of Yeates` body!

*"I couldn`t believe it the way Yeatesy put his shoulder out but he did stupid things like that sometimes. Aidy got very ill with food poisoning after the Tranmere game and it became clear that he would miss the last three games. It was a blow but I had confidence in Dean Gerken. I always rated him and he came in and played without fear."*

So, it would all be decided at Yeovil`s Huish Park on Saturday 6th May 2006. Colchester could be champions, just promoted or dumped into the Play Offs. In truth, nobody was all that concerned about being champions. That would be icing on the cake. What mattered was going up to the second tier for the first time ever, whether it be in first or second place.

| 1 | Southend United | 45 | 22 | 13 | 10 | 71 | 43 | +28 | 79 |
| 2 | Colchester United | 45 | 22 | 12 | 11 | 58 | 40 | +18 | 78 |
| 3 | Brentford | 45 | 20 | 15 | 10 | 70 | 50 | +20 | 75 |

Southend were hosting Bristol City, and Brentford would be going to Bournemouth. So all three clubs were against teams who had nothing obvious to play for, although individual players would be playing for contracts and there was prize money at stake.

Bournemouth were eighteenth and were safe by virtue of an excellent point secured at Nottingham Forest`s City Ground in front of nearly 27,000. Yeovil were sixteenth and had made themselves safe with that great win at Huddersfield. Much fancied Bristol City had endured a poor season in the bottom half until a late revival took them to the edge of the Play Off zone after they replaced Brian Tinnion with Gary Johnson. In fact, it was technically still possible for them to reach the Play Offs, but their draw at home to Swindon left them needing a set of perfect results and shifts in goal difference which would amount to a mathematical miracle. They were out of it.

No-one can ever calculate what "having nothing to play for" is going to mean for a team`s performance. It can relax them into giving one of their better performances, or it can leave them lethargic and vulnerable. One thing was certain. There would be no unchewed nails in the away end at Yeovil.

Brentford were promoted to the second tier in 1992. That had been the first time they had played at second tier level for forty five years and they only lasted one season. They had since missed out four times in the Play Offs, and in one of those seasons had been minutes away from securing automatic promotion. The former BBC Director-General Greg Dyke was now chairman. They had been there or thereabouts all season, and were desperate not to miss out again.

Southend had previously had one spell at second tier level, which followed their promotion from the Third Division in 1990/91. They surprised many by having six seasons at that level, before being relegated in 1996. So Southend and Brentford were virtual strangers to second tier football. Colchester were total strangers.

For Colchester, there was only one aim and that was promotion. If it was done as champions, then so much the better, but no-one bothered to calculate the permutations which might bring about that outcome. It was better to keep things simple. If we avoided defeat, we would go up. A win or a draw would see the dream of Championship football achieved.

If we lost we could still be automatically promoted, but only if Brentford failed to beat Bournemouth. So apart from the match in Yeovil, all the focus of U`s fans was on Dean Court, Bournemouth. What happened in Southend could only influence whether the League One title came to Layer Road.

Whoever missed out from Colchester or Brentford would, of course, get a second chance in the Play Offs, but this was not an inviting prospect. Only one from four would make it, and in all likelihood it would mean battling against clubs the size of Huddersfield, Swansea and Nottingham Forest, and the latter had won six of their previous eight.

It was Colchester v Brentford being played out as Yeovil v Colchester and Bournemouth v Brentford. Clearly the odds were in favour of the U`s. Of all the possible permutations, only a Colchester defeat coupled with a Brentford victory could cause a deep depression over Colchester. We were sorry for the Londoners. We knew they had been just missing out on a regular basis since the early 90s but they would just have to take their chances in the Play Offs. We were so close to the prize we could smell it. Surely we could not give it away now!

For the second time in the season, a vast surge of humanity was making its way out of the town in support of its football club. Nothing else in England could cause such a phenomenon. Only football. The thousands unable to get tickets were preparing their radio sets. This time it would not be a little jaunt up the A12 to London. The coaches had to leave at 8am as the car drivers checked their tyre pressures and oil levels. The remainder contemplated a four and a half hour rail journey.

It had been sixty eight years and nine months since their forebears had made the same journey for Colchester United`s first ever match at Yeovil`s previous home, The Huish. Then the rail journey had cost thirteen shillings and sixpence. It cost a little more in 2006, even with a network card! Yeovil and Petters United, as they were then called, triumphed 3-0 and U`s fans did not want any of that nonsense this time around.

We already knew that we would be without two key players. Aidan Davison was still ill, and Mark Yeates humerus was having only a distant relationship with his scapula. We arrived at Huish Park to be greeted by even more disturbing news. The players were warming up, and there was no Wayne Brown. The king pin of our defence. This was too awful.

It was getting ludicrous! First Davison, then Yeates and now Brown. It would have been easier to take if these players had been lost to football injuries, instead of bad shell fish and a badly executed standing piked dive with twist. Now it looked like Wayne Brown had just failed to turn up! Perhaps he had to go to a wedding. Or perhaps his wife insisted he help her with the monthly shop. Or had Greg Dyke had him kidnapped? It is amazing what directions the stressed mind can go in.

Maybe Brown had strained himself lifting all those Player of the Year awards. We had able deputies, but there was only one Wayne Brown.

Jamal Campbell-Ryce came in for Yeates, and Pat Baldwin for Brown. White, Duguid, Chilvers and Baldwin lined up in front of Gerken. Halford was on the right, Campbell-Ryce on the left with Danns and Watson in the middle. Vernon partnered Iwelumo up front. Cousins, Richards, Izzet, Thorpe and Clarke were on the bench.

The match started and finished after about ninety minutes of play. There is not much more to be said about it beyond recording the final score. Any neutral observers probably wished they had stayed at home to watch their own grass grow! In terms of entertainment it was probably one of the worst games since The Freemasons Tavern in Great Queen Street, London, hosted the inaugural meetings of the FA in 1863. But you would have been hard pressed to find a U`s fan who gave a stuff about the entertainment level.

For the record, both Halford and Danns came close to giving United the lead in the first half, and Gerken had to be alert when turning a Phil Jevons shot on to the post. News came through that Sam Sodje had put Brentford in front at Dean Court. We had to hang on. The half time whistle was sounded, and according to the jungle drums Bournemouth had equalised. Yes! It`s now been confirmed over the tannoy.

Early in the second half a tremendous cross field move ended with David Poole putting the ball just wide of the Colchester goal, when he perhaps should have scored. Iwelumo then shot narrowly wide and Kevin Watson had a penalty appeal turned down. Then horror of horrors. Brentford have re-taken the lead through Andy Frampton, and there is still 20 minutes to play here. The whole season was now teetering on a knife edge. In fact the 70 year history of the club was! A Yeovil goal and the dream was probably over. Distress signals were being fired from the away end!

With the likes of Gerken, White and Baldwin playing beyond their years. With Duguid playing a captain`s innings at left back and Chilvers making sure Brown`s leadership was not missed, the U`s had firmly slammed the door shut. Yeovil huffed and puffed, but there was never going to be a goal.

Andre Mariner put the whistle to his lips and sounded a symphony so beautiful it would have brought tears to a glass eye. To him, it signalled the end of another ninety minutes. To Yeovil it sounded the end of a decent season. To Colchester United`s players, officials and supporters it was the music of the spheres.

All those damp Tuesday nights playing Darlington in front of 2,761. Arriving home with no feeling in the feet and wondering if it was worth it. In this moment it was worth it. The decades of speculation about how far Colchester United could go. Seeing clubs like Cambridge, Southend, Wrexham, Hereford having spells in the second tier. Why can`t we? The near misses of 1957 and 1980 when big finishes were needed, but could not be found. The utter misery of that day at Cambridge in April 1990, when we were relegated out of the League. Would the club survive?

These were the kind of thoughts which went through the mind, when that whistle was blown. Some thought of friends and relatives no longer with us and how they would have loved that moment.

We had done it. The manager. His back room staff. The owner. The Chief Executive. The girls in the ticket office. The groundsman. The coach driver. The fans. And yes, even the much vaunted tea lady, so often spoken of at every football club and yet never seen, probably because she doesn`t exist. And above all, the players. We had all done it. And by God we deserved it.

Total strangers hugged each other. Women cried. Certain men seemed to get something in their eye as well! For ten minutes the words would not come. The mouth opened but nothing came out. Many of us had waited forty or more years to see this. With the changes in football making this sort of success more and more difficult for small clubs it was a moment which seemed to have moved further away. So far as to almost seem unattainable. Trying to explain one`s feelings at that moment to a Surrey based Manchester United fan would have been like explaining the rules of cricket to an American, or House of Commons procedure to a Martian.

We had just seen happen what we had waited decades to see happen and now never thought we would see happen. And boy, did it feel good!

I think it was at the moment, when a six feet 4 inches twelve stone goalkeeper passed body surfing over my head, that I heard a stunned voice in the melee say, "we`re in the Third round of the Cup!"

| 1 | Southend United | 46 | 23 | 13 | 10 | 72 | 43 | +29 | 82 |
|---|---|---|---|---|---|---|---|---|---|
| 2 | Colchester United | 46 | 22 | 13 | 11 | 58 | 40 | +18 | 79 |
| 3 | Brentford | 46 | 20 | 16 | 10 | 72 | 52 | +20 | 76 |
| 4 | Huddersfield Town | 46 | 19 | 16 | 11 | 72 | 59 | +13 | 73 |
| 5 | Barnsley | 46 | 18 | 18 | 10 | 62 | 44 | +18 | 72 |
| 6 | Swansea City | 46 | 18 | 17 | 11 | 78 | 55 | +23 | 71 |
| 7 | Nottingham Forest | 46 | 19 | 12 | 15 | 67 | 52 | +15 | 69 |
| 8 | Doncaster Rovers | 46 | 20 | 9 | 17 | 55 | 51 | +4 | 69 |
| 9 | Bristol City | 46 | 18 | 11 | 17 | 66 | 62 | +4 | 65 |
| 10 | Oldham Athletic | 46 | 18 | 11 | 17 | 58 | 60 | -2 | 65 |
| 11 | Bradford City | 46 | 14 | 19 | 13 | 51 | 49 | +2 | 61 |
| 12 | Scunthorpe United | 46 | 15 | 15 | 16 | 68 | 73 | -5 | 60 |
| 13 | Port Vale | 46 | 16 | 12 | 18 | 49 | 54 | -5 | 60 |
| 14 | Gillingham | 46 | 16 | 12 | 18 | 50 | 64 | -14 | 60 |
| 15 | Yeovil Town | 46 | 15 | 11 | 20 | 54 | 62 | -8 | 56 |
| 16 | Chesterfield | 46 | 14 | 14 | 18 | 63 | 73 | -10 | 56 |
| 17 | AFC Bournemouth | 46 | 12 | 19 | 15 | 49 | 53 | -4 | 55 |
| 18 | Tranmere Rovers | 46 | 13 | 15 | 18 | 50 | 52 | -2 | 54 |
| 19 | Blackpool | 46 | 12 | 17 | 17 | 56 | 64 | -8 | 53 |
| 20 | Rotherham United | 46 | 12 | 16 | 18 | 52 | 62 | -10 | 52 |
| 21 | Hartlepool United | 46 | 11 | 17 | 18 | 44 | 59 | -15 | 50 |
| 22 | Milton Keynes Dons | 46 | 12 | 14 | 20 | 45 | 66 | -21 | 50 |
| 23 | Swindon Town | 46 | 11 | 15 | 20 | 46 | 65 | -19 | 48 |
| 24 | Walsall | 46 | 11 | 14 | 21 | 47 | 70 | -23 | 47 |

**Parky during his early ColU days, feeling it like the fans.**

William McGregor, founder of the
Football League, he of keen eye and
bushy beard.

Where ColU fans could usually find their promotion hopes. Referee Dermot
Gallagher presiding.

JC offering thanks to JC. Jamie Cureton celebrates another goal during his successful loan spell. Chris Iwelumo and Neil Danns give chase.

The scoreboard at Stamford Bridge. Please blow the final whistle now!

Colchester United make a rare splash in the national press.

The final whistle has just blown at Yeovil.
Colchester United are a Championship club!

Next stop, The Coca Cola Championship!

Manager and Captain, Phil Parkinson and Karl Duguid.

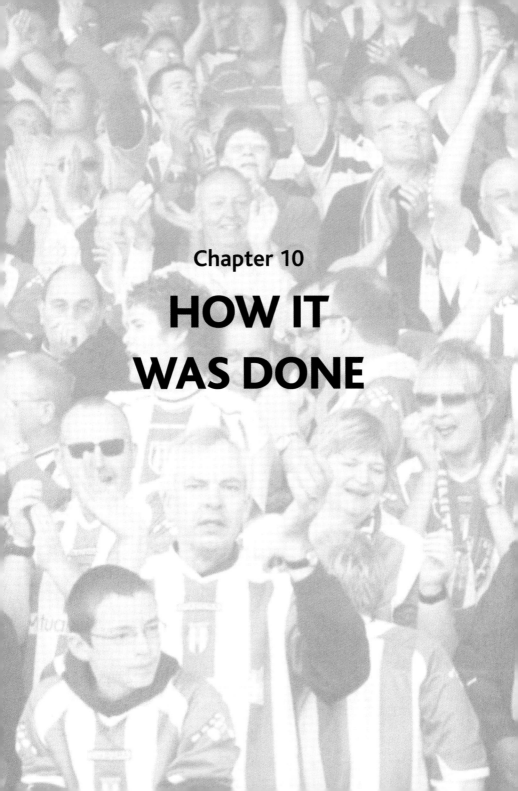

Chapter 10

# HOW IT
# WAS DONE

# Chapter 10
## HOW IT WAS DONE

Geraint Williams looks back to how history was created,

*"There were many people who made vital contributions to that success but of course it was led by Phil Parkinson. As soon as he arrived, he started to persuade players to sign for the club. I have no doubt that his energy and enthusiasm transmitted itself to those players, who were all hungry to improve. Stuart Ayles probably got them fitter than they had ever been, and I like to think that I contributed on the training field, as did Phil and all the staff. It didn`t happen overnight and not every signing was a success, but most were. You build gradually by bringing in three or four every year, you work to improve them and to gel them with the players already at the club, and then you have a team. Provided you have time, it can be done without a massive budget. As well as playing ability, you have to look for the right characters and again, this was where Phil was so good. He realised we needed more experience, and he persuaded Aidan Davison and Kevin Watson to sign. They were both great characters.*

*Aidy was a massive character at the club. Mental, but in a good way. Dean Gerken used to idolise him. Aidy would have him doing weights before training and then take him for a "greasy spoon" as a reward. Dean would not be the goalkeeper he is today without the work that Aidy put into him.*

*Kevin was tremendous on the ball, too good quality for League One level. He was one who had to constantly work on his fitness, and with Aylesy behind him he did. Kevin knew that as well as using the ball in the classy way he did, he also needed to be able to get round the pitch so he dedicated himself to his fitness.*

*The 04/05 season was a bit disappointing but injuries, loss of form, sometimes just bad luck, do happen. We can now look back and call that a blip. They do happen in football. It`s not always plain sailing. There`s too many variables and things you can`t control.*

*I certainly thought something was building going into the 05/06 season. Phil was gradually getting the squad the way he wanted it. It was full of good characters. We couldn`t be certain how good the squad was, nor could we be sure about the standard of the division, but I expected us to do well. Although 04/05 hadn`t been as good as we`d hoped, we were confident the squad was strong and didn`t need any major surgery. That`s why there was very little transfer business during the 2005* summer.

The club's policy in regard to agents could cause us problems. There were occasions when it prevented us from getting a player. However, I could see Mr Heard's point of view. He felt that giving money to an agent was a waste. I've had situations where an agent has wanted to agree his fee before the player's terms had even been mentioned, and that isn't right.

It took us a while to get going in 05/06, and it was Jamie Cureton coming in with his goals which sparked us off. The staff had discussed it, and we thought that we were drawing games that should have been won. We thought we could be more attacking without losing the defensive solidity we had.

Jamie was not having a good time at Swindon, and I think he was handled differently at Colchester. His fitness and nutrition were not as good as they could have been. When he came to Colchester he had a very positive manager telling him that he was the best goal scorer in the division, and he had a fitness coach telling him what to eat. Phil knew how to motivate Jamie, and I don't think the people at Swindon did. Equally, I think Jamie knew that at Colchester there was a manager and a staff who were going to get the best out of him.

We had two great runs of results either side of Christmas, but the Chelsea match seemed to knock the stuffing out of us for a while. We were constantly telling the players to concentrate on the next game, and the cup game will take care of itself, but you have to remember that a lot of those players had never played at anywhere like Stamford Bridge before. I suspect that, subconsciously, they were worrying about getting injured and missing the experience.

We had lots of team meetings where everyone was entitled to their say, but they were never used as an opportunity to criticise individuals. It was all about the team. However, Phil might well have had strong words with individuals in private. Eventually the form turned round, and of course Dannsy came on strong with his goals. To get sixteen from midfield is a hell of an achievement.

If you are going to be successful, you will have "must win" games, and some of the games towards the end of the season were certainly that. You then need your big characters to drive the rest on. Aidy missed the last three games but we had plenty of other leaders in the team. Obviously we wouldn't have chosen for Aidy to miss those games, but he thought Dean was a good young keeper and we knew he had a good temperament. He came in and did well.

What happened against Rotherham was typical of Yeatesy! Later we could laugh about it.

*The preparation for the Yeovil game was all about keeping things normal. It was a big blow when Wayne Brown was injured the day before. That we were able to get a clean sheet, despite missing both Wayne and Aidy, shows the spirit that was in the club. The players had belief in what Phil was trying to do, and it meant that players could come in and do a job. Liam Chilvers was always a good talker in the back four, and with Wayne out he was re-assuring Pat Baldwin and Dean. The players called Liam "the rock", and he certainly was that day.*

*When the Yeovil match finished, I remember a mixture of elation and relief. I`m not one for swallow diving in front of the fans, but I felt a huge sense of pride. I remember looking at Parky`s face, and as well as joyful, he almost looked amazed! We all went back to Colchester and celebrated in the town, and in the small hours I remember being responsible for making sure our manager got home in a cab!*

*Looking back, I don`t think League One that season was as strong as it often is. Nottingham Forest were the only genuinely big club, and they were massively in decline. There were Huddersfield and Swansea, but they hadn`t quite taken off yet. The points tally needed for promotion was relatively low, and these things coincided with Colchester having a good manager who had spent just over two years building a team. It was the right group of players at the right time. But these things should not detract from what was a magnificent achievement to get a club of Colchester`s size into the Championship."*

In a management world obsessed by target setting, the leadership at Layer Road seems to have been remarkably relaxed. Peter Heard remembers,

*"I never had any long term goals for the club. Taking each match as it came is a cliché, but I think that is what we did. We never had any expectation of reaching the Championship. Perhaps that helped in not creating pressure around the club. I suspect we always thought it unrealistic to expect us to be promoted from League One. My role was to set the environment in which the players could perform to their best, and the club could do as well as it could.*

*Phil had fostered a remarkably good atmosphere in the dressing room and no-one was agitating to leave the club during the promotion season,2005/06. The Chelsea match was something of a defining game during that season. Living in London it was a home match for me. I travelled to it on the Tube.*

*Jose Mourinho caused a lot of trouble during my time as Chairman of the professional referees. He was in the habit of having a drink with the opposing*

*manager after games, and it has always been my suspicion that he turned Phil Parkinson`s head somewhat that day. Phil was no less committed to our cause after that match, but I did feel that he was different somehow.*

*I have met Roman Abramovic, but I didn`t see him that day. He went straight to his box to watch the match and did not socialise with the Colchester directors. I thought that was poor considering it was our biggest match for many a year.*

*The match at Yeovil will always be a great memory, although it was not an entertaining game! Our team were terribly nervous. We got the point we had needed before the game, and it was very pleasing. Yeovil`s directors were very decent and put champagne on ice for us. I remember Phil coming into the board room and having a drink with us, which was unusual for him. I then went down and walked through the team coach shaking hands with the players and congratulating them.*

*I remember thinking how far we had come since those first chaotic days when I was invited on to the board by Mr Bowdidge. I think it was an exceptional achievement for Colchester United to reach the Championship.*

*On the night of the Yeovil match I was staying in an hotel outside the town with the other Colchester directors. After enjoying the hospitality of the Yeovil board we went to the hotel where I was giving a dinner for our board. It transpired that also staying at this hotel was the owner of one of England`s larger football clubs. We knew each other. He was "entertaining" a lady who was most certainly not his wife at this quiet hotel in the wilds of Somerset. His face was a picture when I walked in, followed by the Colchester United board of directors!"*

Parkinson`s main job leading up to the Yeovil match was to keep the player`s feet on the ground. Not easy, as he says that both staff and players had a clear sense of the history they were trying to make,

*"Wayne Brown pulled a hamstring while we were training at Reading on the day before the Yeovil game. Pat Baldwin had to come in alongside Liam Chilvers. Pat and Deano both did so well in that game and it illustrated what a good squad we had. This was the key to our success.*

*It`s not enough to have a good starting eleven. You`ve got to have good players on the fringe as well. Often that means having to have experienced players on the fringe, but that doesn`t work at a club like Colchester. You can`t afford it for one thing. Also, senior players tend to get miserable if they are not playing, and that can bring the whole squad down. I`ve seen it happen. We had a good crop of young players* *who didn`t expect to be playing week in week out, and didn`t expect big wages. They were, however, good enough to do the job when called upon. I`m thinking of people like Deano, Pat, George Elokobi, Gary Richards and John White.*

*They all had great attitudes which were infectious, and if they came in for an injured player it could sometimes give the established players a kick up the backside. It made them realise that they had to be playing with an edge or they would lose their place.*

*Not everything went to plan at Yeovil. With Browny out, I`d decided to have Gary Richards on the bench. This meant George Elokobi wouldn`t be in the squad. Somehow George Williams got this mixed up when he wrote out the team sheet for the referee, and Elokobi read that he was to be on the bench. I only realised this when I noticed that Gary wasn`t getting changed! I had to pull Elokobi aside and apologise to him as he was going to miss out that day. George Williams and I laughed about it later, but at the time I didn`t really need any more stress!*

*Jamal Campbell-Ryce came in and he was a good lad. He was caught in the middle of a dispute between his parent club Rotherham and Southend, who he`d been loaned to. That`s how he became available. He`d already agreed to join Southend for the start of the following season. I had some misgivings about playing him against Yeovil in case he had a conflict of interest regarding his connection with Southend, but George thought he would be fine and he was. He celebrated promotion with us and then went off on Southend`s open top bus tour!*

*I`ll never forget those moments after the final whistle for as long as I live. All my family were down there and it was just brilliant. For me, it was the culmination of building things gradually over three years. For other people at the club it had been a lot more than three years` work, and as well as being delighted for myself I was delighted for them.*

*I think the players deserve huge credit for the way they conducted themselves. I told them that, in years to come, you`ll return to Colchester and you`ll be remembered. There were some great personal stories in there. Dugy coming back from being out for over a year and thinking that his career might be over. Browny contracting skin cancer. He had to have a big lump cut out of the top of his head, but almost straight after the operation he was insisting on making a return. He was a vital player for us but I had to hold him back until we got the official all clear.*

*We had the lowest budget in the Division, and we`d been promoted. There`s no doubt in my mind that we would have won the title, but for the FA Cup run."*

It was about an hour after that wonderful whistle that we staggered out of Huish Park. During the evening, someone mentioned that Bournemouth had scored an injury time equaliser. So we would have gone up even if we had lost! Football! Don`t you just love it!

Southend beat Bristol City 1-0 and so were champions. A prize that would surely have come to Colchester but for that FA Cup run. However, they had beaten us twice and they deserved the crown. It was an Essex one-two and we were happy to be the two.

It had been a fantastic season of competition in League One and no-one would have thought it would finish with Southend and Colchester in the first two. It was the sort of unpredictable outcome no longer possible at the top levels of the game, where the purchase of success is the only way forward. In League One it was still possible to be successful through honest endeavour, good scouting, good coaching a will to win and no little skill. Southend and Colchester had proved this.

There was an open top bus tour and a civic reception. An estimated 7,000 people crowded into the High Street to hail their heroes lined up on the balcony of the Town Hall. Flags were waved, horns were blown and street lights were climbed. Unfortunately, no-one thought to rig up a PA system or provide a loud hailer. So speeches were not possible, and the manager and players could only wave at the fans. We did however have the comedy of the hapless Mayor trying to address the throng by shouting!

Barnsley had sneaked past Nottingham Forest into the Play Offs. Poor old Brentford didn`t even make it to the Play Off final, beaten by Swansea, who were themselves beaten in the final by Barnsley.

So how had little Colchester United finally made it to the second tier of English football? There had been a fantastic run of results through November and December. When that finished, there was an immediate bounce back and an even better run through January and early February. Then the wheels came off under the bright lights of the FA Cup but, through shrewd handling of the squad, Parkinson had been able to get the show back on the road and produce the strong finish which eluded his predecessors in 1957 and 1980.

The Board had appointed a good young coach. One who was hungry for success. He had inherited some good players. Some who had started at the club and others who had existing links with the club.

Wayne Brown had links with the area and knew the club. He might have signed whoever the manager was. Similarly, Liam Chilvers looked on his way regardless of the identity of the manager. Karl Duguid, Kem Izzet, Pat Baldwin and John White were already here. So was Greg Halford, and perhaps Parkinson was fortunate to profit so much from his emergence and the rejuvenated return of Duguid after long term injury. However, Parkinson created the conditions in which these players could thrive and develop.

He made the spine of the team, partly through his playing contacts. He had played with Aidan Davison and Kevin Watson and also with Jamie Cureton, whose two month sojourn was the catalyst for the first of those great runs. The spine also came from Parkinson persisting in his courtship of Chris Iwelumo even after the big Scot moved to Germany in preference to Colchester, and unlike many managers, recognising that Wayne Brown was a centre back and not a full back.

He then topped off the cake with the flair players, the ones who could unlock a packed defence, Neil Danns, Richard Garcia and Mark Yeates. All great finds.

So in broad terms, about half the squad had been introduced to the club by Parkinson. The rest were either products of the youth system or had been introduced by the previous manager. But, regardless of how the players came to the club, it was Parkinson, ably assisted by Geraint Williams, who honed their talents, blended them into a team and turned them into winners. The coaching and scouting contributions of Brian Owen and Paul Dyer should also be recognised. Football men to their core who were willing when necessary to tell the manager if they thought he was going wrong.

It did not happen overnight. The board had given him time. Over two seasons before the historic one. There were times when the boat seemed to be off course, but Phil Parkinson kept his eye on the ultimate goal and somehow instilled belief into a bunch of youngsters and free transfers that "little old Colchester" could do it.

They had one of the smallest average attendances in the Division, one of the smallest financial turnovers in the entire League and played out of a tumbledown stadium that had seen better days before Phil Parkinson was even born. But they did it, and not only was it a great achievement for the club, it was great for football.

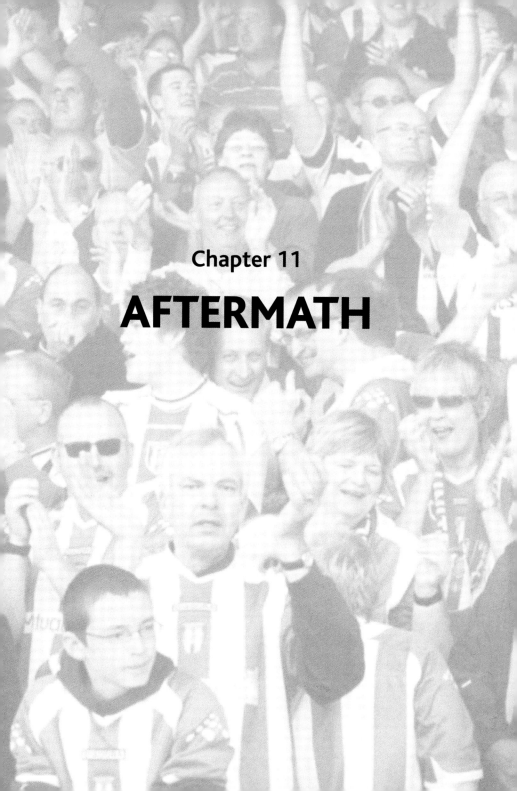

Chapter 11

# AFTERMATH

# Chapter 11
## AFTERMATH

Phil Parkinson was a long way from being an Essex boy. Colchester United had barely figured on his radar until Peter Heard made that call back in February 2003. However, for just over three years he moved to the area and put his heart and soul into the club. A small part of him will always be in North Essex, and he will always follow the fortunes of the club. He speaks with such passion about that period, that one could almost imagine that he is still the Colchester United manager. The smallest details are remembered, and the true significance of what was achieved is clearly understood.

As well as pride at his own achievement, he is at pains to convey the crucial parts played by everyone at the club both on and off the pitch.

*"I have always said how proud I am of what was achieved at Colchester while I was there. However, it would not have been possible without the excellent people I had around me. I have already mentioned a number of people on the staff, but I think Marie Partner deserves a special mention as she was tremendous in her role at the club. She had so many connections in the town, and she built a spirit amongst the non football staff in the same way that I was trying to do with the team. They were all people who loved the club, and it was much more than just a job to them. Equally, there was always good leadership from the board. We all worked very well together.*

*Mr Heard was very clear about the size of the budget and that it was not going to change. I always knew exactly where I stood. When you were negotiating with players even saving £10 could make a difference! It gave you more money to spend somewhere else.*

*I think things were run very well. Mr Heard oversaw the budget from London, but it was myself, Marie and the in house accountant Janie Pitt (now Gregory) who ran it on a day to day basis. Mr Heard just came in for matches and the monthly board meeting. The three of us would regularly sit down and calculate what we had left to spend. It was managing on a shoestring and it taught me a lot. It`s a fantastic education for any manager.*

*Mr Heard was never in a position to put big money into the club, but he was clever. In every other way he backed me in putting the building blocks in place so that we could maximise the budget we had. In this way, we improved things gradually in as many areas as we could. If you do that, and get the foundations right, it gives you a great chance to be successful."*

Parkinson is a professional football man to his core, and it would be easy to make the mistake that when he is managing a football club he is just doing a job. One which comes to a natural end and from which he moves on without a backward glance. In fact, during our talk it became clear that the immense pride with which he justifiably looks back on his time at Colchester, is tinged with a little regret about the manner and timing of his departure. He says,

*"The circumstances of my departure from Colchester were unfortunate."*

Parkinson's work at Colchester had been attracting the interest of bigger clubs from at least January 2006. He could have forced his way out of Layer Road when Leicester City made their formal approach, but he preferred to see the Colchester job through. It was obvious that the phone would be ringing red hot once the season was over.

Parkinson was under contract and all approaches should have been through the club, but it would be naive to think things always happened in that way. The strategy of the bigger club is usually to first make the approach in the correct manner, and then if rebuffed to encourage the manager to resign, thereby weakening the small club's negotiating position on compensation.

Rules and ethics are ignored even when the clubs are neighbours! Colchester United have been the victims of this on more than one occasion and have had to go through Football League Tribunals to secure appropriate compensation. When they have appointed managers, they have generally either been out of work or have been appointed from within the club. On the rare occasions that a manager has joined the U's from a smaller club, it has only happened after compensation has been agreed.

Within two weeks of that great day at Yeovil things were turning sour. On the following Thursday Joe Royle resigned at Ipswich, and they were immediately being linked with Parkinson as were Derby, where there had been no permanent manager since Phil Brown's sacking in the aftermath of their FA Cup defeat at Layer Road. However, it seems that the only club to make a formal approach to interview Parkinson were Charlton Athletic, then of the Premier League. Alan Curbishley had just resigned at the Valley.

Charlton were refused permission to speak to Parkinson. A statement from the board said, "While recognising that Mr Parkinson must have ambition, it is vital that we look to retain him for the future interest of everyone connected to Colchester United at this critical stage."

It certainly was a critical stage. Neil Danns had turned down the offer of a new contract and seemed to be heading to Birmingham. Meanwhile, Liam Chilvers was looking for a move to a northern club as his partner wanted to return to her roots, and Mark Yeates would be returning to his parent club, as would the three short term loans, Campbell-Ryce, Clarke and Vernon. So new recruits were going to be needed, and Wayne Brown needed to be tied down to a new contract.

Phil Parkinson recalls,

*"I had no burning desire to get away from Colchester. I had already started preparing for the new season. I was busy setting up the signings of Jamie Cureton and Johnnie Jackson. When Charlton made their approach, there was a board meeting, and I told them I was happy at Colchester and my family were settled in the area, but that I would like to speak to Charlton. Although I was aware of interest from Ipswich, I said I would not speak to them as they were the local rivals.*

*I particularly wanted to speak to Charlton as they were in the Premier League, and for a young League One manager to be linked with them was quite an honour. In fact the vibes I`d been getting through my agent were that Charlton thought I probably wasn`t ready for the Premier League, but nevertheless wanted to speak to me.*

*I expected my request to be granted, but the next day Mr Heard rang me to say the board had unanimously turned it down. I felt let down. I felt I had done the right thing regarding Ipswich and the Leicester approach in January, after which I had told Mr Heard that I might want to follow up opportunities in the Summer. It is very rare for a League One manager to get the chance to speak to a Premier League club, and to be denied that opportunity after what I`d done for Colchester really got to me. I`m sorry to say that things then got very messy."*

U`s fans hoped against hope that the matter had been put to bed, and that Parky was putting aside his disappointment to concentrate on taking Colchester United into the unknown. Things were looking up as we moved into June, Wayne Brown signed a new two year contract and Jamie Cureton was transferred from Swindon.

Sadly, the sticking plaster that had been placed over the managerial position came off on Wednesday 14th June when it was announced that Phil Parkinson had left Colchester United. He had submitted a letter of resignation. The board said they were refusing to accept it and they urged Parkinson to reconsider his position upon his return from holiday. They expected his contract to be honoured but it was clear that the writing was on the wall.

*"Obviously the world knew that I was unsettled and I was getting lots of approaches through agents. In the end I spoke to Hull City, and was offered the job there which I accepted. I resigned at Colchester and there was litigation which I very much regret."*

It was at this point that the lawyers got involved and a war of words broke out between Colchester United and Hull City. Hull were an ambitious club with a good following and a new stadium. After two consecutive promotions, they had just finished a disappointing eighteenth in the Championship.

The managerial merry-go-round was rotating furiously. It begins with Charlton fans becoming dissatisfied with regular top half finishes in the Premier League, and a growing belief that Alan Curbishley can take them no further. He resigns. Ian Dowie pulls the heart strings of Chairman Simon Jordan at Crystal Palace by saying that he wants to be released from his contract so that he can return closer to his family base in Lancashire, only to then turn up at Palace's south London rivals Charlton Athletic! They appoint him, having just been rebuffed by Colchester. Peter Taylor decides he has no future at Hull, and takes the vacant Palace job. Now Hull need a new manager, and guess what? There's one in North Essex looking for a move.

So when the music stopped, the one left standing was Alan Curbishley. He should really have completed the circle by taking over at Layer Road, but the next step up for him would either have been the England job (which went instead to Steve McClaren) or a Champions League club. In the end he had to settle for West Ham.

One would have to be pretty naive to think Parkinson had not been illegally approached by Hull, and certainly no compensation had been agreed when it became clear that he was bound for the KC stadium.

The players had no idea that Parkinson was intending to resign, including Jamie Cureton who had just signed for the club. Kevin Watson said, "We had no idea this was going to happen. As far as I knew the manager was staying."

The Colchester United board was being both realistic and steadfast, "should we be unable to stop him resigning we will do whatever is necessary to protect the club." After this statement, it should have been no surprise when the club obtained a temporary High Court Injunction preventing Parkinson's move to Hull. It was clear that they were not going to be pushed around by a bigger club, and of course this strengthened their negotiating position.

Hull chairman Adam Pearson said "It seems shockingly vindictive of Mr Heard to prevent Mr Parkinson from making a living when he has done so much for Colchester United and there is a large amount of compensation on offer already." However, Colchester had described the compensation offered as "modest".

Colchester was claiming the moral high ground, and Peter Heard had no intention of rising to Pearson`s personal attack. A club statement said, "The directors, management and fans continue to hold Phil in the highest regard. The decision to seek an injunction to prevent him tearing up his contract is partly in a vain hope that he will change his mind. However, it is in truth more about the principle of ensuring that the process of a football club losing an excellent manager is conducted in the appropriate manner. Colchester United is taking this bold move because it fundamentally believes that even the football world must take employment contracts seriously. The injunction is about making a stand, but it is also a very clear signal to Phil Parkinson and any club making him an approach, that Colchester United puts a very high value on the manager that led the club to success this year- a very high value indeed."

It is notable that at no time during this sad interlude was there any direct rancour between Colchester United and Phil Parkinson, or between Peter Heard and Phil Parkinson. Sabres were being rattled and it was all about one thing, compensation.

Neither party had anything to gain from the prolongation of this dispute. It effectively rendered both managerless, just when they should have been preparing for the new season.

A level of compensation was finally agreed, with Hull admitting it was in excess of the £300,000 they had received from Crystal Palace for Peter Taylor. They had first offered £150,000 and then £250,000. A statement from the U`s said, "A sum in the region of £400,000 has been paid, plus recovery of legal costs." Crucially, the club also secured an agreement that Hull would not seek to employ any employee of Colchester United for a period of 12 months. Parkinson would not therefore be able to take any of the players or staff with him.

Phil Parkinson was formally announced as the new manager of Hull City on 30th June. Geraint Williams started his second spell as the caretaker manager at Colchester on the same day.

Parkinson`s reign at Hull, which had started in such controversial circumstances, was destined to last for only five months. About £100,000 in compensation and legal costs for every month! He was given £2 million to spend on players and expected to deliver immediate success. Second from bottom with four wins from twenty one games, and nine goals shipped in the last two, (including five at Layer Road) did not look much like immediate success to Adam Pearson. The manager he had claimed to have tracked for two years before his appointment, was jettisoned with another compensation payout.

Parkinson now looks back philosophically,

*"I think I was a bit impetuous, and perhaps badly advised. Hull was not the right job for me, and with the benefit of hindsight I think I should have bit my lip and stayed at Colchester. We had a good side and I think I could have improved it. It was not dissatisfaction with the budget that made me leave. I had no intention of leaving. I'd already signed Jamie Cureton and Johnnie Jackson for the coming season. As anyone can see from my playing record I don't move around willy nilly. It was just that refusal of permission to speak to a Premier League club had alienated me.*

*I really wish it hadn't ended up in court because that's not what I'm about at all, and it was a very stressful time for me and my family. I'm delighted to say time has healed the breach though. Peter Heard and I get on very well when we see each other.*

*I felt I left behind a good structure and a good squad of players. I was thinking we could establish ourselves in the Championship for a couple of years and then kick on from there with the new stadium, but it wasn't to be. That's football, managers and players move on."*

How it ended was indeed regrettable. We will never know how things would have panned out had he stayed. In the opinion of this writer the club's successful spell in the Championship would have been sustained across the move to the new stadium, and Parkinson would eventually have moved to a middle ranking Premier League club and might by now be in the Champions League. However there is still time for that.

What we can do is look at the contrast between Phil Parkinson and two other managers who have reneged upon contracts to walk out on Colchester United. George Burley and Paul Lambert both walked out only months into their contracts, after substantial sums had been spent on their players and staff, and before they had any opportunity to justify those investments with success. They are rightly looked upon with approbrium by all U's followers. Phil Parkinson was at Layer Road for over three years, during which he grafted with dedication, and no little inspiration, to deliver more success than anyone had a right to expect.

He should be feted whenever he visits the Weston Homes Community Stadium.


## THE KING IS DEAD (WELL, BUGGERED OFF TO HULL ACTUALLY) LONG LIVE THE KING.

Geraint Williams found himself in temporary charge once again, and his first job was to welcome two old friends signed by the old manager. Neither Jamie Cureton nor Johnnie Jackson needed directions to Layer Road, having both enjoyed good loan spells at the old place. However, he had to bid farewell to Neil Danns, who could not resist the lure of a much bigger club when Birmingham City came calling. In late June the fixtures were announced, and in one of those strange twists, Birmingham would be the first opponents. Liam Chilvers departure was also confirmed, as he signed for fellow championship side Preston.

The release of the fixtures started to bring home to U`s fans that what had happened six weeks before really had happened. The first matches being looked for by most were those against the farmers of Ipswich.

The U`s search for a new manager went on for almost the whole of July, just when work was needed on strengthening the squad. It is an unfortunate fact that the best way to keep the gap between managers to a minimum is to poach someonelse`s. If your manager is poached, you can do nothing about a replacement until the legal wrangling is over. Furthermore, Peter Heard always refused to be hurried over the appointment of a manager. No one could accuse him of not being methodical. Applications were formally invited. Certain individuals or clubs might be approached. Two rounds of interviews were held, and after due consideration an appointment was made.

The former Gillingham manager Andy Hesentahler was known to have applied, and the club had reportedly approached Birmingham City for permission to speak to Eric Black, who was assistant to Steve Bruce at St.Andrews. However, permission was refused and very little else leaked out of Layer Road as to who the likely candidates were although John Fashanu, Teddy Sheringham and Paul Gascoigne were among those linked, but it was no more than speculation. The only certainty was that Geraint Williams was on the short list, and as the month wore on there was a certain inevitability about his appointment, which was finally confirmed on 28th July. Chief executive Marie Partner did however say that the club had another option, which explained why a week passed between the final interviews and the announcement. According to the Eastern Daily Press that option was the former Kilmarnock, Hibernian and Plymouth manager Bobby Williamson.

Peter Heard takes up the story of the 2006 close season,

*"Not long after the Yeovil match I received an approach from Richard Murray, the Chairman of Charlton Athletic, wanting to speak to Phil Parkinson. I said no, he wasn`t available and he said he wouldn`t persist with it. I told Phil about this. He was under contract, and I told him that I thought it best for him to remain with us at that time. I have no clear memory of any approach by Derby, and if there was an*

*approach from Ipswich it never got to me. I think they would have been wary about tangling with us again after what happened with Burley.*

*Somebody from the BBC or ITV rang to tell me that Hull wanted our manager. I spoke to their Chairman Adam Pearson, who said it wasn't true. I then saw a different side to Phil's character. He resigned, and it immediately became apparent that he was going to Hull. These things are very fraught, and there were some heated words. There was a very strong bond between Phil and the board, and sadly that was fractured.*

*Replacing Phil took a long while because we had a lot of applications to go through, and certain complications developed. Sean O'Driscoll was one of those interviewed. Others were Craig Levein, Stewart Robson and Bobby Williamson. Levein withdrew his interest after the interview. We offered O'Driscoll the job and terms were agreed. He knew that Geraint Williams had applied for it, and at his request we told Geraint that we had decided to give it to O'Driscoll. He then changed his mind! This obviously put us in a difficult position with Geraint, who had also missed out on the job when we gave it to Phil Parkinson. The season was almost upon us. We offered the job to Geraint and fortunately he took it on.*

*Geraint is a very nice bloke whose loyalty had impressed us, and the only real doubt we had about him was his lack of experience as a manager. O'Driscoll had been manager at Bournemouth for six years. He had brought them up from the fourth tier and established them in the third. He had done it with very limited resources. However, we thought Geraint had earned his opportunity, and after what happened with O'Driscoll we decided to give him a chance."*

Geraint Williams gives his memories of this time,

*"Phil kept me informed of what was going on regarding approaches made for him. I know he was very frustrated when the club turned down his request to speak to Charlton. We always felt it was wrong to hold back a player who had the opportunity to move on to bigger things, and I couldn't see that it should be any different for a manager. By this time we had a very strong personal and working relationship, and when he resigned to join Hull he wanted me to go with him. I told my wife and she wanted to know how far away Hull was. I told her five hours, and knowing Parky I wouldn't be home for weeks on end as we'd often be working Sundays. There was no question of the whole family moving up there.*

*After thinking about it, I decided to stay, although at that time there was no* way to be sure what my future at Colchester was going to be. Things seemed pretty chaotic at Colchester as I think they had expected Phil to stay.

I was told I could apply for the job, but that there would be other applicants. I was asked to run pre season training while they were looking at things. There were some sessions when we only had six or eight players training, with the Championship season starting in a few weeks! Most of the players had never played at that level before. I had to tell Karl Duguid to try to keep the morale of the squad up, and to tell them that things would be right by the start of the season. He was great at doing this.

A lot of players had left since the end of the previous season and we had a tiny squad. The main concern was not to pick up any injuries during pre season. None of us knew what was going on at the club, and the situation dragged on for weeks. The season was getting closer and closer, and it was getting beyond a joke to be honest. I kept telling the players that things would get sorted, but it was starting to get embarrassing. It was a very difficult time. Joe Dunne helped a lot, without him it would have been impossible.

At one point I was told that Sean O`Driscoll had been offered the job, and that he was happy to keep me on as assistant. I was then asked if I would try to persuade him to take it. It was a strange situation. I was being asked to talk someone into taking the job that I was hoping to get! My wife couldn`t believe it, but I did try. He asked me if I thought we had a chance of staying up. I said I thought we did as we had a core group of twelve seasoned pro`s, but that we needed to bring another five or six in.

It looked like Sean would be coming. A press conference had been arranged to announce him but he slept on it and decided to turn it down. He later joined Doncaster in League One. I was offered the job, and I have to say that I was not at all sure about taking it. It felt to me like no-one wanted it. By now the first game of the season was only about a week away. Birmingham away. It doesn`t come any harder. I said I`d think about it. I think that surprised Mr Heard.

I discussed it with the family. I had also been made a decent offer to stay at the club as assistant. Financially, the offer of the manager`s job was derisory, given that there is a massive difference between being manager and being assistant manager. So what was going through my mind was, why should I put my head on the block for such poor money in a job I have twice been overlooked for, and where everyone seems to think we are going to go down?

I like a challenge though. That side of me came out. I thought, I`ve told Sean

*O`Driscoll that we can stay up so I must believe it, and I can do it. The offer was improved and I took it.*

*I didn`t feel daunted by the challenge. I had played international football. I had been to top clubs as a player and won, so that didn`t worry me. Far from it, I was relishing the idea of going to places like Sunderland and Wolves. I thought back to one of my managers, Arthur Cox. Nothing fazed him. You turn up at a big stadium and you don`t cower. You pump your chest out. The Chelsea game had given me a taste of that and I wanted more, but there was a lot of work to do behind the scenes.*

*Parky had set up the signings of Jamie Cureton and Johnnie Jackson. I had to finish off the Jackson signing, he certainly knew Parky had gone when he signed. I can`t remember whether Curo knew. I think he wanted to sign regardless of whether Phil was still at the club."*

Williams quickly got to work by signing eighteen year old midfielder Lawrie Wilson from Charlton. Hardly earth-shattering though, and there was a worry that the squad looked light for the massive challenges that lay ahead. Williams said, "We have a list of players that we`d like to sign but they have to be good enough to improve the squad and be of the right character. There`s money there to bring players in, but there`s not a pot where you can go out and bankrupt the club and we`ll be sensible." The Danns deal had been worth £850,000, but some was dependent upon appearances so Colchester were still having to search for bargains.

Other players to leave Layer Road during the summer had been Gareth Williams to Weymouth, Sam Stockley to Wycombe, Tony Thorpe to Stevenage and Stephen Hunt to Notts County. The remaining squad consisted of sixteen players and some untried youngsters! At this rate the bench would be resembling a kindergarten, and the squad looked considerably weaker than the one that had finished the previous season. It had also been shorn of its manager, and at this stage Geraint Williams was working with no permanent number two. Whatever had happened over the summer the U`s knew they would be up against it at Championship level, but this year they could have no complaints about being everyone`s strong favourite to finish bottom.

The season was upon us, and it was a season many thought they would never see. Colchester United in the second tier of English football! The club sold more than double its normal number of season tickets, and Layer Road had been spruced up and now looked ready to enter the 1960s!

By Championship standards, the club`s budget also belonged in the 1960s, and we looked around for clubs we might have some miniscule chance of competing with over the course of a season. Which three clubs could we target to finish above and so survive in the Championship? As fans, it was best not to linger on that search for long. One`s extremities started to tremble, and before long a small but steady stream of saliva was emanating from the corner of the mouth. We needed to start working hard on our belief in fairies, goblins and elves. There was Southend and Barnsley, what about Luton and Plymouth? They were only about two or three times our size in financial turnover. Along with us these were the minnows of the Division! We would be facing six clubs who we had never before met in the League, including Leicester and Sunderland who we had never played before in any competition.

It was important that we had ambition for the 2006/07 season. To achieve you have to aim high. The record for the fewest number of points in a Football League season is shared between Loughborough and Doncaster, who respectively managed eight points in the 1899/00 and 1904/05 Second Division seasons. Loughborough conceded one hundred goals in their record equalling season and were immediately dissolved. However, this was quite a tight defensive display compared with Darwen who let in one hundred and forty one in the thirty four games of the 1898/99 season. An average of just over four per game over a season in which they also set the record for the number of consecutive defeats at eighteen.

So there we had it. Realistic aims were hard to come by going into the 2006/07 season. If we could achieve at least eight points, let in fewer than one hundred and ninety goals, lose fewer than eighteen in a row and still exist in July 2007, we would have a platform to build upon!

Bring it on!

Chapter 12

# THE SECRET WEAPON

# Chapter 12
## THE SECRET WEAPON

Members of Geraint Williams` squad going into the 2006/07 season must have felt a bit like the British Army defending Rorke`s Drift in 1879. Hopelessly outnumbered and outgunned. However, the squad had one member whose presence must have been reassuring.

This squad member was a bit frayed around the edges, the old bones creaked and better days had certainly been seen. Many thought this squad member should have been put out to grass many years before.

Like an old Dowager Aunt, she bestowed favours upon her family while disapproving of all change. Unloved by her neighbours, she looked with disdain upon any showing excessive familiarity, and appeared positively unwelcoming to guests.

She was called Layer Road, and had been born as a football ground in 1907. At some time during the 90s, she ceased to be a football ground and laughingly became a "stadium". She even acquired a Stadium Manager. You know, like proper stadia, those that were more than a collection of rust ridden cow sheds.

Layer Road was the sixth home of the amateur club Colchester Town. Before they moved in, there had been a pitch let to the Army by the owner, one Arthur Cant. It was described as "a bleak spot on a cold and rainy day with no cover". This problem was addressed with the building of a covered stand which was opened on 28th April 1910 with a friendly match against Woolwich Arsenal.

With the outbreak of World War One, the ground was handed back to the Army and used as a drill ground. Colchester Town purchased the ground from the Cant family in 1919. At this time, the dressing rooms consisted of a converted railway carriage with a tin bath.

When Colchester United was born in 1937 the initial plan was that they would share Layer Road with Colchester Town, but "The Oysters" would soon fold. By this time, a main stand had been built with dressing rooms installed and "banking" on both sides of the ground had been improved. A cover had been erected at the Layer Road end, and capacity was increased to 14,000 of which 5,000 could be under cover. Unfortunately most of this roof was blown away in a storm a few months later.

During the Second World War the ground was taken over by the Auxiliary Fire Service, who agreed to keep the pitch and buildings in order. It did host some football during that time, with famous players like Frank Swift and Tommy Lawton playing there for Army teams.

Ownership of Layer Road had passed from the now defunct Colchester Town into the trusteeship of Colchester Council, and shortly after the War the main stand was extended and adjoining land (which later became the Sporting U`s area) was acquired.

By now, the ground consisted of two ends called the Layer Road end and the Spion Kop end, the latter also later becoming known as the Clock end and the Open end. The sides were the Main Stand side and the "Popular" side. The latter was also called "the Barn", and eventually became known as the Barside, a name which stuck despite the demolition in the 60s of the bar on which it was based. The housing estate which now occupies the site of the football ground includes a road called "Barside Terrace".

The covered area on the "Popular" side was demolished and replaced in 1946, with timbers from it being utilised in the reconstruction of the Layer Road end and some of the standing areas on the main stand side. Some of the work was carried out by Italian prisoners of war. At this time, one third of all fans travelled to matches on bikes! Terracing replaced the "banking" at the Spion Kop end, and the capacity was now 16,000. There were subsequently games when this was significantly exceeded and in the late 40s the official capacity rose as high as 20,000.

Shortly after Football League status was achieved in 1950, a scheme was considered for the floodlighting of Layer Road. This would have made the U`s the first club in the Third Division to have floodlights. However, money was tight and the scheme was turned down, as were a number of subsequent schemes.

A clock was installed in the Spion Kop end in 1953, causing a change in the name by which that end was known. In 1956 a roof was put over the terracing between the main stand and the Layer Road end. A year later the same thing was done over the terracing between the main stand and the Clock end.

In March 1959, work was finally started on the installation of floodlights. The cost was just under £10,000 which was financed from the proceeds of an FA Cup run and in particular crowds of 16,000 and nearly 63,000 for Fourth round matches against Arsenal. The bigger crowd was of course at Highbury, but the U`s would have received a handsome share of the gate. Local residents, so often "sniffy" about their Football Club neighbour, petitioned against the floodlights. Some considered them ugly, others were worried about noise created by evening matches. On this occasion the club were supported by the authorities. The first Layer Road match under lights was against Grimsby Town on August 24th1959. It finished 2-2 with a local reporter commenting that "The lights were first class but United did not shine so brightly."

Layer Road`s first televised match took place on October 13th 1962, when the Anglia TV cameras showed the U`s being beaten 2-1 by Crystal Palace.

Ownership of the ground had been the subject of some debate and legal investigation for a number of years. Colchester United had paid rent to Colchester Council since the collapse of the Colchester Town club in 1937. The Council were the trustees, but their ability to sell was never fully settled. Despite this, sell they did, to Colchester United in 1969.

In 1972 the floodlights were replaced, and this was also the year when serious discussions began about leaving Layer Road. An application for planning permission to build a social club had been rejected, and the ground was hindered by other covenants and planning restrictions. The old lady had been feeling her age for a number of years. No improvements had been made to the fabric of the ground for fifteen years. It had been thought to be on borrowed time, and spending money on improvements seemed like money wasted. However, it was not until 2008 that the ground finally closed.

Plan after plan to build a new stadium fell by the wayside through the 70s and 80s. Out of necessity, serious money was finally spent on Layer Road in the late 80s. £85,000 worth of work had to be carried out to keep it open. This included new concrete terracing in the Layer Road end, and work on the roof of the Barside. Prior to this, patrons had to comically brush falling rust out of their hair whenever a ball hit the roof.

Jonathan Crisp`s six years of ownership had seen the club`s debt massively increase to a point where it`s very existence was in question. Eventually it had to bow to the inevitable and sell Layer Road back to the Council.

When Colchester United returned to the Football League in 1992 a new stadium appeared to be no closer. The existing one was in a sorry state. There was even doubt as to whether it would be considered satisfactory for League football. A lot of work (much of it voluntarily carried out by fans) had to be completed over that summer, and the Open end, which was crumbling and unsafe, had to be closed. An area of uncovered terracing between the Barside stand and the Layer Road end had already been condemned.

By the turn of the century there was nothing 21st century about the match day experience at Layer Road. The capacity had been falling with each safety inspection. The perimeter walls were considered unsafe to have spectators near them and the capacity came down to 6,320. If the Layer Road football ground had been a dog, it would long since have been put down to save it from further suffering.

This was the "stadium" from which the U`s announced their arrival in the Championship. It bore little resemblance to the stadia occupied by United`s competitors. Let us consider those stadia.

Many had a capacity in excess of 30,000. Sunderland`s Stadium of Light was 49,000. Most were either newly built or newly renovated. Some were considered regional centres, with genuine ambitions to become Olympic or World Cup venues. Multi millions had been spent on them. Coventry City had just finished their first season in the Ricoh Arena which cost £113 million.

These stadia offered facilities unfamiliar to patrons of Layer Road. They had club megastores, restaurants, fast food outlets, hotels, offices, undersoil heating, control rooms, media suites, giant TV screens, skate parks, indoor arenas, libraries, community learning zones, health and fitness suites, cyber cafes and corporate hospitality boxes galore. Most seemed to have been played by Elton John. By contrast, even the most humble Elton John tribute act would have refused to don platform shoes for a concert at Layer Road, even if the planning restrictions allowed it.

Although time had clearly passed Layer Road by, the Time Team called in. Tony Robinson and his Time Team filmed at Layer Road during a match in 2005 in connection with the discovery nearby of the largest Roman Circus outside Italy. This was the sports stadium of its day, and is estimated to have had a capacity between 8,000 and 15,000. From the corner of the pitch at Layer Road, Robinson said it was" the Roman equivalent of Colchester having a world class stadium like Old Trafford". Oh, the irony, the sarcasm. Did the old lady take offence? On seeing Tony Robinson at the ground, many just saw it as a reflection of Layer Road having long since become a museum piece.

## LET`S TAKE A TOUR!

So let us drink in the experience of visiting this 21st century sporting venue. As we walk up Layer Road past Ralph and Rita Martin`s emporium, we can immediately see that it would not have been suitable for Roman chariot racing. It just wasn`t big enough. Furthermore, the pitch would have been rendered a fearful mess!

You go past the Layer Road megastore. A portakabin with rusted guttering and a faded blue awning making it look like an ice cream outlet in off season Great Yarmouth.

You can enter on either corner of the Layer Road end. Until the arrival into the League of Barnet it was the only ground accessible from only one end. During the 50s there had been a proposal to create an entrance into the Spion Kop end from Wavell Avenue, but planning permission was denied.

If you entered on the corner of the Barside, your senses were immediately assailed by the smell of gently simmering burgers and onions. If you had any sense, smelling was as far as you took that experience. There was a caravan behind the condemned terracing staffed by some willing boys and girls on the minimum wage. The fact that they were dressed in the sort of clothing used to tackle a contamination scare at a nuclear power plant should have given something away. There was no question that this structure on wheels constituted a significant explosion hazard, but this was as nothing compared with the danger posed by the culinary offences perpetrated therein. What manner of livestock had given their lives to stock the caravan was the subject of some speculation as well. There had to be an E. coli convention going on in there.

So far as smells went, this was about as good as it got. As you passed behind the Barside stand, taking care not to lacerate the arms on jagged pieces of rusted corrugated iron, your nostrils would take in Chateau de Portaloo. A fragrance produced from the mixture of low quality lager and various digestive juices.

The barside portaloo, otherwise known as "the George Burley urinals", was a structure it was best never to venture into. If you did, it was unlikely that you would be yourself for some considerable time. As well as urinals, there were also cubicles, although it was said that no-one had ever sat down in them. Actually, one fan did in 1997. He has been institutionalised with post traumatic stress disorder ever since!

There were a variety of unexplainable phenomena at work in that portaloo. The same cigarette butt resided in the corner of one urinal for upwards of three years! To the extent that there was water flow, it was of a similar complexion to that washing around on the floor. It flowed from the taps at a variety of speeds which bore no relation to one`s operation of the mechanism and into a basin which had been designed for a colony of pygmies. The less said about the functionality of the locks or the paper the better.

The best thing about the portaloo was its suspension, which could have got you up the M1 at 80mph in complete comfort. Quite why this was necessary, given the function of the place, was always a mystery. It was hardly DDA compliant, (Disability Discrimination Act). You had to pull yourself up a rickety detached set of steps to get in.

It was just best avoided. Men would enter with a spring in their step, joy in their heart and an optimistic glint in their eye. They would emerge with a pallid and haunted look, and a feeling of self loathing as if they had carried out some grubby act, or witnessed something which no civilised person ever should.

The provision of ladies toilets at Layer Road is a subject beyond the expertise of this writer. In fact, extensive research has failed to reveal whether there were ladies toilets at Layer Road. Members of the fairer sex were never in abundance, especially on the Barside. Those who did attend would surely not have demeaned themselves by entering a toilet area if it was anything like the Gents.

So having relieved ourselves of matters gastronomic and colonic, we gratefully move ourselves away from that portable chamber of horrors and take our place for the match. First we must bounce up some wooden steps into darkness, so that we can emerge into the further darkness of the Barside terrace. The word darkness here is not only a comment on the light. It was not always a place to be spiritually uplifted. In fact darkness is also a reflection of much of the behaviour which went on there. A sort of unreconstructed laddishness, which made it no place for women, children, or anyone of a sensitive disposition.

Profanity and blasphemy were rife, while the less salubrious borders of the Anglo Saxon language were pushed back. If you preferred not to hear fruity language, you were definitely in the wrong place. You could see little, therefore the hearing sense was enhanced.

In the less enlightened times of the 70s and 80s there would be male chauvinism, racism, jingoism, hooliganism, sexism, sectarianism, with good side orders of xenophobia and homophobia! However, these things improved as time went on, which allowed humour and togetherness to flourish.

Sometimes the atmosphere was electric on the Barside but let us not pretend that it was a good place to watch football. To the left there was rubble. To the right there was a huge wire fence, separating the boisterousness of the Barside from the delicate sensibilities of the family enclosure. This made the one group appear to the other like SS guards peering at concentration camp inmates!

No matter. You had brought yourself to this place to look forward at a football match. Unfortunately, the terracing was so shallow that the act of looking ahead brought you little except an examination of any scalp complaints suffered by the person in front. That is unless you were above six feet in height. You could then see a glimpse of green, although anything occurring on the nearside of the pitch was a mystery, and if the ball went more than eight feet in the air, it was like you were looking at a "spot the ball" photograph. It was like trying to watch a match from inside a post box, or through a tank driver`s slit.

Walking down to the front allowed you to look across to the full majesty of the main stand. With an incongruous camera platform teetering on a mildew infested roof, this was little more than double the size of the dug outs at the Stadium of Light.

A fairly regular piece of Layer Road theatre was the half time charity collection. Four intrepid individuals would walk around the perimeter of the pitch each holding the corner of a blanket. Fans were asked to throw any spare coins into the blanket. It simply would not have worked at a bigger ground or at any modern swept back stadium. You would have needed the throwing arm of a javelin gold medallist. At Layer Road it was a great opportunity for target practice. The blanket, of course, was much too easy a target. So everyone aimed for the collectors. Bloodied but unbowed they would press onward, and a few weeks later be there again in aid of another worthy cause. This wonderful piece of audience participation fizzled out in the 90s, probably the victim of Health and Safety legislation.

There was also something "very Layer Road" about the annual Peter Heard address. Mr Heard did not become a football club owner in order to raise his personal profile. Indeed some of us knew him as "Mr Unheard" so rare were his public pronouncements. He did however deem it appropriate to take to the pitch at the final home match so as to thank the fans for their support during the season. He would emerge purposefully from the main stand and make for the centre circle. Unfortunately this would always prove to be beyond the range of his radio mike, and with no more than two words in every five being audible what transpired was an extended Norman Collier impersonation!

As we continue our tour around old lady Layer Road, we find an area of open terracing between the Barside enclosure and the Spion Kop end. In reality, this progress was impossible. The wire fence and various other hazards saw to that. The ability to circumnavigate the ground was a thing of the distant past, courtesy of 1970s hooliganism, and in particular some running battles with Sheffield Wednesday fans.

Entering on the corner of the Main Stand side enabled you to take in the office area and another of those fine blue awnings, this time below a board advertising the next match and constituting the home of several million termites. A good example of 1960s urban blight, enough to turn Frank Lloyd Wright away from a career in architecture.

You would walk into a symphony of crumbling concrete, rotten wood, peeling paintwork, exposed cabling and ill fitting corrugated panels. There were lights so obscured by dirt and spider`s webs that they lit nothing, and guttering which defied the laws of gravity. There were interesting contrasts of old and new, with rust covered metal clippings which would surely have greeted Ted Fenton when he came in for training, sitting alongside satellite dishes and CCTV cameras.

There were poorly lagged pipes held together with duct tape, lime scaled taps which would pour no more and mysteriously painted over air vents.

This side of the ground was a botanical talking point. There are twelve thousand species of moss and most could be found on the Main Stand side, either on the iron and asbestos coverings or encroaching triffid-like from Rainsborowe Road. A small tree had somehow transferred itself from Rainsborowe Road and appeared to be growing out of the Vice President`s lounge.

One of the great joys of standing on this side was the ability to move at half time, so that you were nearer the goal being attacked by the U`s. When United first went to Wembley in 1992, some fans seemed surprised when they realised this could not be done at the national stadium!

When on the terracing of the Main Stand side, one had to contend with interrupted sight lines. There were a small number of areas on both terraces where it was possible to see the entire pitch without having to peer around a pillar. They were much sought after and it was necessary to arrive at least fifteen minutes before kick off to get into one of these areas. Unlike the Barside, the terracing on this side was of a very good quality and sufficiently steep to allow sight over the person in front. However, just like those on the Barside, most in these stands had their view obscured by something and on occasions were grateful for it!

It was rare for there to be chanting from either of the terraces on the Main Stand side, but they did have their own atmosphere. Especially in the late 70s, when most matches seemed to be pulled out of the fire with late goals inspired by the marauding overlaps on the Main Stand side of Mickey Cook.

As we walk behind the Main Stand to the back of the dressing rooms, the smell of liniment invades the nostrils. Here there is an entrance to the Main Stand, and if you run down it and jump the wall you will enter the field of play near the half way line. From here you can walk up the "tunnel". It was difficult to see how the "tunnel" fitted the definition of that word. It was just a walk way which took you into the bowels of the Main Stand through a canvas concertina, which was supposed to protect the players and officials from irate fans.

The splendour of the dressing rooms was such that many players might have preferred to run the gauntlet. Bijou was the word for them. Tea cup throwing managers could not be employed at Layer Road, because any flying crockery was likely to ricochet and take out half the first team squad. The dressing rooms were so small you had to step outside to change your mind!

So that completes our tour of "the Layerdome". She was ninety nine years old going into the unscaled heights of the 2006/07 season. She was an unhygienic, smelly collection of rust ridden memories but she had a playing surface that was second to none, and it was only as the season got into full swing that we realised what a powerful weapon she would be in Geraint Williams` armoury.

It is a little known fact that the ghost of comedian Les Dawson was invited to comment on the Layer Road football ground. He said

"It was so decrepit, vandals broke in one night and decorated it.

I don`t know when it was last painted but rumour has it that Rembrandt did the first coat.

The dressing rooms were so small, mice had to sellotape their whiskers to walk through.

When the railway sleepers at the Layer Road end were taken out, the woodworm spoke Latin after the ancient Romans who made them.

When it was demolished, many parts of Layer Road had to be repaired so that they were safe to pull down.

The Barside portaloo was so dirty it had to be sprayed with DDT before the flies would go in." And so on and so forth...

The full majesty of Layer Road`s main stand, supporting some hardy media folk.

A serene vision of Old Lady Layer Road. But don`t be fooled.
With 6,000 people inside and eleven in blue and white stripes,
she could become a burial ground for big clubs.

Promotion to the Championship meant ground improvements at Layer Road. Additional seating for away fans. Borrowed from Henley Regatta perhaps?

**The annual Peter Heard address. It was so Layer Road!**

**Layer Road sight lines. Better tune into the radio to find out what is happening on this side of the pitch.**

Can`t even understand why we built a new stadium!

The Barside Portaloo. It was best to have a strong bladder. Failing that, you would need a strong stomach.

Layer Road catering. This area has been designated a crime scene and evidence must be gathered!

Chapter 13

# "LET US THEREFORE BRACE OURSELVES"

# Chapter 13
## "LET US THEREFORE BRACE OURSELVES"

To compare the task faced by Colchester United in August 2006 with that faced by the United Kingdom in June 1940 is taking things a little too far. In fact it is getting things entirely out of perspective. However, as Geraint Williams assembled his threadbare squad in the dressing room at St.Andrews, he must have hoped for some Churchillian inspiration. Or, given his background, perhaps he was thinking of Aneurin Bevan.

He had been asked to climb Everest with little more than a walking stick, a leather helmet and a stout heart! As he glanced across at Birmingham City`s backroom staff filing one by one into their places he must have thought "I need an assistant, a physio wouldn`t be a bad idea either". Stuart Ayles having left the club shortly after Phil Parkinson.

David Geraint Williams (known to most as George) was forty four years of age. Born in the Rhonda Valley, he had made his debut as an eighteen year old for Bristol Rovers, where he made one hundred and forty one appearances before a £40,000 transfer to Arthur Cox`s Derby County in 1985. He missed very few games with the Rams, helping them to consecutive promotions to the old Second and First Divisions. In 1989 they finished fifth in the First Division, which was their best in more than a decade, and only missed playing in Europe due to the Heysel ban. Unfortunately, they were relegated back to the Second Division two years later.

After making three hundred and thirty one appearances at Derby, Williams was transferred to Ipswich Town in 1992. John Lyall paid £650,000 for him to boost the side which had just been promoted to the newly formed Premier League. After three seasons at that level, Ipswich were relegated and Williams spent a further three seasons with them as they battled unsuccessfully to return. After two hundred and sixty three appearances at Ipswich, and aged thirty six, Williams was allowed to join Colchester for an undisclosed fee in July 1998. Signed by Steve Wignall, he was one of a number of ex Ipswich players moving down the A12 around this time.

Williams` playing time at Layer Road was turbulent. The U`s had just been promoted to the third tier and were finding life difficult at that level. Wignall resigned part way through the season, to be replaced by Mick Wadsworth, and Williams experience in midfield played a vital role in keeping the club up. During the following season, injuries were making it clear that the Welshman`s playing days were over, and in March 2000 he announced the end of a successful playing career in which he had won thirteen international caps.

By this time Williams had accepted Wadsworth`s invitation to take up a coaching role at Layer Road, although it would not be long before he was working for Steve Whitton, a former playing colleague at Portman Road and now in the Colchester hot seat. He became Whitton's number two, and later Parkinson's.

Williams looks back on his playing career, and how he started in coaching at a club he very nearly did not join at all,

*"I was born in a village called Cymparc. When I was young, there was a pressure to play rugby, if you refused you weren't allowed to play any sport. Everyone in my age group loved football, we never lost at football and never won at rugby. The teachers soon realised that we were useless at rugby so they arranged us football matches instead.*

*My football career started at Bristol Rovers. They had a fantastic scouting network around South Wales, whereas Cardiff and Swansea didn't really get round the valleys. Bristol Rovers had a nursery team in Cardiff called Clifton Athletic. They would play the best teams from the valleys on Sundays. I was eleven playing for the local under-14 team and we were winning the league. The Rovers nursery team came to play us, it was like a trial match, and if you did better than the players you were up against then you would be invited to go and train with Clifton. This led to me playing for Clifton. It was quite a commitment. It meant getting a train to Cardiff twice a week for training in the evenings, and then again on Sundays for games. Twice a year, we would go to Bristol and play one of the Bristol Rovers boys teams, and the Rovers manager would be watching. At this time Bristol Rovers were in the old Second Division and they had six or eight Welshman in the team every week, so you can see how important the Welsh network was to them.*

*Harold Jarman was one of the youth coaches at Rovers, he was an early influence on me. He was a great coach who wanted you to work hard but enjoy yourself. Eventually I became a young professional. My most influential manager at Rovers was Terry Cooper, the former Leeds and England full back. He was very enthusiastic and would always be telling us how good we were and that we should relax and play. When you are eighteen and playing in the first team, you need managers to have that confidence in you.*

*We were relegated from the Second Division in my first season as a first team player. A lot of youngsters had been thrown in at the same time. To add to our problems the main stand at Eastville burnt down, so it seemed to be a cursed season. In the next few seasons we were usually up near the top of the Third Division but never quite able to get back to the Second. We were always strong at home but sometimes struggled away. Similar to Colchester, there was a core support who would always be there, the famous five thousand as they were called. I was involved with Rovers from age eleven until I left at twenty three, and I have many fond memories of them.*

*In 1985 I had just bought my first house and I was still settling in. We had got a good draw at Derby and I played quite well. The Rovers manager, Dave Williams, told me the club had accepted an offer from Derby for me. So I went to speak to their manager Arthur Cox. Like most players then, I had no agent but it must have been clear that I was disappointed with the offer of personal terms, as they improved it and threw in some carpets as one of the Directors had a carpet company!*

*Arthur Cox was the manager throughout my time at Derby. He was a fantastic man. He had such a passion for the game. When some managers faced an obstacle they would try to find a way round it. Arthur would just stick his head down and run at it and we would all follow. He had no fear. He would take on anyone. We could go to any stadium and believe that we could win. In my first full season we were promoted from the Third Division and in the next season we won the Second Division title. In our second season in the First Division we finished fifth but missed out on Europe due to the Heysel ban. That was the year when Arsenal won the title with the last kick at Anfield, and we doubled them that year, so we were a decent side. The club was owned by Robert Maxwell, and his financial support dwindled. Players like Mark Wright and Dean Saunders were sold and we were relegated in 1991.*

*In 1992 we reached the Second Division play offs but missed out. I`d been averaging about forty games per season in the first team and when my contract finished John Lyall of Ipswich was showing an interest in me. I was thirty by this time, and Ipswich had been promoted to what was now to be called the Premier League. John Lyall was very impressive in the way he spoke to me, about how he wanted the team to play and me to play. He was a great thinker about the game. Very different to Arthur Cox. I had been at Derby for seven years with a manager I liked, so it was a wrench to leave but I never regretted it.*

*John Lyall did great things with the players at Ipswich. He made them all better. He made me a better player at the age of thirty. His knowledge of football and his openness were the things that impressed me. He would never just tell you to do things. He would always reason it out. It was John Lyall who opened my eyes to the benefits of good coaching, although I still didn`t have any real intention of going in that direction when I finished playing. I had scored well in a mensa test and done courses in computer programming and accountantcy. This is the sort of thing I saw myself doing. I had six great years at Ipswich.*

*In 1998 Colchester had just been promoted. I was thirty six, and Ipswich had* *offered me a one year contract, but George Burley said I wouldn`t be first choice because they had Keiron Dyer coming through. Steve Wignall said Colchester had a lot of young players, and they needed someone to sit in midfield and make sure they were solid. I went training on the Monday and they hadn`t done the contract. They asked me to sign a blank piece of paper. I said no, but terms were agreed, and as I was leaving Steve got me to shake hands on the deal and said "I know you`re a man of your word".*

*That night I got a call from Frank Burrows, the manager of Cardiff City. He said he was desperate for me to go there. They were my boyhood team and my wife was very keen on a move back to Wales. Nevertheless I had to say that, although I had signed nothing, I had shaken hands and given my word that I would join Colchester. My wife wouldn`t speak to me for a couple of hours and in fact it was a tough couple of weeks in the Williams household! If Steve hadn`t got me to shake hands, I would definitely have gone to Cardiff.*

*Steve resigned during the 98/99 season and Mick Wadsworth came in. That was a big change because there had been an "all for one, one for all" ethos with everyone on bad money. He brought two or three in on much better money, and it got a bit fractious. However, to be fair to Mick he went very attack minded. He went to win games so as to stay up, and it worked.*

*I had to have a knee operation, and while I was recovering Mick suggested that I take charge of the reserves. I`d had no thoughts of going into coaching and I hadn`t taken my badges. The reserves were mostly the youth team with a few senior pros. I`d never taken a training session before, but they seemed to enjoy it and so did I.*

*When Steve Whitton became manager, I became number two. I was very lucky because I had virtually no experience but Steve wanted someone he could trust".*

By 2006 Williams had been working behind the scenes at Layer Road for six years, and was clearly ready to make the step up. No-one could have criticised him, however, if he had felt somewhat daunted at the challenge facing him.

At 3pm on Saturday 5th August 2006 Colchester United`s first ever match at second tier level began. The moment that must have been dreamt of by Maurice Pye and his colleagues when they formed the club in 1937. A moment that the writer had been waiting forty years to see. And one which he missed, due to the attractions of the Purity Mad Goose in the Wellington on Bennetts Hill and a complete misjudgement as to how long it would take to travel from there to St.Andrews!

About 1300 U`s fans made it on time, knowing what a massive challenge the team faced. Birmingham City had just been relegated from the Premier League, and following a summer clear out had brought in a raft of high quality players. Six would make their debuts in this match, including Nicklas Bendtner on loan from Arsenal and Cameron Jerome a £4 million signing from Cardiff, where he had scored twenty goals in the previous Championship season. They had spent over £3 million on other players (including Neil Danns) and within a fortnight would part with another £4 million to bring Gary McSheffrey to St.Andrews. They were amongst the hot favourites for promotion, along with Sunderland and West Brom. Colchester had won six of their seven pre season friendlies, but you had to wonder whether AFC Sudbury at King`s Marsh was the best preparation for Birmingham City at St.Andrews!

In keeping with recent tradition, Colchester United had spent precisely nothing over the summer. Some needed reminding that they were watching a league match as it had the feel of a cup tie with a big club hosting plucky opposition from the lower leagues. Williams had to remind his players that they had earned the right to be there and were entitled to compete.

Even with so few players to choose from, the manager had a couple of selection conundrums to contend with. Most of the team picked themselves, but he had to decide between John White and George Elokobi at left back, and also between Chris Iwelumo and Richard Garcia to partner Cureton up front. Elokobi and Garcia started. Iwelumo was carrying a slight knock. The departed Chilvers and Danns would be replaced by Baldwin and Izzet.

It was the main match on ITV`s highlights show "The Championship" and the U`s gave a very good account of themselves in front of nearly 25,000. Neil Danns made his debut for the Midlanders, waving to the Colchester fans as he took an early corner.

A DJ Campbell header gave the home side a half time lead, but there was no sign of the visitors being overawed. They came into it more and more as the game wore on, and it was no surprise when the equaliser came in the fifty first minute. A tremendous cross field pass from Halford found Duguid in space. Cureton was denied from his cross but the ball ran loose to Garcia who hammered home. Sadly, it could not last. In the seventy ninth minute the U`s defence allowed Bendtner perhaps twelve inches of space in the penalty area. The Dane, who would later be the holder of fifty six international caps at the age of twenty five, superbly controlled a Stephen Kelly cross, before drilling past a helpless Aidan Davison.

After sixty nine years the U`s had made their bow in the second tier of English football. They had been beaten, but had not looked out of place. Later, ITV pundit Andy Townsend achieved, for him, the rare feat of delivering his post match analysis without using the phrase "all of a sudden" as he commented on the U`s good organisation and said "they will be alright". The manager summed things up very well when he said "our starting eleven can live with anyone in this league". The ninety minutes at St.Andrews had shown that, but everyone knew there would be injuries and suspensions. The U`s needed to strengthen, both on and off the field, and they needed to do so quickly.

Most U`s fans would have seen any points taken from Birmingham as a bonus. In contrast, the next two fixtures were the kind of games from which points needed to be taken if the side were to stay out of the relegation zone. Plymouth and Barnsley at home looked like opportunities not to be missed. Plymouth had finished fourteenth in the previous season`s Championship while Barnsley were fifth in League One and were promoted through the Play Offs.

Plymouth Argyle on Tuesday August 8th 2006 was the first second tier match ever played at Layer Road, and the writer extracted himself from the Dragoon in time to see it kick off! The match looked as winnable as any in this division ever would. Under Ian Holloway, Plymouth had spent £400,000 on bringing in Sylvan Eubanks-Blake and Barry Hayles over the summer. Small beer compared with Birmingham, but exactly £400,000 more than Colchester had spent!

There had been activity away from the pitch. On the day before the Plymouth game, it was announced that Geraint Williams` former Derby County team mate Mick Harford would be joining the club as his assistant. An England international, Harford had previously been manager at Rotherham. Tony Flynn would be the new physiotherapist, while Donough Holohan would be joining as the club`s first ever sports scientist/fitness coach. Sports scientist? At Layer Road? We had visions of some mad professor mixing up potions as thunder claps ricocheted around the kit room, but it seemed these were all the rage now. Every club had one!

Would the club`s burgeoning backroom staff necessitate the installation of bigger dug outs? How would this be possible without restricting the view of half of the main stand? It all seemed a far cry from the days of Dennis Mochan running on with water sloshing out of a pig`s bladder, ready to apply the dreaded wet sponge.

The unchanged U`s played well against Plymouth, but took nothing from the match, which was decided in favour of the West Countrymen by a Luke Summerfield strike in the thirtieth minute. Amongst a number of near equalisers was Garcia`s volley coming back from the woodwork and Cureton`s follow up producing a great save from McCormick in the Plymouth goal. Except for their goal, Plymouth had threatened very little and admitted being fortunate to get all three points. Geraint Williams said "They took their chances but we didn`t take ours".

So we moved on to Barnsley. Still there had been no more acquisitions on the playing front, and the transfer window would be closing at the end of the month.

The referee would be Graham Poll of Berkhampstead. Why are referees always from such unregarded places? He was being rehabilitated into the game following his much publicised blunder at the World Cup finals in Germany. After showing Josip Simunic of Croatia a second yellow card, he failed to send him off. Obviously not realising that it was a second yellow. He then showed the player a third yellow card at the final whistle for dissent, and this time followed it with a red. He was the only British referee at the World Cup finals, and the mistake ended his international refereeing career.

Colchester v Barnsley was an interesting choice of match to return Poll to the English game. He was no stranger to Layer Road having, for example, refereed the final match of the triumphant 1991/92 season against Barrow when Colchester had clinched the Conference title. If the FA thought that putting him in charge of two of the least heralded Championship clubs might keep Poll out of the spotlight, they were wrong. The national media descended on Layer Road to see how the mighty had fallen.

Fans are always full of sympathy for a referee`s misfortune! Noticing the media circus and knowing how much Mr Poll used to like the limelight only increased the fan`s empathy! Poll was barracked throughout, and, in a classic example of Layer Road humour that even he would have appreciated, many held up yellow cards with the number three printed on them!

With Richard Garcia still being preferred to Iwelumo up front, Colchester went into the match desperate to get their season started. Young Gary Richards was brought into central defence, with Baldwin dropping to the bench. Barnsley had enjoyed a good summer, with the ex Celtic Irish international midfielder Colin Healy the most notable among a number of additions. They also beat off interest from other clubs in their ex Scunthorpe striker Paul Hayes. They had lost on opening day, but were fresh from a tremendous 3-2 win at Hull`s KC stadium.

Inevitably, Graham Poll showed three yellow cards during the game, but fortunately they were to different players! Shortly before half time Jamie Cureton showed that he was much more than just a goal poacher when he hung up a superb cross at the far post for Halford, still forward from a corner, to head home. Would this be the first win? Sadly, the U`s were lacklustre in the second half as goals by Marc Richards and Brian Howard sent the points to Yorkshire. The only bright spot was an encouraging substitute appearance by nineteen year old Jamie Guy who worried the Barnsley defence with his penetrative running late on. In a way though, this summed up the problem. If United wanted to make a change during a game, they were looking for teenagers without a league start to their name to come on and spark the team. And that was with an almost fully fit squad.

Williams was no longer expecting plaudits for a plucky performance, "The second half was the most disappointing performance so far, the game plan we had just didn`t happen. It`s proving to be a very steep learning curve in the Championship and we`re not learning quickly enough". With the next match being at unbeaten West Bromwich Albion, there was no doubt that fast learning was needed.

For the trip to the Hawthorns, Colchester at last had an experienced new signing to welcome. Twenty six year old left back Chris Barker came in with more than three hundred first team appearances to his name at Barnsley and Cardiff. It was a four month loan, that was eventually extended to the end of the season. A model of consistency Barker had been the supporters` player of the year at Cardiff for the 04/05 season. He was Mr 7 out of 10. Nothing flashy but you knew what you would get from him.

West Brom had spent their recent history bouncing yo-yo like between the Premier League and the second tier. They had been in the Premier League for three of the previous four seasons, being relegated in two of them. Former player Bryan Robson was in charge, although he seemed to be on slippery ground after the previous season`s relegation. Perhaps a symptom of his weak position was that the only summer business they had done was of the relatively cut price variety. They were however interesting signings, John Hartson and Kevin Phillips. Both coming towards the end of their careers, but top quality nonetheless. Mostly they were hoping that the players they had come down with would take them back up.

Barker came straight in, replacing the suspended Elokobi, while Johnnie Jackson missed out through injury. Garcia dropped back into midfield to replace him, with Iwelumo making his first start in attack.

In the eleventh minute Hartson showed all his experience letting go of Wayne Brown`s shirt for just long enough to fall earthwards in the box. Not only did referee Taylor buy it, he invested it on the stock market and watched his capital grow handsomely while he lived off the dividend income for years! Doubtless it was an honest mistake, but it was one of the worst decisions given against the U`s for a long time, and not what a squad which cost nothing needs when battling against £25 million worth of players! Ellington converted the penalty, and Ronnie Wallwork made it two just before half time. The U`s were shell shocked. An electrifying volley by substitute Jamie Guy halved the arrears, but there were only seven minutes left and it was too little too late.

Colchester United going into the Championship was always going to be one of the biggest mis-matches in football, whatever the circumstances. We knew that when the final whistle sounded at Yeovil. However, we did not then know that we were going to lose our manager, our physio/sports scientist and ten of our players! Ok, not all ten were great losses, but some were key members of the squad which had won promotion.

The consensus was that if Colchester United were to have even a small chance of survival, they had to have a decent home record and they had to make a reasonable start. Four games in and the scorers were still waiting to be troubled by the Layer Road boys. Played four, lost four. And how is that home record going? Er, well, played two, lost two actually, both against unfancied teams. They had also lost to what was in effect an MK Dons reserve team in the Carling Cup.

Most had thought of twenty fourth being the club`s natural position in the Championship all the way through the season. Amazingly, we had not yet found our way to that position despite the four consecutive defeats. Our goal difference was one better than promotion favourites Sunderland, who had also lost their first four.

A lot of work had needed to be done behind the scenes, and it looked as though the summer turbulence and the length of time taken to appoint a manager who was already at the club had fatally holed the ship, at least for the first few weeks of the season. There was no doubt that things could only get better, the question was whether the U`s could recover from such a poor start in such auspicious surroundings.

The bottom of the table after the West Brom game,

| 13 | Stoke City | 4 | 1 | 2 | 1 | 4 | 3 | +1 | 5 |
|----|------------|---|---|---|---|---|---|----|---|
| 14 | Queens Park Rangers | 4 | 1 | 2 | 1 | 5 | 5 | 0 | 5 |
| 15 | Preston North End | 4 | 1 | 2 | 1 | 4 | 4 | 0 | 5 |
| 16 | Sheffield Wednesday | 4 | 1 | 2 | 1 | 3 | 3 | 0 | 5 |
| 17 | Derby County | 4 | 1 | 2 | 1 | 4 | 5 | -1 | 5 |
| 18 | Leeds United | 4 | 1 | 1 | 2 | 3 | 4 | -1 | 4 |
| 19 | Leicester City | 4 | 1 | 1 | 2 | 3 | 4 | -1 | 4 |
| 20 | Coventry City | 4 | 1 | 1 | 2 | 2 | 4 | -2 | 4 |
| 21 | Hull City | 4 | 0 | 1 | 3 | 3 | 7 | -4 | 1 |
| 22 | Ipswich Town | 4 | 0 | 1 | 3 | 2 | 6 | -4 | 1 |
| 23 | Colchester United | 4 | 0 | 0 | 4 | 3 | 7 | -4 | 0 |
| 24 | Sunderland | 4 | 0 | 0 | 4 | 4 | 9 | -5 | 0 |

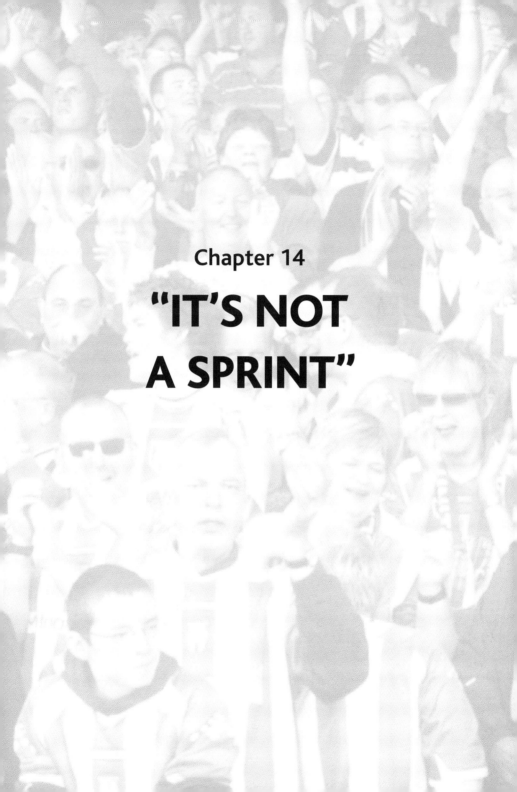

Chapter 14

# "IT'S NOT A SPRINT"

# Chapter 14
## "IT'S NOT A SPRINT"

Any Football League season is a marathon, not a sprint. The problem was that Colchester United had not even started to jog! Four league defeats, not a point on the board and dumped out of the Carling Cup. We did not even have the "Paint Pot" to fall back on. We were so high in the pyramid we did not qualify for it. Furthermore, the FA Cup did not start for us until January. It was hard being such a big and glamorous club!

Shortly there would be more comedy. Colchester United would have a blank weekend due to the international break! We should pause for a moment while we let that sentence sink in...... We didn`t have any international players of course, but most of our opponents did.

As August 2006 neared its end, many were surprised that Greg Halford was still a Colchester United player. He would surely have left over the summer if we were still in League One, and many expected there to be an offer the club could not refuse before the transfer window closed, or "slammed shut" in the language of the great God Sky TV! He was being scouted by all and sundry, with Premier League West Ham said to be heading the queue.

Halford was now twenty one, and in conjunction with his agent felt he had to prompt the situation. He said he was desperate to play in the Premier League, and that Colchester had turned down a big offer from Sheffield United who were then in that league. He put in a formal transfer request, and the club insisted that any interested club would have to "dig deep". This was all very well, but the feeling was that, whilst we needed an influx of new players to compete at this level, most of the talk concerned the possible departure of one of our best players. Perhaps the sale of Halford was the only way we would have a budget to spend.

Geraint Williams remembers those difficult early days in 2006/07,

*"I spoke to Mick Harford about being my assistant. What I liked was that the first thing he wanted to know was how we were going to play. Not how much was he going to be earning, as I`m sure he knew the money would be poor. He came to watch us at Birmingham and agreed to take the job. He wanted to be with the right person at the right club, and he wanted to be associated with attacking football. He turned out to be a very important acquisition.*

*We lost the first four games but only closely. Little things had cost us. We then went to MK Dons in the Carling Cup. I wanted to get the confidence up with a win*

*and we played a near full strength team. We played them off the park, and lost to a wonder goal in extra time.*

*I remember sitting alone in the dug out after the final whistle, trying to think of what I was going to say to the players. I was starting to doubt myself and I was thinking that perhaps I should have stayed as a number two. Mick came up and said "What do you think?". He could see how down I was. I said "It`s so tough, we keep losing to the odd goal!" He said, "Gaffer, we are so close, we`re doing the right things, it`ll turn." I needed to hear that at the time. He said, "Get yourself in there, those boys are looking to you and they want you". I wasn`t sure but as I walked into the dressing room every head instantly looked up at me. At that point I knew I still had them, and that was massive. They still believed in what we were doing.*

*The following Saturday we beat Derby, despite having extra time in our legs, and that was the start of winning eleven consecutive home games. This shows how important it is to have the right assistant. The right words at the right time. Mick had a fearsome reputation as a player. He is a tough man who doesn`t have to prove it and he was actually a very calming influence. The players loved him.*

*I boosted the numbers by signing Chris Barker and Kevin McLeod, but the squad was still very small. It was therefore vital that we kept people fit. Donough Halohan came in as sports scientist and he, Mick and I were all singing from the same hymn sheet which was very important. Provided we didn`t have too many injuries, I saw the smallness of the squad as a strength.*

*Chris Barker was a very important signing. He was on good money at Cardiff and we had to take over his contract which took up a good chunk of the budget, but he was worth it. He and Browny were the two big characters in the dressing room. Chris was a fantastic pro who always trained well. He always gave 100%, but he also had quality. He helped bring on Pat Baldwin and Greg Halford.*

*A big problem in the early part of the season was that Greg was desperate to get away. I sat down with him and his agent and asked him to give me a good six months and then I`d get him a good move. I told him I could make him a better player by bringing him back to right back. I felt that his size and athleticism made him better at long running. He could break from the back and be unstoppable, but he didn`t have the pace over four or five yards to take somebody on. I wanted him to get forward from right back into the gaps created by Richard Garcia coming in off the line."*

Halford`s form had shown no signs of him losing focus. He had been Man of the Match against Barnsley, and, although he did not want to stay for the whole season, he seemed just as determined as anyone to get the club going in the Championship.

Geraint Williams would certainly not have wanted any distractions as the U`s now faced another massive challenge in the shape of Derby County coming to Layer Road. This Derby County would be a very different proposition from the one which had exited the FA Cup at Layer Road in the previous January. Since then, the board, the manager and many of the players had changed. They had been linked with Phil Parkinson, but they had plumped for Billy Davies as manager after he had done so well at Preston, who he had twice taken to the Championship Play Offs.

Davies was re-shaping the squad. He had brought in goalkeeper Stephen Bywater from West Ham, and had paid £1 million for Steve Howard from Luton. He had also borrowed Arsenal`s highly rated young striker Arturo Lupoli on a season long loan. Not content with adding Howard and Lupoli to his strike force, he had also been trying to prize Freddy Eastwood from Southend.

The Rams had made a steady start with five points from their opening four games and arrived confident. Content with the second half performance at West Brom, and with Johnnie Jackson still injured, the only change made by Williams was to return Baldwin to the defence at the expense of Richards.

Jamie Cureton had so far been goalless, and he had not often gone as many as four games in his career without scoring. That all changed in a golden three minutes in the first half. First he volleyed home after Iwelumo`s aerial strength had caused chaos in the Derby defence. Then the little man popped up to head in a perfectly placed Kevin Watson free kick. Lupoli got the visitors back in the game just before half time with a shot through a crowd of players.

It was a pulsating game, and four minutes into the second half a superb catch and throw by Aidan Davison released Garcia on a long mazy run, which finished with him being brought down for a penalty by Lewin Nyatanga. This was the first time the Championship would see Chris Iwelumo`s somewhat individual way of taking a penalty. With the ball on the spot, he would stand on the edge of the area facing his own goal. When the whistle sounded he would turn, jump three steps to the left and run in to strike the ball. He rarely missed, and that was 3-1 to Colchester.

In the sixty seventh minute there was another triumph for direct football as Iwelumo headed on Davison`s kick. Cureton was waiting, and he lobbed first a defender and then the goalkeeper for his hat trick. A magnificent exhibition of goal poaching, and surely nothing could now deny United their first points of the season. However, there was still time for some anxious moments as the Rams did not give up. The Italian Lupoli scored his second in the eightieth minute, and then in the eighty ninth substitute Paul Peschisolido took advantage of slack marking to head home. Without a point to their name, and now only one goal in front, stoppage time was going to last forever. However United saw out the final moments, and from the cheer at the final whistle you might have thought that promotion had been won again!

Afterwards it was easy to detect relief in the words of Chris Iwelumo, "We have shown now that we can hold our own in this division, and everyone knows that they are good enough." He also commented on the unique Layer Road atmosphere which would come to the fore so many times during the season, "We thought it might be a bit quiet after the last four weeks but the fans were right behind us from the opening whistle. It is like having a twelfth man on the pitch and makes such a difference to have support like that."

There was more good news for U`s fans as the end of August arrived. Left sided midfield player Kevin McLeod arrived on a free transfer from Swansea City to give Geraint Williams another option and the squad a little more depth. The 26 year old had previously been with Everton and QPR, and had over one hundred and twenty first team appearances to his name. Perhaps the best news, though, was that Greg Halford was still around, as he would be now at least until the New Year when the transfer window re-opened. A late bid from Sheffield United, reported at £1.25 million, was turned down.

Despite this, the squad still looked painfully thin, and some fans were critical of the club for a perceived lack of ambition during the transfer window. Chief Executive Marie Partner said, "Geraint has the total support of the board and knows the budget available to him. He`ll only sign players who are right for the club, rather than for the sake of increasing the size of the squad."

It was an unfortunate fact that as the club moved up the pyramid, they found that players likely to be capable of thriving at Championship level were looking for longer contracts. Many preferred to remain where they were on their existing contracts, even though they were out of the first team picture. Offering three, four or five year contracts would have been financial madness for a club of Colchester`s size, and could have brought about complete meltdown in the event of relegation.

Although the permanent transfer window was closed until January, loans were still available and this was to where Geraint Williams` focus now turned. Loans offered clubs like Colchester the sort of flexibility they required. Williams said, "There are possibly one or two places that need strengthening."

The most dramatic news during the international break was that the ownership of the club had changed. It was announced that Peter Heard`s controlling interest had been sold to Tiptree based multi millionaire Robbie Cowling. Cowling was not new to the club having invested £30,000 as shirt sponsor in 2000. Heard would be staying on as Chairman, as would the remainder of the current board. Cowling expressed his admiration for the job they had done, and said that he would be adopting a purely "observational" role for the time being.

While this role continued, it did not appear that there would be any injection of cash. He said, "I`ve never run a football club and that is why I want Peter to maintain his role as Chairman. He has done very well with Colchester, and I could not think of a better person to learn from." For the longer term he said, "My big aim is to try and establish the club in the Championship, and ensure a smooth transition to the new stadium."

Typically modest, Peter Heard refused to accept too much praise for the progress of the club from the fifth to the second tier during his period of influence, "I`m pleased with the progress the club has made. A Chairman of a club can set the guidelines but I don`t put the ball in the net, the players do that." With reference to the new owner he said "I believe he and I have similar philosophies. He is a lot younger than me. He is a very successful businessman. It`s a very important day for the club. I will be 68 next month and nothing goes on forever."

It was the end of an era and perhaps the opening of an exciting new era, albeit that the style in which the club was run would not change in the immediate future. Peter Heard now says,

*"Robbie Cowling had approached me a few years before about buying the club but at that time I did not want to sell. In 2006 I felt we needed someone with deeper pockets than mine. There was one other person showing interest but he quickly dropped out. Robbie came to see me on his motorcycle and we did the deal.*

*At Robbie`s request I carried on as Chairman for about a year, but having run the club for so many years I found it difficult not having authority to make decisions. So this arrangement was quite shortlived."*

Geraint Williams remembers,

*"Robbie Cowling brought a new dynamism to the board. He was full of ideas, and he couldn`t believe how well we were doing on the budget we had. I don`t recall any immediate change in the club`s policy on dealing with agents, although we didn`t sign many players to find out!"*

Back on the field, the team were putting their poor start behind them. Some of the good fortune which had deserted them returned at Burnley`s Turf Moor and Kenilworth

Road, Luton. In Lancashire the U`s found themselves two up despite spending most of the match on the back foot. Kevin Watson converted another Cureton cross in the first half and then in the fifty fourth minute Colchester were awarded a somewhat debatable penalty. Although Burnley scored late, an excellent "smash and grab" was completed. Burnley manager Steve Cotterill thought of it as a piece of banditry, as he referred to Colchester riding out of town with their sombreros on!

The 7,609 at Luton on the following Tuesday witnessed a remarkable goalkeeping display by Aidan Davison. It wasn`t so much the quality of the saves he made as the sheer quantity. Block after tip over after catch must have exhausted the thirty eight year old, and a Luton fan calling BBC Radio 5 afterwards described it as the finest goalkeeping he had ever seen!

Sam Parkin headed Luton into a deserved lead on thirty one minutes, but soon after another combination between Iwelumo and Cureton ended with an equaliser by JC. Most of the second half took place in the Colchester penalty area, with Davison at the centre of things. There was yet another harsh penalty, when the air turbulence caused by Kem Izzet`s blinking eye lash sent Richard Langley to the turf. Shaken up by this vicious assault, the same player could only strike the crossbar! The U`s were now unbeaten in three, during which they had picked the same starting eleven.

The next two games would be against sides who had made poor starts, and the unbeaten run was stretched to five. QPR arrived at Layer Road with only one win. They had been in the doldrums for some time. Although thinking of themselves as a Premier League club, they had not been there since 1996 and in 2001 had been relegated to the third tier where they spent three seasons. Their recent history had featured administration, unsustainable borrowing and boardroom scandal.

They were not heavily fancied going into 2006/07, but for all their difficulties they would have expected to make short work of Colchester United. In common with a number of teams visiting old lady Layer Road during that season, they looked around at their surroundings and were still asking themselves what they were doing there when they found themselves behind.

The U`s had to make one change. Davison`s exertions at Luton saw him miss out, and Dean Gerken make his first appearance of the season. It was 2-0 after only eighteen minutes courtesy of Iwelumo and Garcia. Colchester continued to dominate and missed a number of chances to further extend their lead. Despite pulling a goal back in the seventy sixth minute, QPR never looked like getting anything from the game and never deserved to. Three days later, QPR manager Gary Waddock was sacked.

On 23rd September, United made their first visit to Leicester City`s Walkers Stadium.

Probably one of the best stadiums they would visit, it had opened in 2002 at a cost of £37 million and there were 22,449 present for the visit of the humble Essex boys. This included nearly a thousand in the away section. Davison returned in goal, and chances were few and far between. It finished goalless with neither side having done enough to have expected to win. It was however Colchester who had more to be satisfied about. It was their first clean sheet of the season and it took them up to fifteenth.

The season was now nine games old, and after that terrible start results had improved immeasurably. We had jumped over our fellow promoted sides Southend and Barnsley. We were just below mid table, with local rivals Ipswich and Norwich in our sights. Cardiff were the early pace setters followed by Birmingham and Southampton and guess who was bottom? Phil Parkinson`s Hull City! The early fears about the thinness of the squad had so far proved unfounded. Physio Tony Flynn was facing redundancy! There had hardly been an injury.

## THE BATTLE OF THE A12

Next it was the one they had all been waiting for. Well, all at Layer Road anyway. The first League match between Colchester United and Ipswich Town since that infamous match nearly half a century before. There is not enough space to fully describe the depth and character of the rivalry between these clubs. It would justify an academic study all of its own. It was unique, because it was almost entirely one way.

Ipswich Town would have been as surprised as most Championship clubs to find Colchester United occupying the same division as them. Although only eighteen miles apart geographically, it had been so long since the two clubs had moved in the same orbit that most Ipswich fans, and even some Colchester fans, had forgotten how to hate each other! Ipswich had much bigger fish to fry, while some Colchester fans could only muster hatred for teams we played regularly. Some would say, "we will never play Ipswich, so they are not our rivals." There was even a small number of deluded people who claimed to support both clubs. In their ravings these people would say, "it`s always nice to see the local teams doing well."

Those with their compass calibrated correctly saw no connection between regular meetings and rivalry. They took our supporters, they took our managers, they took our players. They did far more damage to us than Southend or Wycombe, who were just small clubs trying to survive like ourselves. Ipswich sold merchandise in our Tescos! Their players visited our hospital at Christmas. We could not even call our sick children our own!

They took support from all over North Essex and beyond. Why? Because they had been successful. What sort of reason is that to support a football club! That success was a long time ago, but we now had 20-somethings travelling up the A12 on Saturdays because their fathers had before them. The A12 had not been thick with southern bound tractors on Friday 29th September 2006. Few in the away end at Layer Road had travelled from Ipswich. A huge percentage had CO postcodes. This tyranny had to be stopped, and the usual eleven had been charged with the responsibility for doing so. The battle would be broadcast live by Sky TV.

Layer Road was sold out. If you could have plugged the national grid into the atmosphere in the ground that night, you could have lit up the whole of North Essex. Most of the abuse (or should we call it banter?) was flowing from both sides of Layer Road towards the Ipswich fans (we will not call them travelling fans!) looking and feeling strangely out of place in the Layer Road end. Most of it was about "local club", and how those Ipswich fans might like to support it instead of someone else's club.

As a former Ipswich player, Geraint Williams was feeling the rivalry as much as anyone. His good friend Jim Magilton would be leading the opposition and, despite the atmosphere, Williams was anxious for his players to maintain focus, "we need fire in our bellies and our heads in the fridge" he said.

Sky's desire to cover the match must have been pretty strong when you consider the difficulties that the old lady presented. She would not have taken kindly to these young upstarts buzzing around her with their cables, dishes and trucks. There would be eight miles of cabling, six trucks and twelve cameras at the game.

They brought a crew forty strong, and a combination of temporary scaffolding and four by twos had George Gavin and Steve Claridge sitting precariously above the open terracing in the "sporting U's" corner of the ground. Their unease would have been nothing compared with that faced by commentators Bill Leslie and Chris Kamara.

Used to the more salubrious surroundings of Old Trafford and White Hart Lane, one can imagine them examining their contracts when they are handed crampons, boots, harnesses, rope and cord for an attempt on the north face of the main stand. When they were told to go and broadcast on the col, they would have thought it a reference to the home team rather than a mountaineering term. Nevertheless, they would have found themselves picking their way through the flora and fauna in search of the lost passage that would deliver them to the commentary position on the roof. Now in touch with Gavin and Claridge, all four must have had as much interest in the likely lifespan of the structures supporting them as they did the football.

Only this insecurity could have explained the "expert" punditry of Claridge, as he expressed the expectation that Colchester would struggle in this league and would lose this match. Obviously it had escaped his attention that the U`s had the better goalkeeper. He also failed to notice that Ipswich had no-one of Halford`s quality, no defender as dominant as Wayne Brown and lacked the goal scoring potential of Cureton and Iwelumo.

Ipswich arrived in excellent form, they were unbeaten in six of which they had won four. As the teams came out, George Gavin said that Layer Road "was making noise for a ground five times its size".

When the home fans took a break from abusing the away fans, attention was turned on the Ipswich players. In Darren Currie there was a player who had built upon the crime of playing for Wycombe by signing for Ipswich. He also had flowing blonde locks, leaving the Barside without any inspiration for their angle of attack!

Alan Lee, in common with many of the Ipswich fans, had "travelled" to the game from within the borough of Colchester. Dedham in his case, where he endured a difficult relationship with local cyclists from the confines of his Porsche, "He`s blue, he`s white, he`ll knock you off your bike" would go the chant.

As the game kicked off, the mind went back to all those pre season friendlies/Willhire Cup games between the two sides. It seemed to be an annual event in the late 70s and early 80s for Ipswich to come to Layer Road in August with a team of internationals and run rings round the U`s. The score would always be kept respectable by the brilliance of Mike Walker. These games always seemed to be his busiest and best of the season. Seeing the two teams competing on level terms, in the same division, seemed like the stuff of fantasy then, but now we were seeing it happen and it quickly became clear that if this was to be one sided it would not be in favour of the Tractor Boys!

The fire that Williams wanted to see was immediately in evidence, with Colchester players feeding off the energy coming from the terraces. They were running and tackling as if their lives depended on it. Whatever Jamie Cureton`s faults as a player might have been, being shot shy was not amongst them. In the fourth minute, he audaciously tried to lob Lewis Price in the Ipswich goal from the right touch line but the ball finished bouncing down Layer Road! It was though, a statement of intent.

Four minutes later, Cureton made space for himself twenty five yards out and let fly. Like most of Cureton`s shots it was never going to win goal of the season but it needed stopping. It had Price sprawling to his right, where he could only palm it out. Karl Duguid was thinking ahead of the Ipswich defenders and he reached the loose ball first. With defenders converging and Price recovering his position, Dugy managed to thread it through the small gap and in. It was a much better finish than it first appeared, and whilst it must be admitted that the roofs at Layer Road were not held on by much, they were sent skywards by the delirium of the fans.

This was the cue for Colchester to take control. They began to threaten a second, with the crowd singing "who needs Phil Parkinson, we`ve got George Williams". A superb dribble by Cureton finished with a shot inches wide and the keeper struggling. A few minutes later Izzet`s header set up Cureton with a half chance on the edge of the box. His brilliant volley across Price missed the other post by inches. He was clearly bubbling with confidence, and it was hard to believe that he would end the night goalless.

Although Cureton was everywhere, it had to be said that Chris Iwelumo was getting little change out of Jason Devos, Ipswich`s big and ugly Canadian centre half. In the thirty ninth minute Ipswich posed their first serious threat when Lee half volleyed just wide from a tight angle. When half time came, there was no doubt that United had been well worth their one goal advantage.

During the break, the Sky cameras focused on a fan wearing a truly magnificent and bejewelled sombrero above a blue and white striped waistcoat. It was in fact the town`s MP Bob Russell, although this was obviously unknown to Sky as they made no mention of it.

The forty eighth minute saw perhaps the game`s most crucial moment. With Brown and Baldwin troubled by a long ball from the keeper, Alan Lee burst into the penalty area where he was denied by a brilliant save by Davison. Jon Macken followed up to prod over the line, as the United keeper tried to gather the loose ball. Referee Lee Probert decided that the ball had been kicked out of Davison`s hands, and awarded a free kick. The replay suggested that Mr Probert should be bought drinks whenever he visits Colchester! With Ipswich still arguing about this, play quickly switched to the clock end where Iwelumo forced Lewis Price into a brilliant point blank save.

With tempers boiling over, Karl Duguid decided to test Macken`s composure. For a long time, Duguid had specialised in "winding up" overwrought opposition players. It had often been possible to watch the temperature of such players going northwards as they came under Duguid`s onslaught. A sly comment here, a rough tacke there. Eventually the player would take matters into his own hands with some ill judged retaliation, followed by the inevitable yellow and sometimes red card. Warren Feeney of Bournemouth was one who had to see red after an exchange of views with Duguid at Layer Road. Macken looked like becoming another, until pulled away by the referee just before he did something irretrievable.

While Colchester had dominated the first half, the second was proving to be very even. The farmers were starting to pass the ball with some aplomb but in the sixty second minute it was time for the home side to be looking at the referee. Situ, in attempting to volley clear, succeeded only in scything Iwelumo down in the penalty area. Mr Probert waved play on as he did six minutes later when Naylor appeared to handle in the area. Maybe we`ll hold that drinks order Mr Probert!

Colchester`s former loanee Billy Clarke was brought on to try to rescue the game for the visitors, and this very nearly proved to be an inspired substitution by Jim Magilton. Lee headed on and Clarke swivelled to volley at goal. Aidan Davison employed all his experience. He read the situation as it developed, advancing from his line at just the right moment to make a brilliant block. He had to be at his best again in the seventy ninth minute when turning round a Legwinski volley.

From this moment, the Ipswich players seemed to sense that it was not to be their night. They became increasingly desperate and started to argue amongst themselves. There was now chanting coming from every area of the stadium except those occupied by away fans. Every Colchester header and tackle was met with thunderous noise from the home support. With Iwelumo back defending as if his life depended on it, and Davison dominating the box. With Captain Marvel Karl Duguid covering every blade and Izzet nipping at every Ipswich heel, and with Halford, Garcia and Watson denying Ipswich precious moments of possession, the clock ran down.

Could it be that good was about to triumph over evil? That Colchester were about to beat Ipswich for the first time in fifty four years? The final whistle sounded, and it was almost as good as that whistle at Yeovil. Geraint Williams had tried to keep things in proportion by saying that it was just another game with three points at stake. It did not seem that way, as Layer Road witnessed its most raucous cheering since that famous Leeds match in 1971. Everything shook from your fillings to your toe nails. It was not a moment to be suspended twenty feet in the air above some hastily thrown together temporary structure. George Gavin and Steve Claridge must have been contemplating an alternative means of employment. It was not a moment to be on the roof of a main stand held together by rust and rampant foliage. With helicopter rescue unlikely, and with abseiling and parachuting unwise the faltering voices of Bill Leslie and Chris Kamara signed off and plotted their uncertain descent.

U`s fans wended their happy way into the night discussing their ascent of the Championship table. They were now thirteenth and the only way was up!

| 1 | Cardiff City | 10 | 7 | 2 | 1 | 22 | 8 | +14 | 23 |
|---|---|---|---|---|---|---|---|---|---|
| 2 | Birmingham City | 10 | 5 | 3 | 2 | 14 | 11 | +3 | 18 |
| 3 | Preston North End | 10 | 4 | 5 | 1 | 11 | 8 | +3 | 17 |
| 4 | Crystal Palace | 10 | 5 | 2 | 3 | 13 | 11 | +2 | 17 |
| 5 | Southampton | 10 | 4 | 4 | 2 | 15 | 11 | +4 | 16 |
| 6 | West Bromwich Albion | 10 | 4 | 4 | 2 | 14 | 10 | +4 | 16 |
| 7 | Plymouth Argyle | 10 | 4 | 4 | 2 | 15 | 12 | +3 | 16 |
| 8 | Wolverhampton Wanderers | 10 | 5 | 1 | 4 | 8 | 10 | -2 | 16 |
| 9 | Derby County | 10 | 4 | 3 | 3 | 15 | 13 | +2 | 15 |
| 10 | Luton Town | 10 | 4 | 3 | 3 | 15 | 15 | 0 | 15 |
| 11 | Burnley | 9 | 4 | 2 | 3 | 14 | 11 | +3 | 14 |
| 12 | Ipswich Town | 10 | 4 | 2 | 4 | 14 | 13 | +1 | 14 |
| 13 | Colchester United | 10 | 4 | 2 | 4 | 13 | 13 | 0 | 14 |
| 14 | Sunderland | 10 | 4 | 1 | 5 | 14 | 14 | 0 | 13 |
| 15 | Coventry City | 10 | 4 | 1 | 5 | 8 | 8 | 0 | 13 |
| 16 | Queens Park Rangers | 10 | 3 | 3 | 4 | 12 | 14 | -2 | 12 |
| 17 | Norwich City | 9 | 3 | 2 | 4 | 14 | 14 | 0 | 11 |
| 18 | Barnsley | 10 | 3 | 2 | 5 | 15 | 21 | -6 | 11 |
| 19 | Leicester City | 10 | 2 | 4 | 4 | 6 | 9 | -3 | 10 |
| 20 | Leeds United | 10 | 3 | 1 | 6 | 9 | 15 | -6 | 10 |
| 21 | Stoke City | 10 | 1 | 6 | 3 | 9 | 11 | -2 | 9 |
| 22 | Southend United | 10 | 2 | 3 | 5 | 9 | 17 | -8 | 9 |
| 23 | Hull City | 10 | 2 | 2 | 6 | 8 | 14 | -6 | 8 |
| 24 | Sheffield Wednesday | 10 | 1 | 4 | 5 | 6 | 10 | -4 | 7 |

Chapter 15

# THE MORE
# THINGS DON'T
# CHANGE...

# Chapter 15
## THE MORE THINGS DON'T CHANGE...

Geraint Williams was named Championship Manager of the Month for September. It might have been argued that he had little to do, as he didn`t have any selection decision to make during the entire month! He brought in Gerken for the injured Davison for one game, and maintained the same outfield ten for all the games. He said he had cash to bring in loan players but clearly saw no urgent need to do so. The entire squad were fit, except for long term absentee Marino Keith.

On the field, things were going swimmingly, and all the manager had to do every week was phone in the same team selection. No doubt this is doing a disservice to our Welsh wizard, who with his constant entreaties for positivity had brought the team through the early difficulties and instilled real belief in a squad with little experience of this level. Wayne Brown seemed unimpressed by standards in the Championship, "People say it is the Championship, only one step below the Premiership, but if you look at the teams on paper, big teams like Wolves with big reputations and see the players they have, you have to think `hold on they aren`t any better than us` so you go into every game thinking there is no team we can`t beat".

Sadly, it transpired that Wolves were a team we couldn`t beat! At least not on 14th October, when a goal by future England international Jay Bothroyd earned all three points for the home side at Molineux. It was the first defeat in seven, and a case of Manager of the Month curse? It was a tight game in which Williams felt that Colchester deserved a point. Despite the defeat, Ipswich dropped below Colchester in the table on goal difference. Town had been beaten 5-1 at home by West Brom.

The U`s would quickly have a chance to put this result behind them, as four days later Sheffield Wednesday would be visiting Layer Road. Wednesday had made a faltering start to the season, and used to the cavernous Hillsborough would have been one of those teams not relishing the confines and unfriendliness of old lady Layer Road. They arrived with hopes of turning round a poor recent record against United.

The U`s dominated throughout although it took until the twenty eighth minute for them to take the lead. Wednesday`s highly rated Algerian international defender Madjid Bougherra would later in the season be sold to Charlton for £2.5 million, but he was unable to cope with the pestering of Jamie Cureton. He misjudged a bouncing ball and allowed Cureton his one hundred and fiftieth league goal.

The lead was doubled ten minutes into the second half. When Greg Halford had his shooting boots on, being a goalkeeper could be a dangerous occupation. So could being a net! If his aim was slightly off, it was best not to be a spectator in the vicinity of the goal. If asked, he could probably have made an early start on the demolition of Layer Road. On this occasion he was content with beating Sheffield Wednesday. Unwisely given space 30 yards out, he wound up his right foot to deliver a hammer blow. The surely punctured ball flew past an unmoving goalkeeper into the top right hand corner, leaving a knot of spectators behind the goal to offer a prayer of thanks to the net manufacturers for saving their lives!

Five minutes later Chris Iwelumo decided to get in on the act. Having won back possession himself, he took a pass from Garcia and drilled home from twenty two yards. Duguid then completed the rout with another thirty yard stunner past an unsighted keeper. That was now four consecutive home wins. The old lady was starting to exert her influence.

Colchester moved to tenth and were now top of the unofficial league of East Anglia. It was almost unheard of for there to be as many as four East Anglian clubs playing in the second tier of English football, but such was the case in 2006/07.

On the following day the Board of Directors at Hillsborough re-evaluated their business plan. Noticing that it had no reference to a 4-0 defeat in a collection of cow sheds, they sacked Paul Sturrock.

After the demolition of the Owls, Colchester travelled to Coventry full of confidence and with an unchanged starting eleven yet again. The match was to be live on Sky, and had been moved to the Monday night as a result.

The team coach caught fire on the way home, and unfortunately this was not a phrase that could be used to describe Colchester`s performance. Both Kevin Watson and Richard Garcia were forced off by injury in the first half, and the team`s pattern of play was clearly effected. The U`s found themselves two down going into the final quarter of the game. Just as at West Brom, Jamie Guy had been introduced in the hope of saving the game. Once again, he notched in the last few minutes but it was not enough.

The outfield ten had now been unchanged for nine games and there was no doubt that having such a settled line up had contributed to the team`s good run. They had picked up five wins and two draws over those games. There would however have to be some change for the visit of Southampton. Watson was injured, while Garcia was both injured and suspended. Johnnie Jackson and Kevin McLeod, who had both been waiting so patiently in the wings, would come in. So far, McLeod had been restricted to occasional substitute appearances. The same had mostly been the case for Jackson, although he had started the first three games. As well as these two, Halford, Cureton and Brown had all picked up knocks at Coventry, although they would be fit to start against the Saints.

These worries had sent Geraint Williams to the phone lines in the hope of recruiting some cover. His efforts were initially unsuccessful, but on the day before the match Ritchie

Jones, a young Manchester United midfield player, arrived on a month's loan. Marie Partner said, "We have signed Ritchie in order to cover us for the different injuries that were picked up in the match against Coventry. Ritchie has signed for a period which takes us up to the Hull match, and this is the anticipated time frame for the injured players to return to fitness".

This episode illustrates very well how Colchester United were still operating as a small lower division club even now they were in with the big boys. Even the smaller clubs in the Championship were operating with squads in excess of twenty five. The bigger ones had thirty to thirty five. Sunderland had more than forty in their squad!

Colchester had a squad of twenty. At this time you needed five substitutes so your match day squad was sixteen. It would not therefore take a huge number of injuries to cause difficulties at Layer Road. After the Coventry match Watson, Garcia and Keith were out, and at Colchester this constituted a full blown injury crisis! The thinking was that, if players were absent, loanees could be brought in at short notice and for the short term. But of course this presupposed that the right sort of player could be found at the relevant time, that his club were prepared to release him, and that the player wanted to come. If a player could be secured, he would have little time to get accustomed to his team mates, their mode of play or the coaching of the manager and his staff.

Ritchie Jones had just turned twenty and was yet to make a first team appearance in a League match. Could he really replace Kevin Watson? Note the words of Marie Partner, Jones would be there only for as long as it took for the unavailable players to get fit. There was no question of retaining additional players on staff to offer greater competition for places or to address potential injury or suspension problems. Colchester could not afford to be proactive. They had to wait for the problems to occur and then address them.

Southampton were ninth, five places above Colchester. They had been relegated from the Premier League in 2005 after twenty seven consecutive seasons in the top flight. Like many Championship clubs they boasted a multi million pound squad, including a fledgling Gareth Bale.

As Colchester endured their three player injury crisis, it is worth looking at the difference in resources of these two clubs as represented by the respective benches. Southampton's substitutes included three internationals, and had players with a total of 1153 league starts to their name. Thanks mainly to John White being a regular during the previous season, Colchester's substitutes were able to boast 85 league starts between them.

Southampton were managed by "spawn of satan", George Burley. A former Ipswich player he had been given his start in English management by Colchester United in 1994. He resigned on Christmas Eve, less than six months after his appointment and half way through a promising season at Layer Road. This followed an approach from Ipswich to whom he moved as manager. In the pre internet age most fans knew nothing of it until arriving at Layer Road for a Boxing Day fixture against Northampton.

After a poor start under Burley, Colchester had been rising steadily up the Division Three (fourth tier) table and sat sixth on Boxing Day, which was a play off position. A good second half to the season could see a push for automatic promotion. In the midst of the off field turmoil caused by Burley and Ipswich, the Northampton match was lost and the club slumped to finish tenth. Substantial compensation and costs were eventually prised out of Ipswich after protracted legal proceedings.

Burley`s time at Ipswich is often viewed as successful. When he arrived they were struggling in the Premier League. Despite having more than half a season to turn things round, he failed to do so as they were relegated in bottom position. He then took five seasons to get them back to the Premier League, where they had one outstanding season before being relegated again. Burley was then sacked.

Burley can now look back on a long career. He made 628 league appearances as a player and won eleven international caps. He managed eight clubs and the Scottish national team. His twenty one year management career was punctuated with acrimony and turmoil. He was sacked by Crystal Palace after six months, and by Apollon Limassol after two games. He did have two good seasons at Ipswich, and there is no doubting that he had been an outstanding player. He is unlikely to count among his highlights the Layer Road song which bears his name, followed by an intimate area of the female anatomy, nor the naming after him of the Barside portaloo urinals!

Twelve years had passed since his departure, but football fans have long memories, and anticipation of his appearance in the dug out in charge of Southampton added a frisson of antipathy. We ached to see him leave pointless, almost as much as he had ached to leave the moment he got a better offer.

Under the Parkinson and Williams regimes, Colchester loved to tear into opposition early at Layer Road. This match was a prime example as the early stages were dominated by United`s collection of free transfers. An exchange of passes in the third minute between Iwelumo and Cureton had the Bristollian running with the ball. He stood up a tremendous cross at the far post where McLeod, making his first start in the blue and white stripes, ghosted in to power a header past Kelvin Davis. Davis then had to pull off some fine saves to keep the Saints in the game.

Burley made changes in the second half. He even took off the free scoring Pole, Grzegorz Rasiak. The £2 million signing from Tottenham had been blunted by Wayne Brown and Pat Baldwin. Bradley Wright-Phillips, and the Czech internationals Skacel and

Licka, were introduced. Davison and the U`s defenders had to be at their best to maintain the lead. The keeper`s excellent point blank save from Kenwyne Jones being a highlight.

In the eighty third minute Southampton had strong penalty appeals waved away and must have been cursing their luck when Jamie Cureton was sent through on the keeper by a pinpoint pass from Halford, just as stoppage time was beginning. With the coolness of a gunslinger, he waited until he saw the whites of Davis`s eyes before smashing home to leapfrog United over Southampton and into tenth in the table. Burley left Colchester just as he had in 1994, with the appreciation of the Layer Road faithful ringing in his ears!

The curtain on October was brought down by another East Anglian derby. Over fifteen hundred U`s fans made their way to Carrow Road for a Tuesday night fixture, with some early arrivers having a tour around what is the real ale capital of eastern England. Norwich City versus Colchester United had been a regular feature of 1950`s Third Division South life, but it had not been seen for forty six years. Norwich had been promoted to the Second Division in the1959/60 season, and had since spent all their time either in that division or in the top flight. They had been relegated from the Premier League in 2005, and in the previous season had finished ninth in the Championship.

They had ambitions to get back to the Premier League, but had not started well. They started October with a 4-1 home defeat against Burnley, which saw them drop to seventeenth. Manager Nigel Worthington was sacked on the same day. Two weeks later Peter Grant was appointed. He started with wins over Birmingham and Cardiff, but the wheels had come off at Stoke on the previous Saturday as they lost 5-0.

Unsurprisingly Geraint Williams saw no reason to change a winning team, and there were no injuries from the Southampton game. Once again, Colchester made a lively start in front of 25,065, the biggest crowd to watch them so far. In the first half both sides had decent efforts on goal and both keepers made saves. An even first half ended goalless.

The match came to life early in the second half when Iwelumo typically caused consternation in the Canaries` defence with his height. The ball was transferred to Jackson, who let fly from twenty five yards. Gallacher in the Norwich goal made a good save, and the ball rebounded to Duguid who had the presence of mind to spot Cureton unmarked. He lashed into the net, and then walked away with an expressionless face as his team mates celebrated. He had started his career at Norwich, and had vowed not to celebrate any goal as a mark of respect. At this time he was our hero, and we loved him even more for retaining affection for a former club. Subsequent events caused us to look upon this incident in a different light!

Twenty minutes later, Dickson Etuhu ended a passage of possession around the Colchester box by arrowing a twenty five yard shot into Davison`s bottom left hand corner.

It was a goal which deserved to earn Norwich a point, and so it did.

We were now one third of the way through the season and were absolutely amazed and delighted to be twelth. Bottom of the top half! Above Ipswich on goal difference. Cardiff were four points clear at the top and Hull had moved off the bottom where they had been replaced by Southend. And it would be the Welsh table toppers, supported as a boy by Geraint Williams, who would be the next opponents.

Jamie Cureton took stock of the season so far. He said the team`s expectations of themselves had changed due to the early results and performances, "We now expect to win games that going into the season we probably wouldn`t have done". He also issued a note of caution, "We know we can compete at this level and beat top sides so I think expectations are a bit higher, but we are also realistic in our aims. To stay up is the main aim. We are aiming for 50 points as I think we will be safe with that. We want to finish mid table, so the first aim is to get those points on the board and go from there".

On a personal note he said, "I`m delighted with my own form. I couldn`t have asked for more. I feel I am playing as well as I have ever played". He had scored seven in fifteen matches. He had also been making goals for colleagues. The team had gained twenty one points from those fifteen matches and so were well on target to achieve their aims.

Cardiff City were one of those clubs often described as a "sleeping giant". In fact their glory days were as long ago as the 1920`s when they had been runners up in the First Division and reached two FA Cup finals. In the 1923/24 season they battled it out with Huddersfield for the League title, eventually finishing behind them due to having a slightly worse goal average. If it had been decided by goal difference they would have been champions. In 1927 they were the first club to take the FA Cup out of England. They were relegated in 1929 despite, bizarrely, having the best defensive record in the division. This was the start of a decline which had never really been arrested.

They had two brief spells in the top tier in the 50s and 60s but mostly struggled in the second. Between 1985 and 2000 they were mostly in the third and fourth tiers. In 2003, under the ownership of Sam Hammam, they had been promoted to the second tier, where they had been around mid table for the previous three seasons. They were now £40 million in debt and in the midst of an acrimonious take over by a new consortium which intended to deliver a new stadium. Despite this they were having their best season on the field for over forty years.

Dave Jones was in his second season in charge of Cardiff and, along with Colchester, they were the surprise packets in the Championship. No-one expected them to be struggling near the bottom but, equally, no-one expected them to be four points clear at the top going into November. Finances were tight at Ninian Park and in the summer Jones had been forced to sell Cameron Jerome to Birmingham for £4 million. However, they still boasted a squad which had cost around £4 million, and in Michael Chopra had one of the best strikers in the division who had scored ten goals from fourteen games so far.

Colchester`s only line up change was forced on them by the terms of Chris Barker`s loan agreement. He was not allowed to play against Cardiff, who were his parent club. George Elokobi deputised. It was a cagey first half. The U`s did have the ball in the net, but it was ruled out for offside against Iwelumo.

Early in the second half Kevin Campbell rattled the home side`s cross bar. Almost immediately, Cardiff were unable to clear a Halford cross. Jackson passed and McLeod buried a shot from inside the box. The lead lasted for just over a quarter of an hour. Pat Baldwin then found himself unable to clear a Cardiff cross and Chopra had a tap in.

A draw now seemed the most likely outcome. "Bring on Jamie Guy" was the chant and Geraint Williams obliged in the seventy sixth minute, Iwelumo giving way. Guy was his usual bundle of energy, and just seven minutes later Izzet headed into his path just inside the box. He muscled past the attentions of Cardiff`s million pound captain Darren Purse to divert the ball beyond Alexander in the Cardiff goal. The home fans went wild as Guy presented himself to the away fans in a manner unlikely to endear him to the local constabulary. It was his third goal in eight substitute appearances.

Not content with this, Guy then set up the other substitute, Ritchie Jones, for a run on goal. He was brought down and with regular penalty taker Chris Iwelumo off the field, Cureton converted to seal the points.

Another giant had been slain, and this one was top of the table! If there was anyone left not taking the U`s seriously as a Championship force to be reckoned with, they would be now. Williams felt that the fans had helped to turn the game, "When it was tight, when we needed their support, that was when the atmosphere really lifted. The lads were driven on by that and they wanted to get the win for the fans".

We were now up to ninth, and things were starting to get ridiculous! It was being pointed out that a win in the next match could propel the U`s into the top six and a play off position! To add to the feeling of exaltation, Colchester Council approved the funding for the new Community Stadium. A crowd cheered as Marie Partner made the historic announcement from the Town Hall steps, "You`ve got your stadium".

The next match was Leeds United at Elland Road for the first ever league meeting between the two clubs. Laughably, Colchester were, in theory at least, favourites in this match because Leeds were second from bottom!

This was an interesting fixture, because it pitted what was the object lesson in how not to run a football club against probably the best run club in the League.

Colchester United under the careful leadership of Peter Heard had no debt, refused to pay agents and budgeted conservatively, never assuming that income which had the slightest doubt surrounding it would be received. Accordingly, they budgeted on the assumption that every cup competition would be exited in the first round, and that no transfer income would be received. When the ITV Digital collapse occurred many clubs had already spent the money and now found themselves in administration. Colchester United had never budgeted to receive the money, and were not therefore inconvenienced. For a number of years Colchester United were a byword for good practice in football and a model which many other clubs, such as Blackpool and Scunthorpe, sought to follow as they achieved their own triumphs.

Many of the profligate clubs would have accused them of a counsel of mediocrity, but events proved otherwise. Steady year on year improvements eventually delivered stunning success, proving that it was possible in football to combine success with proper financial planning.

Leeds United went about things in a different way. Perhaps the start of Leeds` troubles was in 1996 when they saw fit to appoint a manager who had just finished a ban from the game for receiving illegal payments from an agent, one George Graham. Graham soon left to be replaced by David O`Leary, following which Leeds had one of the most successful periods in their history. They consistently finished in the Premier League top five, and reached both the UEFA Cup and Champions League semi finals.

While some of this success had been based upon the development of young players, it had also been financed by large loans which depended on continued success to be repaid. In particular, repayment depended upon ongoing qualification for the Champions League. After finishing fifteenth and nineteenth in the Premier League, the latter resulting in relegation, there was financial meltdown and a fire sale of the players, the stadium and the training ground. A spiral from which the club has not recovered to this day and which caused them to endure three seasons in League One.

Chris Barker returned to the line up, but there had to be a change in the other full back position due to an injury to Halford. John White came in. Future Colchester defender Matt Heath took his place in the Leeds defence, having just arrived on loan from Coventry.

It might have been that thought of a play off position, but whatever it was Mr Reality came calling as Colchester slumped at Elland Road. They were never at the races from the moment they fell behind to a Robbie Blake goal in the thirty sixth minute. For once, they looked like a small club playing at a big ground rather than ninth place visiting twenty third. Richard Cresswell headed in the second three minutes after the break, and matters were sealed when Blake got his second from the spot after another terrible penalty decision, this time for a" foul" by White on Cresswell. Not even the late introduction of Jamie Guy could lift the visitors. It was the first time Colchester had lost a game by more than one goal since that hammering at home to Southend eight months before.

The first ever meeting between Colchester United and Sunderland was up next, at the Stadium of Light. Sunderland had made a poor start under the "temporary" management of Chairman Niall Quinn. Roy Keane took charge and immediately signed six players in the August window including his former Manchester United team mates Dwight Yorke, and Liam Miller. They were starting to creep up the table.

Geraint Williams was looking for a reaction to the poor result and performance at Leeds. Perhaps to encourage this, he surprised many by dropping Iwelumo to the bench in favour of Jamie Guy. The Carrow Road attendance was slightly exceeded but, despite the return of Halford, things did not go well for the U`s. They looked a little overawed by the magnificent surroundings and uncharacteristically prone to giving their opposition too much respect. There was little sign of United taking the game to their hosts the way they had at Norwich, until they fell behind at least.

Stephen Elliott ruined the U's fans` half time cup of tea with a swerving shot, and then added another eight minutes into the second half after a fine move. It was no more than Sunderland deserved. Iwelumo replaced Guy with twenty minutes remaining and fully embraced the super sub role when prodding home in the seventy ninth minute. Unfortunately hope sprang only until the ninetieth minute when David Connolly settled it for the Black Cats. Away from Layer Road, Colchester were finding Championship life very challenging as they searched for a method that could deliver results.

A Saturday/Tuesday home double now provided an excellent opportunity to get the show back on the road. Both had added spice. The first was the latest edition of the Essex derby, and that was to be followed by Hull Ciity, which meant the return of Parky.

Every member of the squad went into these games with a shaved head! This was in honour of a young fan who had passed away with leukaemia. A touching tribute, and an outward sign of just how tight knit the squad had become.

Southend had failed to maintain the momentum from the previous season in the way that Colchester had. They had deservedly been champions and had managed to keep hold of their hot goal scoring property Freddie Eastwood, but they now sat bottom of the table.

The Shrimpers were enduring what would become an eighteen match run without a win in the League. They had not won away since their visit to Layer Road in the previous March, but there were some optimistic signs. They had picked up decent draws in their previous two matches, and conceded only one goal in their previous three. As one of those had been in the Carling Cup against a Manchester United side including Wayne Rooney and

Cristiano Ronaldo, it was especially creditable. They had beaten ManU 1-0 at Roots Hall to earn a quarter final tie at Tottenham, so surely they could account for their little Essex cousins whose two consecutive defeats seemed to suggest the bubble might be bursting.

Geraint Williams added to his squad by acquiring West Ham`s eighteen year old winger/striker Hogan Ephraim on a one month loan. However, like Ritchie jones, he was yet to make a senior appearance for anyone, so how much impact could he be expected to make? He would make none against Southend as he was not selected in the match day squad. Williams was impressed by Iwelumo`s response to being dropped and he returned in place of Guy. Otherwise he stuck by the same team which had lost at Sunderland. Kevin Watson had now sufficiently returned to fitness to take a place on the bench.

What a great four days in late November they were. The Southend match exploded into life in the fifty first minute. With play in another area of the pitch, Karl Duguid decided to exchange pleasantries with Kevin Maher who inexplicably tensed his body in Duguid`s general direction. This act of unprovoked aggression quite understandably sent Duguid falling to the turf clutching his face. Indeed, it was clear from Maher`s whole countenance that he was intent on inflicting terror on the entire population of North Essex, and that only Duguid`s selfless flop of thespian magnificence had prevented an appalling outrage. Even Maher knew this. Before departing the shadow cast by the referee`s red card, he bent over Duguid`s prone body to express his gratitude for being brought back from the pages of notoriety!

Five minutes later Duguid saw in the eyes of Mark Gower another soul who needed to be saved. Gower made a move towards the pumping legs of the U`s skipper right in front of the Barside. His next appointment would be with the Layer Road bath. As they surveyed the wreckage of the Southend team the home fans could only admire Duguid`s evangelical zeal while at the same time hoping that he felt his work was done. At this rate of progress the crustacean worriers would be down to six by the seventieth minute and the game would be abandoned!

The final twenty minutes proved that Southend needed more than nine men. Halford, Baldwin and Cureton scored without reply as proud Tilson`s army were sent homeward to think again. Chris Barker decided that he didn`t need to see Cureton`s goal, as he joined Maher and Gower on the naughty step five minutes from time.

When Parky`s Tigers came to town, feelings were still a little raw regarding his departure. They were second from bottom but had picked up eight points from their previous five games. Most U`s fans just wanted to see their team win, and there was little hostility towards the former manager although this was put to the test in the sixteenth minute. Nicky Forster shot Hull into the lead, with Parkinson running down the touchline punching the air in celebration.

Elokobi had to replace the suspended Barker at left back, while Ephraim was on the bench in place of Ritchie Jones, who had returned to his parent club having only made substitute appearances. It was one of the occasions when the spirit in the Colchester camp became evident. The ability to bounce back from a set-back which had been so important in getting promotion. In particular it was a red letter day for Chris Iwelumo.

The U`s went into turbo charge, and Hull had no answer. Their lead had lasted only three minutes when they presented the big Scotsman with a free header just outside the six yard box. He made no mistake. In the second half you almost had to feel sorry for the visitors. They became increasingly desperate and chaotic in the face of Iwelumo`s aerial power and the interplay between him and Cureton. Iwelumo finished with four and Colchester with five, Cureton scoring the other from an Iwelumo flick on.

Afterwards, Iwelumo seemed to have bitter sweet feelings. Delight at scoring four goals, tinged with regret about what it was doing to the man who gave him a platform back in English football. The continuation of Parkinson`s stay in the East Riding was looking tenuous, and it seems likely that the decision to sack him was taken after this result, albeit that the deed was not done until the following Monday. If so, he was the third manager in two months to get the bum`s rush after a visit to the Old Lady. She just didn`t like some people!

What this reflected, of course, was just how little some Chairmen thought of Colchester United. To watch their expensively assembled squads dismantled and made to look like idiots by a collection of free transfers, at a ground that smelt more of wee than success, was too much to bear. So down came the axe.

They were going to have to get used to it though. United had now recorded eight consecutive home wins which is a pretty formidable platform to build any season on. Despite the less impressive away results, and the portents of gloom expressed by the "expert" pundits at the start of the season, it was now clear that there would not even be a flirtation with relegation.

In terms of league position, the Hull win brought about a new high. Seventh place after twenty games, although that became eighth after Southampton won on the following night. Chris Iwelumo and Jamie Cureton were the heroes of the hour, and it was obvious that the potency of their partnership had taken the Championship by surprise.

"I don`t think there`s a more effective partnership in the Championship" said the big Scotsman after the Hull triumph. Considering the multi millions spent by other clubs on their strikers this was a bold statement. It was hard to argue with though. They now had nineteen goals from twenty games between them to add to the sixteen notched between them from eleven games in the previous season. Iwelumo had eighteen of these to Cureton`s seventeen with the big man being helped by his somewhat quirky penalties. "If anybody had said I would have nine goals under my belt at this stage of the season I wouldn`t have believed them" he added. "It`s always good to score goals, and I love scoring them, but most of all I`m really honoured to be part of a team that is playing so well".

Cureton said "We`re in the team for different reasons. Chris is the target man, while I`m the runner in the channels. We do different things, but we`re both scoring. It`s unbelievable that we are riding so high". Ironically, after all this talk of scoring goals, the following match would finish goalless.

Geraint Williams took his squad to the Land of his Fathers for the return fixture against Cardiff City. Everything had been going so well for the Welshmen until they had to visit the Old Lady a month before. They were four points clear at the top, and thought they could take liberties. They had been fixed with an Edwardian stare and sent away, tail firmly between legs. They had still not recovered, having picked up only four points from five subsequent matches. They had been knocked off the top by Preston.

There was a feeling that in Colchester`s previous two away games they had been too open as they tried to play as they did at home. They had been cut apart, conceding six goals. It was felt they needed to put up a more solid structure when away from home, and with this in mind Williams decided, unusually, to change a winning team. Kevin McLeod made way for the return of Kevin Watson. The defence would be looking quite youthful, as Aidan Davison was injured and Chris Barker could not play against his parent club. Gerken and Elokobi deputised.

A clean sheet from a game of little incident was a case of job done. It also showed again that the squad had some quality, if not that many numbers. Gerken and Elokobi were two young players who had been brought through by Phil Parkinson and who were proving that they could cut it at Championship level.

The increasing defensive solidity away from home was maintained in the next match which was in front of over 16,000 at Selhurst Park on 9th December. Barker returned to the team and Gerken continued in goal. Garcia took a place on the bench after seven weeks out, and his introduction in the sixtieth minute turned out to be the turning point of the match.

Palace were a disappointing sixteenth in the table but were clearly going to be dangerous opponents. In Clinton Morrison and Shefki Kuqi they boasted two international strikers who had cost them £2 million and £2.5 million respectively. They had Colchester under pressure in the first half, and it needed some desperate defending and fine goalkeeping from the visitors for the game to be goalless at half time.

Williams told his team to go for it in the second half, and they began to take the game to their hosts. Only three minutes after Garcia came on, they took the lead when Cureton`s deflected cross was bundled home by Duguid. Garcia started to be a big influence on the game with his direct running and in the seventieth minute he refused to be shaken off the ball before drilling home from just outside the box.

The U`s were now in complete control, and Iwelumo almost made it three. Against the run of play, and with many home fans having filed out of creaking and uncomfortable Selhurst Park, Morrison caused the 1500 away fans some anxiety when he headed in from a Danny Granville free kick. There was no need for concern. Granville brought down Garcia, and Iwelumo converted the spot kick in the final minute.

Colchester returned to eighth, but in-form Stoke City would be the next side to threaten the impregnability of Layer Road. The U`s appeared now to have addressed their flagging away form. If they could maintain the fortress like qualities of "the Layerdome" a place in the top six was a realistic aim, to the utter astonishment of everyone in football! However, Stoke would be another real test of these credentials.

Stoke were another club who felt they belonged in the Premier League even though they had not been in the top flight since 1984/85. Since then, the only times that they had escaped the second tier had been out of the wrong end. They had twice been at third tier level where they had met Colchester. They had a modern stadium and new investment in the shape of Bet365 founder Peter Coates, who was said to be worth £750 million. One of his first acts was to put Tony Pulis in charge, and they were expected to be a force in the 2006/07 Championship.

They had started poorly, winning only one of their first ten games. This had turned round with a 4-0 win at Leeds, and when they came to Colchester they had nine wins from their previous twelve and had risen to fifth in the table. They breezed into the Old Lady having kept seven consecutive clean sheets, and she saw yet another brash visitor who needed taking down a peg. Geraint Williams saw a big club who, having been introduced to the bijou delights of Layer Road, needed to be attacked from the off. He started with the eleven that had finished at Selhurst Park, and that meant Garcia in for Jackson. It was to be all out attack.

Aidan Davison was fit again, but Williams stuck with young Dean Gerken in goal. He had been impressive at both Palace and Cardiff. He was now twenty two and had thirty two first team appearances under his belt. Davison`s job had been to put himself out of a job by grooming Gerken, and this was clearly going well. Davison was approaching thirty nine, and the Layer Road goalkeeping mantle was being handed over.

Stoke`s highly rated goalkeeper Steve Simonsen had played 656 minutes of football without conceding a goal when proceedings began at Layer Road. He managed to add only one more minute to this impressive record when he was beaten by Cureton`s looping shot from 20 yards. To be fair to him, Stoke could have fielded five goalkeepers and it would still have gone in!

After a start like that the U`s were going to take some holding, and Stoke never looked like being equal to the task. In the seventeenth minute Iwelumo, playing against his former club, flicked on and as the visitors searched for their bearings Garcia lobbed through to Cureton. He was thinking way ahead of Stoke`s multi million pound defenders. As they looked hopefully at the linesman, Cureton buried a close range volley.

Stoke had their moments, and Sidbe was particularly unlucky to have a good looking goal ruled out for offside. However, with the U`s in this mood it would have been no more than a consolation. The issue was put beyond doubt in the sixty third minute when Garcia headed in a Barker cross. The game ran down to cries of "ole" from the Layer Road terraces as the ball was passed around with Stoke chasing shadows. Some went home remarking that it had been very similar to looking at a certain South American national team!

United had been threatening the play off positions for a while, but now it had happened! This 3-0 win had eased Colchester over Stoke and into sixth. It was the half way mark in the season, twenty three matches and thirty seven points. Round about thirty seven more than we thought we would have at this stage! We were the equal leading scorers in the Championship, along with West Brom. A truly remarkable achievement given the multi millions spent by most clubs and the fact that the Colchester squad had cost nothing. This was not a Cup upset. It was not a case of a small team having a good day, or a few good days. It had been achieved over twenty three games.

| 1 | Birmingham City | 23 | 14 | 4 | 5 | 38 | 22 | +16 | 46 |
| 2 | Derby County | 23 | 13 | 4 | 6 | 33 | 25 | +8 | 43 |
| 3 | Preston North End | 23 | 11 | 8 | 4 | 35 | 22 | +13 | 41 |
| 4 | Southampton | 23 | 11 | 6 | 6 | 37 | 27 | +10 | 39 |
| 5 | Cardiff City | 23 | 11 | 6 | 6 | 34 | 26 | +8 | 39 |
| 6 | Colchester United | 23 | 11 | 4 | 8 | 39 | 26 | +13 | 37 |

As we looked forward, it was impossible not to catch a fleeting glimpse of what lay beyond the Football League!

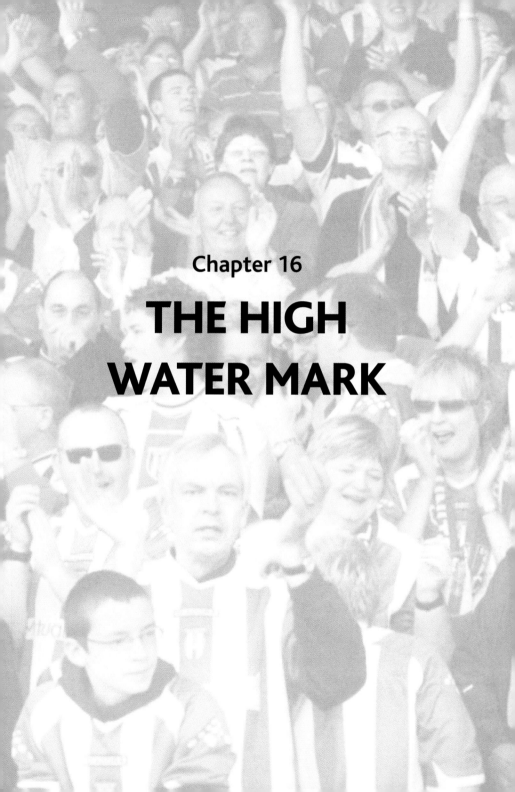

Chapter 16

# THE HIGH
# WATER MARK

# Chapter 16
## THE HIGH WATER MARK

Manager Geraint Williams looks back on how the amazing 2006/07 season was panning out,

*"To start with, our only thought was to try and stay up. However, as time went on and results got better and better, especially at home, we started to believe we could do far better than just stay up.*

*There were certain key games. I`ll never forget the home match against Ipswich. The atmosphere in the ground was magnificent, and for Dugy to score the only goal was almost poetry as he`d been at the club for so long and he wasn`t a regular goalscorer. It was perhaps the greatest highlight in a season of highlights.*

*I also particularly remember Crystal Palace away. In the first half we looked timid. We were dropping off and looking like we were bottling it, which wasn`t like us. We were lucky to be 0-0 at half time. I was angry and ready to deliver a rocket which is unusual for me. As we were walking to the dressing room, Mick said "What are you going to do?". I said "They`re going to get it." He said "We know the group they are. I don`t think they`re bottling it. I think they genuinely don`t know what to do and need help." I thought about it as we walked, luckily it`s a good long walk at Palace.*

*As I got into the dressing room the lads were arguing amongst themselves because they were frustrated. They couldn`t understand what they were doing wrong. So we sat down and had a calm discussion. We changed a few things tactically. I said we needed to hold a high line at the back and that if we got caught out with the ball over the top it`s my fault. I said we needed to be more positive and get "in their face". We went out and won 3-1.*

*Again, Mick`s contribution was vital. The players would have thought about me, "He knows what he`s doing". This builds trust. We started to believe we could beat anyone.*

*The home match against Hull was a very different kind of memory. Parky and I still got on very well, and as much as I was delighted with the result and for Chris, I found it slightly embarrassing. I know that Phil Parkinson would fight for every ball to get a result and I felt that some of his players let him down badly that night. I think some of them chucked it in."*

It is unlikely that the other twenty three clubs in the Championship went into the 2006/07 season with a collective ambition to halt the progress of Colchester United. Although it would not take a huge leap to imagine the club owners in the Premier League using their vast wealth to help those clubs achieve just that. One can picture the furrowed brows of the Premier League owners as they watched the U`s "juggernaut" move Into sixth position at the half way point in the season. They must have exchanged some very old fashioned looks, "Are we really going to have to visit this place, what`s it called, Player Road? Where will we land the helicopter?"

In fact they did not need to worry. Their salvation lay in the Premier League handbook. The ground criteria section was not actually headed "Keep Layer Road out of our lives", but it might as well have been. Let us picture the scene, Colchester United have just been promoted to the Premier League, whose officials arrive for their tour of inspection. They are led by an earnest looking gentleman who really wants Layer Road to pass this audit and he is determined not to be deterred by the massive obstacles in his way.

First he is shown into the dressing rooms tape measure at the ready. It`s a big tape measure as they have to be 30 square metres excluding showers and baths! He asks again for the dressing rooms, believing himself to be in the broom cupboard. On realising there has been no mistake he puts the tape measure away, "Ok, that might have to be an area for special dispensation. At least the special room for Ronaldo`s beauty products is not yet a requirement."

Next he asks for the Police and under soil heating control rooms. Blank looks. "Alright, lets have a walk round outside then.

Erm, the 3000 seats for away fans, they`ve just been taken out for temporary maintenance have they?

Can we move on to the Rules surrounding broadcaster`s requirements. We`ve looked all around the main stand and the whole stadium, we can`t seem to find the principal TV gantry with at least five camera positions, each with at least three seats and at least three metres wide and one metre deep.

It`s up where? Well, it has to have at least three UK TV commentary positions and 15 overseas commentary positions, and it has to be easily accessible by technical personnel without disturbing commentators or cameramen. I think I`d have to be concerned about the screams of a falling lighting engineer coming out on the broadcast.

There has to be full internet connectivity, with total bandwidth of 40 megabits per second, burstable to 100 megabits per second. What`s that, you provide climbing axes and crampons?

We haven`t seen the TV studio either. Oh, it`s over there. How nice. The commentators and anchor man will be able to wave to each other through binoculars. Such nice scaffolding and four by twos. We thought it was a forest fire look out tower.

I was wondering about the seven hardwired pitch side presentation positions, three metres wide. It`s just that there were some glitches when we tested during your pre season friendly, two of our presenters finished up in a heap on the ground with four of your substitutes on top of them. We`ll come back to that.

Yes, thank you for showing us to the tunnel area, because I wanted to bring that up. There needs to be at least five hardwired tunnel interview positions, two for UK broadcasters and three for overseas. There needs to be some distance between this area and the shower area. When we tested here, we found that steam seeping out of the dressing rooms was making the interview look like a scene from the great smog of 1952. We know that you are pleased to be in the Premier League, but we need the interview to be a search for the stories from the game, not a dream sequence from a Fellini movie.

The other area for interviews is the "Mixed Zone". This has to be located between the player`s dressing rooms and their point of exit from the stadium. I`m delighted to say that this is one requirement which you satisfy, although it is more common for the area to be indoors! We are a little concerned about hardwiring and lighting, but there is no question that the stipulation to accommodate at least 20 representatives of broadcasters in this area is fully satisfied, so well done.

Perhaps we`ll come back later to the question of the media working area, media conference room, fifteen radio commentary positions, twenty car park spaces for broadcasters, outside broadcast compound, and fifty press seats, but just before we do that I`d like to walk over to behind that covered area.

So what is this area called again? The Farside? And this mobile contraption is to meet the natural needs of the Premier League spectator. So, let`s have a look in here then. Very good suspension.......... Oh sweet mother of God!! Give me a paper bag".

After a few moments to collect themselves the officials re-assemble, "Yes I`m feeling a little better now thank you" says their leader. "I think the box on my form which says "each club shall provide bright, clean and hygienic toilet and washing facilities for male and female spectators" might have to be another case of special dispensation!"

The earnest looking leader, wearing a genuinely pained expression, would hand the audit report to Marie Partner. Layer Road would have failed almost every area of the Premier League ground criteria despite the provision of a delightful "mixed zone" affording the players the opportunity to show off their sponsored umbrellas.

Promotion was still a fantasy, but the line between fantasy and reality was looking pretty blurred at this stage of the season. Nevertheless, Layer Road, with it`s capacity of 6,120 and it`s corporate facilities for forty people, would not be gracing the Premier League.

It would be some time before the nightmare vision of Colchester United in the Premier League could be banished from the minds of Premier League owners. United would stay in or around the Play Off positions for the remainder of the season. However, this particular stay in the top six would only last a week. An unchanged team took on Liam Chilvers and third placed Preston at Deepdale two days before Christmas, and returned pointless despite a good performance. David Nugent`s thirty third minute goal would end United`s run of four wins and a draw from five matches and see them drop to eighth.

The penultimate Boxing Day fixture at Layer Road would bring struggling Luton Town to Essex. They included Colchester old boys Dean Morgan and Rowan Vine, and future Colchester captain Chris Coyne. Karl Duguid had been injured at Preston and was replaced by Kevin McLeod.

Luton had made a promising start to the season under Mike Newell and were fifth after thirteen games. On the way to playing at Ipswich on 29th October, their defender Sol Davis had suffered a stroke on the team coach. An understandably shaken up team lost 5-0 and went on to lose their next six matches as well.

They arrived at Layer Road in nineteenth position, and were no match for a U`s side back in the comfortable surroundings of the Old Lady. As with so many games during the 05/06 and 06/07 seasons, the visitors had as much possession as Colchester, but they did far less with it. The U`s attacked with verve and penetration, mixing up long and short passing. There was the guile of Watson, the aerial presence of Iwelumo, the tenacity of Garcia and Izzet and the football brain of Cureton. This was a potent mix, and like so many teams Luton had no answer in the hostile atmosphere and confines of Layer Road.

The fun started in the twenty third minute when McLeod showed his goal scoring knack again when nodding in Izzet`s cross. Iwelumo made it two four minutes before half time. Garcia scored on the hour and then it was exhibition time.

Some Championship managers had referred to the size of some of Colchester`s players and the physicality and directness of their game. Whilst it was true that Queen size beds would not have done the job for at least half the United squad on overnight stops, any idea that this was a long ball team who relied on knocking the opposition over was utter nonsense. This team could mix it up. If a long ball was required it was delivered. They had no qualms about getting the ball into the opposition box early so as to apply pressure by exploiting the discomfort that Iwelumo`s height and agility could cause. Equally, they could adroitly move the ball around without it leaving Layer Road`s excellent playing surface and have expensive players chasing shadows.

Luton must have been looking for the white flags in the sixty fifth minute when a six pass movement beginning deep in the U`s half had Cureton sprinting down the right wing. His pin point cross was powered home off the head of Iwelumo. Vine knocked in a penalty five minutes from time, but other than dirtying Gerken`s sheet it made no difference to anything.

Four days later the thirty or so players and staff of Wolverhampton Wanderers had the job of fitting into the Layer Road changing rooms. Before they got that far, and as they came through the player`s entrance and walked behind the main stand, they must have been asking the coach driver why he had brought them to this twilight world. "Please could we be taken to the football stadium in Colchester", they would have been pleading as they squeezed out of the dressing room and up the tunnel. Here they would have been relieved at last to see something familiar, a football pitch. This was not the carefully manicured lawn of Molineux though. "Welcome to Layer Road". As the Wolves surveyed their surroundings, they would have seen a pride of slavering lions in blue and white stripes on a pitch tightly surrounded by 6,000 baying canines with their blood up.

It seemed that nothing in the professional careers of the Wolves players had prepared them for these experiences. They were 1-0 down after four minutes. The unchanged U`s simply carried on where they had left off against Luton as Cureton stroked home a free kick. Then, just before half time, the referee failed to notice Iwelumo`s blatant handball which propelled him beyond Gary Breen to make it 2-0. Wolves managed a consolation goal in stoppage time, but once again this made no difference except to annoy Dean Gerken.

This was now an astonishing eleven consecutive home wins. Twenty wins from twenty four home league games in the calendar year! The U`s returned to 6th.

| | | | | | | | | | |
|---|---|---|---|---|---|---|---|---|---|
| 1 | Birmingham City | 26 | 16 | 5 | 5 | 46 | 25 | +21 | 53 |
| 2 | Preston North End | 26 | 13 | 8 | 5 | 39 | 26 | +13 | 47 |
| 3 | Derby County | 26 | 14 | 5 | 7 | 34 | 27 | +7 | 47 |
| 4 | Southampton | 26 | 12 | 8 | 6 | 43 | 31 | +12 | 44 |
| 5 | West Bromwich Albion | 26 | 12 | 7 | 7 | 47 | 28 | +19 | 43 |
| 6 | Colchester United | 26 | 13 | 4 | 9 | 45 | 29 | +16 | 43 |
| 7 | Stoke City | 26 | 12 | 7 | 7 | 35 | 21 | +14 | 43 |
| 8 | Cardiff City | 26 | 11 | 9 | 6 | 36 | 28 | +8 | 42 |
| 9 | Sheffield Wednesday | 26 | 11 | 7 | 8 | 38 | 35 | +3 | 40 |
| 10 | Wolverhampton Wanderers | 26 | 11 | 6 | 9 | 26 | 29 | -3 | 39 |
| 11 | Burnley | 26 | 10 | 7 | 9 | 32 | 28 | +4 | 37 |
| 12 | Sunderland | 26 | 11 | 4 | 11 | 34 | 32 | +2 | 37 |
| 13 | Plymouth Argyle | 26 | 8 | 11 | 7 | 32 | 33 | -1 | 35 |
| 14 | Coventry City | 26 | 10 | 4 | 12 | 24 | 29 | -5 | 34 |
| 15 | Norwich City | 26 | 9 | 7 | 10 | 33 | 39 | -6 | 34 |
| 16 | Ipswich Town | 26 | 9 | 5 | 12 | 36 | 37 | -1 | 32 |
| 17 | Leicester City | 26 | 8 | 8 | 10 | 26 | 32 | -6 | 32 |
| 18 | Crystal Palace | 26 | 8 | 7 | 11 | 28 | 31 | -3 | 31 |
| 19 | Luton Town | 26 | 8 | 6 | 12 | 35 | 45 | -10 | 30 |
| 20 | Queens Park Rangers | 26 | 7 | 6 | 13 | 33 | 41 | -8 | 27 |
| 21 | Barnsley | 26 | 7 | 5 | 14 | 29 | 45 | -16 | 26 |
| 22 | Hull City | 26 | 6 | 6 | 14 | 25 | 37 | -12 | 24 |
| 23 | Leeds United | 26 | 6 | 3 | 17 | 25 | 48 | -23 | 21 |
| 24 | Southend United | 26 | 3 | 9 | 14 | 19 | 44 | -25 | 18 |

In a sense, the win over Wolves represented the high water mark of the season, and indeed of the club`s entire existence. They would remain in this position for three weeks, despite disappointing results in the next two games and the ending of that incredible win sequence at Layer Road.

The first game of 2007 was at Loftus Road against underachieving QPR. They had lost seven of their previous eight and were sinking into the relegation dog fight. Once again the U`s were not able to take their home form on the bus with them. A 1-0 defeat was a poor result from a poor performance. The goal was scored by Ray Jones, who had been rejected by Colchester as a youth team player, and for whom they would have a £200,000 bid rejected in the following June. A few weeks after Colchester made their bid, Jones was killed in a car accident, three days before his nineteenth birthday.

On a happier note, Chris Barker`s loan from Cardiff was extended to the end of the season. He had been excellent in the left back position and fans were delighted that he would be staying, if a little concerned that the club had been unable to acquire his permanent transfer. We were in the Play Off zone and only four points away from the automatic promotion positions. The vast riches of the Premier League were glimmering on the horizon. What could be done over the final twenty games of the season to maintain or even enhance the challenge? Could we really do that without adding to the squad?

There was a lot of talk about the club having certain transfer targets as the window had re-opened on 1st January. However, the only movement which seemed imminent was the possible departure of Greg Halford. It seemed as though every match might be his last.

The squad was paper thin, and had cost nothing. The biggest transfer fee ever paid by the club was a paltry £50,000.

To enhance the squad now possessed by the U`s, any new players would have to be of a certain quality. To thrive in the upper echelons of the Championship, such players would be likely to cost a massive (for Colchester) transfer fee and command the sort of wages and length of contract which would go along with that.

Even if the club felt it could afford the fee and the wages, there would be the ever present risk that the player might not do well and/or that the club would be relegated while carrying the burden of these big contracts. Much bigger clubs than Colchester had been brought to the brink by taking on such liabilities. The effect on the rest of the squad also had to be considered. They were the ones who had brought the U`s to this level, and they were not on big money. It was a tight knit squad, and the introduction of a few big money acquisitions might have blown it apart.

This must have been the dilemma faced by Geraint Williams and the Board at the beginning of 2007. Financial prudence had been the byword for many years, and it had brought the club to the highest position it had ever occupied. The policy was not going to change now, even as we glimpsed the glittering prize which lay beyond the Football League. After all, the aim for 2006/07 was not promotion. It was survival, and this had already been pretty much achieved.

Near miracles had been performed to bring the club this far. The policy over the final twenty games would be to continue performing those miracles. While Colchester considered the loan market, most of their rivals splashed the cash. Birmingham, for example, spent £2.5 million on Rowan Vine from Luton and £1 million on Sebastian Larsson from Arsenal.

A good Cup run was one thing which might have earned some pennies for use in the transfer market. This opportunity had been passed up with the Carling Cup defeat at League One MK Dons back in August. Now there was another chance. As a Championship club Colchester had been ushered straight through to the third round of the FA Cup.

League Two Barnet had overcome Gainsborough Trinity and Northampton Town to reach this round, and must have been eagerly anticipating a glamorous third round tie when the balls started shaking in the bag. Manchester United at Old Trafford, or Arsenal at the newly opened Emirates perhaps. Colchester United at Underhill was not what the Doctor ordered! No glamour to attract the home fans. A relatively small away support, and being against a good Championship club, they would probably be beaten as well.

United made their intentions clear by fielding a full strength team and at half time the match was going according to plan as Colchester led by a Cureton goal. Things went decidedly off script in the second half as Colchester battled against a strong wind. Barnet scored twice without reply, and a giant (if that can ever be the correct adjective to use on Colchester United) had been slain. So that special feeling of joining the FA Cup in the third round, like a big club, lasted only ninety minutes!

For the home game against Leicester City, Duguid returned in place of McLeod. Unfortunately, a twelfth consecutive home win eluded the U`s. They fell behind to an Iain Hume goal in the nineteenth minute but got back to level terms early in the second half. This was courtesy of one of a number of strange decisions made by referee Danny McDermid. Having already denied Colchester two good penalty shouts, he somehow interpreted Iwelumo`s off balance attempt at a flick on as a foul by Patrick McCarthy. In keeping with most of the penalties given for and against United during this season it was plainly wrong. Iwelumo converted, while Mr McDermid later capped his bizarre performance by showing Duguid a red card for having incurred a second yellow card. The only problem was that the first yellow had never been given to Duguid, a fact pointed out by Duguid and the fourth official! It was Graham Poll`s 2006 World Cup in reverse and the U`s captain saw out the game, as did Leicester, despite Hogan Ephraim netting, a score cancelled out by the ever reliable Mr McDermid!

Although Colchester had exceeded all expectations, it had to be admitted that their away form had not been good. Two wins and ten defeats from sixteen away league and cup matches was poor. For them to be as high as sixth showed just how good the home form had been. A visit to Portman Road seemed like a fantastic opportunity to improve things away from home.

## THE BATTLE OF THE A12, ACT TWO.

Few Colchester fans would ever have expected to see their team in the same division as Ipswich. The win at Layer Road in September was a dream come true. Not only were we in the same division, but we had spent most of the season above our farming friends. We went into the match on 20th January no fewer than nine places and nine points above them.

It was the first League meeting between the sides at Portman Road since 6th October 1956 when 20,431 saw Ipswich win 3-1 on the way to being Third Division South Champions. The two sides had met in the Southern League during Colchester United`s inaugural season, 1937/38. Ipswich had then been elected to the Football League. When Colchester were elected in 1950, the clubs met in the Third Division South over four seasons before Ipswich were promoted. They only spent one season in the Second Division, and there were then two more seasons when the two clubs occupied Third Division South. After that their paths had gone in very different directions.

There are some lovely photographs of steam engines leaving Colchester`s North Station festooned with rosettes and scarfs and packed with fans heading for Suffolk to attend the derbies of the 30s and 50s. There would be no repeat of this in 2007, and it had nothing to do with the discontinuation of the steam locomotive.

Despite knowing that thousands of people would be travelling between the two towns, our lovely railway companies chose this weekend to close the line for engineering works! It was Chelsea away all over again, except this time they had seven months notice of the fixture. It beggared belief, but football fans are not easily put off. The U`s 2,200 ticket allocation disappeared in days, and with many of the home areas also occupied by away fans one could only estimate how many of the 28,355 in attendance were supporting the Essex boys. It was the biggest crowd to watch either Ipswich Town or Colchester United during that season, bigger than either of the Ipswich v Norwich derbies.

Colchester had been very lucky with injuries all season. However, they had to make two changes for the visit to Portman Road. Jamie Cureton was withdrawn with a hamstring strain in the Leicester match and he failed a fitness test on the day of the Ipswich game. He would have been gutted to miss such a big match. It was one of only two games that he missed that season, but what a game to miss! He probably could have played at a pinch, but the fact that he played all but one of the remaining games probably showed what a sensible decision it was.

Pat Baldwin had been excellent all season alongside Wayne Brown. Many thought Liam Chilvers would be missed when he left. No-one had been brought in to replace him, either because no-one of sufficient quality could be found at the right price or because the club had faith in Baldwin and young back up Garry Richards. This would be a chance for Richards to show it was the latter as Baldwin was laid low by a virus.

Cureton's replacement would be Hogan Ephraim. His loan from West Ham had been extended although he had been restricted to substitute appearances. It would be a big ask for these two youngsters in such a big game. Ephraim was eighteen and had not yet started a league match for anyone. Richards was twenty and had only sixteen appearances to his name. Arguably, it transpired that the occasion was a little too much for either of them. Once again, the loss of only two regulars had stretched Colchester's squad to its very limits.

It turned out to be another pulsating derby, especially in the first half. Richards got off to a bad start when he sold Dean Gerken short with a headed back pass. Then, in the fifteenth minute Peters played the ball into the Colchester area where Clarke beat Richards to it. He shot past Gerken, but Richards had got back and appeared to clear it. Ipswich claimed it had crossed the line and as they remonstrated with the officials Colchester broke upfield. A long ball from Garcia found Ephraim. He played it inside to Duguid, who beat Lewis Price with a shot from inside the area.

Ipswich felt that an injustice had been done and they tore into Colchester. Gerken saved well from Roberts, and Richards's eventful game continued as he headed off the line, but it wasn't one way traffic as Watson almost made it two for the visitors. There was more controversy on the half hour. Gavin Williams played it into the Colchester box, where Richards and Alan Lee challenged. Lee went down and the appropriately named referee Mr Laws surprisingly pointed to the spot.

This really was a season where a forward only had to be breathed upon for a spot kick to be given! It had been a slightly clumsy challenge, but it was a very harsh decision. Lee himself converted.

Ipswich were now in the ascendency and Gary Roberts hit the bar with a sweet twenty yarder just before half time. Billy Clarke and Greg Halford were both booked in the first half for protesting the controversial incidents.

The second half began quietly and there was no real incident until the fifty sixth minute when Town took the lead. Legwinski headed in a Williams corner from eight yards out. Soon afterwards Jamie Guy was introduced for Ephraim.

Both sides probed, but there were few clear cut chances. Jackson came on for Izzet in the seventy third minute, shortly after Danny Haynes had replaced Clarke on the Ipswich side. Haynes probably should have done better when bursting from deep to force Gerken into a save.

Ipswich sealed victory in the eighty second minute. Peters passed inside a tiring Garry Richards, and Danny Haynes ran onto it and beat the exposed Dean Gerken. The U`s did not give up. Watson had a good effort deflected wide, and then in the final minute Duguid`s through ball released Halford. He crossed and Price saved brilliantly from Jackson. Iwelumo`s follow up was also brilliantly saved, but not this time by the goalkeeper. David Wright, later to play for Colchester, was this day making his debut for Ipswich. He handled on the line and was sent off for a second yellow card. The ever reliable Iwelumo netted the spot kick. He quickly retrieved the ball and raced with it to the centre spot but there was insufficient time for an equaliser.

A very disappointing day, but in truth Ipswich`s ball retention had probably been better than Colchester and they just about shaded it. As at Layer Road in September, the home side had won by one goal and had just about deserved it. U`s fans were left to ponder what might have been. Perhaps Baldwin`s extra experience would have avoided that first half penalty, and maybe his greater mobility would have seen a tackle made on Haynes for the third goal. We had probably missed him more than we missed Cureton, although the little man was always likely to pop up with an opportunistic goal, and his intelligent runs might have troubled the Town defence more than Ephraim`s pace.

United dropped to eighth. We headed disconsolately to the station for the rail travellers normal weekend activity of catching the "special" bus service. Our mood in no way improved for being outnumbered by Ipswich fans returning home to North Essex!

Geraint Williams, the man from the valleys who stepped into the breach.

**How the TV companies must have looked forward to visiting Old Lady Layer Road!
Were these trucks lowered in by helicopter?**

U`s fans trudge away and contemplate the Premier League!

Karl Duguid and Pat Baldwin celebrate another Layer Road win.

**U`s fans packed in and celebrating.**

**Richard Garcia airbourne after notching against QPR.**

**Dwight Yorke and Jamie Cureton compare notes during Geraint Williams`
favourite match.**

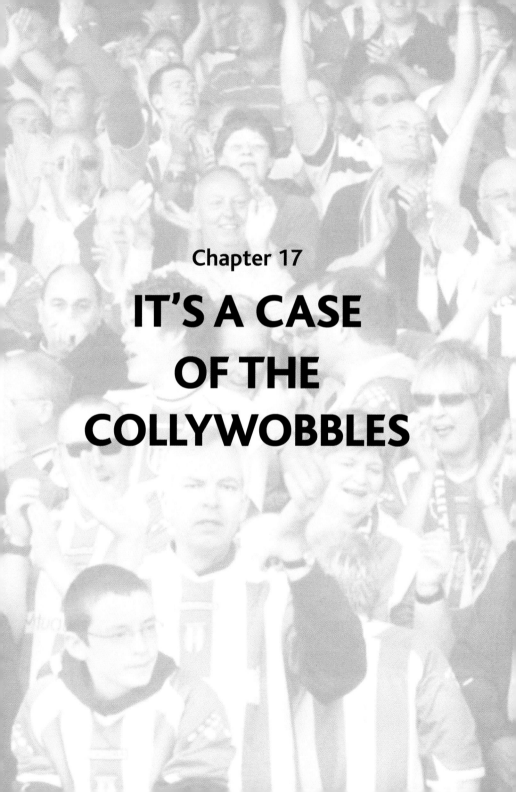

Chapter 17

# IT'S A CASE OF THE COLLYWOBBLES

# Chapter 17
## IT'S A CASE OF THE COLLYWOBBLES

There were seventeen games left, and it would be meaningless to say that Colchester United stood on the cusp of history because this is where they had stood for over a year! Even if they had finished the 2006/07 season rock bottom in twenty fourth position, it would have been the club`s highest finishing position ever.

The transfer window did not slam shut at Layer Road on 31st January. It was closed in a quiet and orderly fashion, albeit with the club`s highest ever transfer fee received.

The departure of Greg Halford had become increasingly inevitable. As a Colchester player he had become an England Under 20 international. He was being compared with Gareth Bale who was just emerging at Southampton. He was being tracked by a host of clubs. He had quietly handed in a transfer request, but had continued to perform very effectively. In no sense had his actions destabilised the team, not least due to his own performances. Reading, then of the Premier League, paid £2.5 million for him. It was a good price and it would have been counter productive for the club to stand in his way. He left with the best wishes of club and fans. His final action was to put in a cross at Portman Road from which a penalty was earned. Not a bad way for any Colchester United player to go out.

When Halford left, the transfer window had twenty four hours of life left in it. Colchester had no replacement lined up. If strengthening the squad in any position relied on receiving money for Halford, one might have hoped that the club would have deals lined up and ready to go as soon as Reading put pen to paper. Such was not the case, and as clubs around them spent millions to boost their squads for the run in, Colchester conducted only one piece of business, the acquisition of defender Mathew Mills on a month`s loan from Manchester City. This could hardly be called squad strengthening. It was a reaction to Baldwin`s virus.

Williams and his staff had been working hard to bring players in, but had mostly been frustrated. Players they had looked at had ended up going for massive fees to much bigger clubs. The manager said, "There is no way we can spend £3 million for a centre forward and pay the wages that go with that, and then give our players higher wages to catch up as you have to be fair to everyone." United were the only Championship club to have spent nothing on agent`s fees. Although ownership had transferred to Robbie Cowling, Peter Heard was still in charge and club policy had not changed in relation to agents. Rather than greasing the wheels, this might have been a spanner in the works. Even more so at the higher level.

Mills was twenty and had already enjoyed loan spells at Coventry and Bournemouth. He had twenty two senior appearances to his name. He would go straight into the side in place of Garry Richards for the next match, which was at home to third placed Preston.

Under the management of Paul Simpson, Preston had taken over from Cardiff as the other surprise packets of the Championship. The Welshmen were never quite the same after their encounter with the Old Lady in November. They arrived at Layer Road top of the table. They had now dropped to seventh and would eventually finish thirteenth. Preston had hit the top in December. They were not big money spenders by the standards of the Championship, but they had been able to hang on to their £6 million rated goal scorer David Nugent. He would later that season become the first Preston player to play for England since Tom Finney.

The mood at Layer Road was quite sombre, due to the departure of Halford which had been confirmed earlier in the day. John White took the right back berth. In all, there were four changes from the Ipswich match, with Cureton returning in place of Ephraim and Jackson starting for the injured Garcia.

Having no FA Cup 4th round engagement the squad had been taken out to Malaga for some warm weather training. To avoid this seeming like a reward for exiting the Cup, and to banish memories of what followed the Portuguese trip a year earlier, the team owed the club a good performance against Preston.

Despite being dropped, Garry Richards found himself in the action. Mills came off with a dead leg after sixty two minutes and Richards became the hero. He headed in a Kevin Watson corner for the game's only goal. It had taken until three minutes from time, but the U's had the edge throughout. After a one game intermission they were back to winning ways at Layer Road. Like so many teams, Preston would go somewhat off colour after calling in for tea with the Dowager Aunt. They departed Layer Road, returned to 21st century surroundings and missed out on the Play Offs.

Birmingham City was not a side that was going to be happy just reaching the Play Offs. They had spent over £14 million since the end of the previous season, and felt they belonged in the Premier League. Neil Danns and Rowan Vine were amongst their buys. They were second when they came to Layer Road on 3rd February.

As we moved into the business end of the season, most of the big boys were muscling in for an assault on the summit. Derby, West Brom, Southampton, Sunderland and Wolves were all in the top ten with Birmingham. Quite what Colchester United in eighth were doing in this company was a question few had an answer to. Another of the big clubs was propping up the division, basket case Leeds United.

In previewing the Birmingham match, skipper Karl Duguid pointed out, "They have signed some very good players since we last took them on, and we won`t be taking them lightly." So it was good to know there would be no complacency against title chasing Birmingham and their £20 million + squad!

The U`s kept the same starting eleven, but for once did not start brightly. They were fortunate not to find themselves behind early on when Gary McSheffrey missed a good chance. As the half wore on Colchester became the most likely to score with Cureton looking constantly dangerous. It was, though, Birmingham who hit the post, and right on half time Fabrice Muamba pulled a good save out of Gerken.

Early in the second half Cureton went close and then on fifty five minutes Iwelumo knocked the ball down for Cureton to swivel and volley from twenty two yards. The ball rebounded from the post and Kem Izzet struck home with the keeper grounded. It was his first goal for three years.

Unfortunately for Colchester the lead only lasted for ten minutes. Gerken had saved superbly from a Jaidi header but from the resulting corner Clemence headed home. Both sides huffed and puffed for the remainder of the game, but neither had done enough to deserve a win.

When the U`s travelled to Barnsley on 10th February they took an unchanged team and an away record that could, at best, be described as patchy. However, there was no sign of away nerves as they tore into Barnsley, as they had so many teams at home. Goals from Duguid and Cureton had them 2-0 up after ten minutes. The Tykes simply never got a look in. Jackson and Cureton both hit the bar before the visitors` domination was confirmed seven minutes from time by substitute Hogan Ephraim`s first goal in senior football. It was the first time United had won at Oakwell since 1980. "That was probably our best away performance of the season" said Geraint Williams.

The U`s now sat eighth, two points from the play off zone, and only five points below the automatic promotion places. They had hit the magic fifty points, which was seen as the number required to guarantee at least one more season at this level. They had done it with three months of the season still remaining. In fact, as few as forty four points would turn out to be good enough for safety in 2006/07 and United had hit that number with the draw against Leicester back on 13th January.

The club`s target had never changed, and that was to stay up. There was never any talk of promotion to the Premier League, or even making the Play Offs. There was a Monty Python character called Ernest Scribbler who one day wrote the funniest joke in the world and then died laughing. The joke was so funny that no-one could read it and live! It was developed as a secret weapon by the Army. It was tested on Salisbury Plain and found to be deadly from anything up to 50 yards. The words written down by Mr Scribbler were,

"Colchester United will be promoted to the Premier League." The reader should now Google "The collected jokes of Margaret Thatcher" for the antidote.

Geraint Williams was very much of the "take each game as it comes" school of football thought. He was never going to tempt fate by publicly stating that the club was now aiming for the Play Offs or better. It could not be denied however. There was a clear glimpse of what lay beyond the Football League, and behind the scenes contingency plans had to be laid. It could not be passed off as a joke by those responsible for running the club when you occupied Colchester's position with only 14 games remaining. Where on earth would the U's play if they went up?

The new stadium would not be ready until August 2008. The idea of Layer Road in the Premier League would have been Mr Scribbler's next piece of work if he had survived. So it would have to be a ground share, and this threw up a very unsavoury prospect. Marie Partner said "Looking at the alternatives it would have to be Portman Road". Was getting to the Premier League worth that? Partner continued, "It's something that's been loosely discussed, and would be something that Ipswich would have to think about, but commercially it's not ideal." So conversations about this fantasy were going on, albeit very low key.

United and the Old Lady now had to intimidate another of those high flying big clubs. The next visitors to Layer Road were third placed West Brom on the following Tuesday. Layer Road should not have come as any surprise to Albion. Two years before, they became the last in a long line of top flight clubs to lose a Cup match at Layer Road.

The Baggies had started the season slowly, but then replaced Bryan Robson with Tony Mowbray. By December they had reached the top six, and were now looking to force their way into the automatic promotion spots. They were unbeaten in five, of which they had won four. The U's were unchanged again. They were defending a fourteen match unbeaten home record of twelve wins and two draws.

It was an even first half with little incident. The match exploded into life immediately after half time, and unfortunately the bomb went off in the Colchester penalty area. Paul McShane headed in a corner, and a minute later Diomansy Kamara drove home to make it 2-0. It was quality finishing that Colchester could not match on the night, although Johnnie Jackson pulled one back with thirty five minutes still left. There were close shaves at both ends in the final half hour, but West Brom were probably worth the win.

So it was a rare occasion when the Old Lady felt hospitable. She had put out the Earl Grey as well as the cucumber sandwiches, and she'd even cut the crusts off! West Brom's good run continued, and United's long unbeaten home run finally ended. Tony Mowbray said, "We have immense respect for Colchester, and that's why we've built this game up to almost a cup final. They`ve done magnificently this season and I`m sure other teams will find it difficult to play against them."

Could Colchester now resume their progress against the Pilgrims? They were off to Home Park on Tuesday 20th February. Plymouth had never been an easy place for Colchester to visit. In fact they had never won there in the League. West Brom had just become the first team to double them, Plymouth would be the second.

The only change in the U`s line up would be Garcia coming in for a suspended Kem Izzet. After spending most of the promotion season on the bench, Izzet had been a mainstay of the team during the historic first Championship season. He had until now started every game. He was effectively a replacement for Neil Danns though a totally different kind of player. He was a box-to-box athlete with a good short passing game. He did not have a range of passing, and what was a keen eye for goal diminished as his career went on. His strength lay in linking the team together and breaking up opposition attacks, and he was doing it well enough in 06/07 to be linked with moves to big clubs.

Those moves never quite happened, but he was certainly missed at Plymouth. The home side were buoyant, having just reached the FA Cup Quarter Finals, and they had no intention of letting United continue to improve their away form. The Home Park pitch was very heavy and would have ideally suited Izzet. Plymouth had the upper hand for most of the first half, and deserved to take a twelfth minute lead through David Norris.

Things did not improve in the second half. The penalty hoodoo struck again on the hour. Wayne Brown fouled Ewbanks-Blake a yard outside the box. Naturally referee Ray Oliver pointed straight to the spot! Ewbanks-Blake himself converted and it was game over. Although Brown was clearly the last man, the referee compounded his error by failing to send the big defender for a much needed early bath. The U`s misery was completed when Gosling made it three. After what had been their best away performance at Barnsley, Williams felt this had been their worst. It was certainly the heaviest defeat of the season so far.

A patchy month came to a low key end with the visit of Burnley. The U`s had now dropped to tenth, their lowest position for nearly three months, and there were always likely to be casualties from the performance at Plymouth. White and Jackson were dropped. Duguid moved to right back and Izzet returned. McLeod took Duguid`s place in midfield. Both sides had been struggling in their recent matches. Perhaps both managers went into the match thinking they would be happy with a point. It was one of the least entertaining games seen at Layer Road during that season. It finished goalless which was a fair reflection of the play.

At last there was a slight wobble in home form. There had been two draws and a defeat from the previous three home games. Teams were now coming to Layer Road and putting the emphasis on stopping Colchester from playing. This was a huge compliment to United`s collection of free transfers and home grown players, and a way to combat it would have to be found.

The U`s now had to go to Pride Park to play third placed Derby County. The Rams had been steadily improving all season as Billy Davies reshaped his squad. In January he spent over £5 million in signing no fewer than seven players, former Colchester striker Craig Fagan among them. How Geraint Williams must have looked enviously at this. They had won six in a row at the start of the year, and a win at Southend on 20th January sent them top of the table. The match had been brought forward to the Friday night as it was to be live on Sky. Travelling U`s fans would be able to take advantage of Derby`s ticket promotion. They would be allowed in for £10 which was to be contrasted with the £31 recently charged by our lovely neighbours from Suffolk.

John White returned at right back, and Duguid went back to midfield. Williams dropped Iwelumo to the bench, and for the only time that season played a lone striker, Jamie Cureton. It was not a success.

The U`s had a night to forget in front of the TV cameras and a crowd of 26,704. They were on the back foot from the beginning, and White in particular had a torrid time against Derby`s exciting young prospect Giles Barnes. It was all over within half an hour as Derby took a three goal lead. Colchester`s new system could not cope with Derby`s running from midfield. The first two were carbon copies. A strong run from midfield, a cross to the far post and a volley in. Barnes mesmerised Brown with his step-overs for the third.

The U`s had nothing to play for in the second half except pride at Pride Park. Williams replaced Cureton with Iwelumo at half time. Hope was restored in the fifty sixth minute when a five pass move finished with a brilliant Duguid cross being headed in by Jackson. The prospect of an unlikely come back was finished six minutes later when White brought Barnes down for a rare thing in the 06/07 season, a correctly given penalty. Steve Howard made it four, and the rout was completed in the sixty ninth minute by a Chris Barker own goal. Derby went back to the top.

Going into the Deby game, United had picked up one point from nine. Clearly Williams had felt the need to shuffle his pack a little, but it had not worked. He explained, "It has been a long hard season and a lot of the players have played nearly all the games. Fatigue is a factor at this time of year. You can stick with the same players if you are winning every game and every player is looking fresh, but if someone is not quite at the top of their form you have to look at why. Has he got a knock? Is it mental? Has he been up all night with the baby and is shattered, but hasn`t told us? We put the heart rate monitors on them and it may be that the player is doing the same things in training but their heart rate is up. So we have to ask `why is he more fatigued than last week?` There are all sorts of things we make team selections on."

Despite the heavy defeat at Derby Chris Iwelumo was upbeat, "It was disappointing to be left out. Me and the gaffer had a good chat. He makes the decisions and I respect that. Things are not going for us in front of goal at the moment, but we have to still be confident that we can make the Play Offs. We have thirty points to play for. If we can get at least twenty we will have a realistic chance."

The next team to come to Layer Road and shut up shop were Coventry City. They had a new manager in Iain Dowie, whose litigation encouraging spell at Charlton had lasted only fifteen games. His first three at Coventry had seen seven points picked up, but they were still down in sixteenth.

The days of Colchester fielding the same eleven seemed distant now. In an effort to rediscover the winning formula Geraint Williams rang the changes. Duguid again dropped back to right back in place of White. Loanee Matt Mills found himself on the bench as Pat Baldwin, long since recovered from his virus, was restored to the defence. McLeod`s attacking qualities were preferred in midfield to Jackson, despite the latter`s goal at Pride Park. The team reverted to its familiar home formation, with Iwelumo partnering Cureton up front.

Colchester applied pressure, but could not make the breakthrough. Coventry also had their moments with Leon McKenzie looking dangerous and Wayne Brown having to head off the line. The second consecutive home match ended goalless, with Coventry`s Adam Virgo having the best game he would ever have at Layer Road! The U`s remained tenth but were now nine points away from the Play Offs. Automatic promotion was no longer in the equation as sixteen points separated United from the top two, with nine games remaining.

An Increasingly tired looking U`s squad set off for Hillsborough on the following Tuesday. They needed to turn results around, as they were in danger of being sucked into the bottom half of the table. It appeared as though the loss of Halford and the inability to freshen up the squad with some quality acquisitions was taking its toll. They were not going to go down, and it seemed that subconsciously the team were switching off as the task set for them had been achieved. The adrenaline which had taken them through to the end of 2006 was no longer coursing. Perhaps the magnificent surroundings of Hillsborough could re-invigorate the team.

Sheffield Wednesday was now managed by Brian Laws and he had seen them up to a mid table position. George Elokobi came in at left back for his first start in over three months, while Mills returned in place of Baldwin. Barker was dropped to the bench.

Surprising changes to a defence which had kept a clean sheet in the previous game. Up front, Cureton was rested and Hogan Ephraim got another start. Williams clearly felt that the sheer number of games being played by certain players was effecting their form.

The defensive changes did not have the desired effect since it was two first half defensive errors that pulled the rug from under Colchester's performance. Brown and McLeod failed to clear, presenting Simek with the first on twenty seven minutes. Eight minutes later Mills, perhaps expecting Gerken to collect a corner, headed into his own net. The U's improved considerably in the second half and often looked like getting back in the game, especially when pepped up by the introduction of Jamie Guy. It would, however, be another pointless journey.

The previous twelve games had brought two wins, four draws and six defeats. They were still tenth but the Play Offs were now looking very unlikely as ten points separated Colchester from sixth while only four separated them from fourteenth. Williams had always felt that the period after the New Year would be the most difficult, and so it proved. With the main objective in the bag, the season seemed to be fizzling out.

| 1 | 2 (P) | Birmingham City | 37 | 21 | 7 | 9 | 54 | 34 | +20 | 70 |
|---|---|---|---|---|---|---|---|---|---|---|
| 2 | 3 (P) | Derby County | 38 | 21 | 7 | 10 | 51 | 38 | +13 | 70 |
| 3 | 1 (P) | Sunderland | 38 | 20 | 7 | 11 | 58 | 39 | +19 | 67 |
| 4 | 7 | Preston North End | 37 | 19 | 8 | 10 | 54 | 41 | +13 | 65 |
| 5 | 5 | Wolverhampton Wanderers | 38 | 19 | 8 | 11 | 43 | 39 | +4 | 65 |
| 6 | 4 | West Bromwich Albion | 37 | 18 | 9 | 10 | 63 | 42 | +21 | 63 |
| 7 | 13 | Cardiff City | 38 | 17 | 12 | 9 | 53 | 39 | +14 | 63 |
| 8 | 6 | Southampton | 38 | 16 | 12 | 10 | 60 | 46 | +14 | 60 |
| 9 | 8 | Stoke City | 38 | 15 | 13 | 10 | 47 | 32 | +15 | 58 |
| 10 | 10 | Colchester United | 38 | 15 | 8 | 15 | 55 | 47 | +8 | 53 |
| 11 | 12 | Crystal Palace | 37 | 14 | 10 | 13 | 45 | 40 | +5 | 52 |
| 12 | 9 | Sheffield Wednesday | 38 | 14 | 10 | 14 | 56 | 57 | -1 | 52 |
| 13 | 11 | Plymouth Argyle | 36 | 11 | 16 | 9 | 48 | 46 | +2 | 49 |
| 14 | 17 | Coventry City | 38 | 14 | 7 | 17 | 39 | 48 | -9 | 49 |
| 15 | 16 | Norwich City | 37 | 13 | 8 | 16 | 47 | 56 | -9 | 47 |
| 16 | 19 | Leicester City | 37 | 11 | 13 | 13 | 40 | 45 | -5 | 46 |
| 17 | 14 | Ipswich Town | 38 | 13 | 6 | 19 | 47 | 52 | -5 | 45 |
| 18 | 15 | Burnley | 36 | 10 | 11 | 15 | 36 | 39 | -3 | 41 |
| 19 | 21 | Hull City | 38 | 11 | 8 | 19 | 41 | 56 | -15 | 41 |
| 20 | 22 (R) | Southend United | 38 | 9 | 11 | 18 | 39 | 58 | -19 | 38 |
| 21 | 20 | Barnsley | 37 | 11 | 5 | 21 | 40 | 63 | -23 | 38 |
| 22 | 18 | Queens Park Rangers | 37 | 9 | 10 | 18 | 42 | 58 | -16 | 37 |
| 23 | 23 (R) | Luton Town | 38 | 9 | 9 | 20 | 47 | 65 | -18 | 36 |
| 24 | 24 (R) | Leeds United | 38 | 10 | 5 | 23 | 38 | 63 | -25 | 35 |

Chapter 18

# IT'S THE FINAL COUNTDOWN, AND THE ENGINE IS KICK STARTED

# Chapter 18
## IT'S THE FINAL COUNTDOWN,
## AND THE ENGINE IS KICK STARTED

The title of this chapter achieves the impossible. It makes the lyrics to Europe`s famous song even worse than the ones they wrote! The question now was whether Colchester United could achieve the impossible and reach the Championship Play Offs, before stepping beyond the Football League into the Premier League. A place where all forms of measurement are distorted by vast riches. A league declared every year by Sky to be more wide open than ever before! Where any team can finish above any team. Where you have no idea who will fill the relegation positions or the top four! Uncertainty. The very essence of sporting entertainment!

Colchester United had eight games to submit their bid for membership of the feeding frenzy, and they needed to get their skates on. For the past ten weeks they had been showing relegation form as they continued to struggle on their travels, and teams at last seemed to be coming to terms with the Layer Road experience. Four defeats and two draws from the previous six games, with only two goals scored, told its own story. Could they now find a strong finish as they had in 05/06?

The run-in did not look all that daunting. Third placed Sunderland still had to visit Layer Road. Otherwise, United had played all the top sides twice. The remaining games included matches against three of the bottom six. One of the toughest was up next. The U`s had to go to Southampton`s St.Mary`s Stadium. Once again there would be a nationwide audience through the medium of Mr Murdoch, and as a result it was a Friday night kick off.

There were more changes as White, Barker and Baldwin all returned to the defence. Mills and Elokobi moved to the bench, and Duguid missed out with a knee injury. The game of musical chairs between Jackson and McLeod was this time settled in favour of the former, and Cureton returned up front. Claudio Ranieri was no longer in England, but his tinkering style seemed to be influencing things at Layer Road! However, except for Halford and Duguid, we were now seeing the restoration of the unchanging outfield line up which had done so well through the autumn.

Like Colchester, Southampton were pushing for the Play Offs but their recent form had been patchy and they had dropped to eighth. They fielded a seventeen year old Gareth Bale who would be sold to Spurs for £10 million at the end of the season and would later become the world`s most expensive player when, at just over £85 million, he moved on to Colchester United. Or was it Real Madrid? Yes I think it was Real Madrid. It was nearly Colchester United but they lost out in a bidding war after it was discovered that everything about Bale was outside their budget, except one of his boot laces!

The U`s had not fared well in their live Sky games since that heady night against Ipswich back in September. Since that experience, Sky had seemed none too keen to renew acquaintances with the Old Lady. They`d found Coventry`s Ricoh Arena and Derby`s Pride Park somewhat easier to deal with, and had covered Colchester`s games at those modern arenas. United had lost both, the latter heavily, and now hoped for a change of fortunes in front of the cameras.

Despite the poor recent form, assistant manager Mick Harford said they were going for the win. This positive approach seemed to surprise the Saints. Only four minutes were on the clock when Jamie Cureton stabbed home an Iwelumo cross. Southampton`s only January acquisition, Marek Saganowski, equalised in the twenty sixth minute, but Cureton struck again almost from the restart. He brilliantly hooked in a Garcia cross. The U`s supporting couple who had just named their new born son Cureton, to join his sister Mercedes Porsche, must have felt vindicated! Their son`s namesake returned to the top of the U`s goal scoring charts with sixteen strikes. We have to be grateful that this family preferred strikers to goalkeepers!

Colchester had to ride out some second half pressure, and needed an excellent one handed save by Gerken to retrieve a Watson mistake. They hung on to claim the points but remained tenth.

March saw some changes in the squad. Marino Keith ended his injury nightmare, but not in a good way. Unable to conquer the achilles injury which had caused him to miss over a season and a half, he announced his retirement from the professional game in England.

At the end of the month, Matt Mills was allowed to return to Manchester City. His spell at Layer Road had been a mixed bag, and had certainly not ended well when he headed through his own goal at Hillsborough. Many had difficulty seeing him as a better option than the virtually home grown Pat Baldwin. Garry Richards would be returning from a loan spell at Brentford in early April, so there was sufficient cover. Mills has gone on to have a good career at Championship level, attracting some big transfer fees.

This was a good time to be coming into form, as United now faced two East Anglian derbies. Next, Norwich would be visiting "the Layerdome", and then we would be celebrating Easter beside the seaside. First there would be another of those strange phenomena, the international break. Most Championship clubs saw their training numbers severely depleted during one of these. Colchester`s rented training ground at Essex University saw no change. The international managers had not yet programmed Layer Road into their sat navs, despite the efforts of Geraint Williams to convince everyone that Jamie Cureton was Welsh!

The Budgies had not had much to chirp about. In fact their heads had been forlornly buried in their wings for much of the season, and their grip on the perch was looking tenuous. Their Championship future did now look secure, but they could only build for the following season as the Play Offs were way beyond them.

Duguid returned at right back in place of White, and United were otherwise unchanged. Again, this was a fixture that took you back to many pre season friendlies in the 70s and 80s when Norwich usually had too much class for Colchester. They had not visited Layer Road for a competitive match for forty seven years. Norwich were promoted that season but still suffered a 3-0 defeat in Essex. History would repeat itself in 2007

The Canaries looked like a side with little to play for, as Colchester quickly took control of the game. In the first half Iwelumo hit the underside of the bar and forced a good save from Tony Warner in the visitors` goal. Huckerby had looked dangerous on a couple of occasions, but the general view at half time was that United deserved to be ahead.

In the second half, the U`s hit a gear unavailable to Norwich. A typically surging right wing run and cross by Duguid had Iwelumo heading back from the far post for a supremely confident Cureton to flick past a defender and volley in. Soon after, it was Jackson`s turn to shine in setting up the second for Garcia. The cats were really in the bird cage now. Norwich looked punch drunk as Andy Hughes tried to head back to his keeper, but only set up Iwelumo. It was his sixteenth goal of the season, but his first for ten weeks.

Situated a convenient five hundred yards from the local HMRC office, Roots Hall Southend is a former landfill site. Some of us in North Essex have on occasions suggested that planning permission for change of use must have been denied when the stadium was built! The tax office has issued Southend United with so many winding up petitions that they know their own way up Victoria Avenue. Every one has been side stepped with all the dexterity of a crab.

6th April 2007 was Good Friday. It was not a collection day, but Jamie Cureton seemed intent on putting the rubbish out. The Shrimpers cast their net and found it full of Cureton`s goals. A magnificent hat trick in the sun shine started in the first minute, with a fine example of the little man`s football brain. Mentally, he was so far ahead of the Southend defenders as he latched on to a dozy backward header by Efe Sodje and drilled passed Daryl Flahavan.

Freddy Eastwood had threatened an equaliser, but celebrations in the packed away end really got under way in the second half. In the sixty third minute Cureton picked his spot from 25 yards. That spot was in the top left hand corner of Flahavan`s goal. In the seventy ninth minute, Cureton`s intelligent movement off the ball was found by Chris Barker. He clipped the ball over the onrushing Flahavan, and we stood and paid homage to an exhilarating display of striking. With these goals, Cureton became the first Colchester player to score twenty goals in a League season since Tony Adcock in 1984/85, and that was two tiers below in the pyramid. The home fans were informed that something was coming over the hill, it was relegation and unlike the later winding up petitions, it could not be avoided.

Colchester were still tenth after the following day`s games. They had not moved up, despite three consecutive wins. However, the gap between them and the Play Off zone had shrunk to only four points with five games remaining.

The build up to the next would see a flood of black and white footage. People would be dusting off their vinyl albums, their old newspaper supplements and their bizarrely coloured match day programmes. The two hundred thousand people who were apparently in Layer Road on 13th February 1971 would recall, as if it were yesterday, a player scoring while on the ground, another scoring with the back of his head. Graham`s Grandads were now Great Grandads, and they no longer wore ties the width of the River Colne. The nostalgia industry would be coming to Layer Road on Easter Monday, closely followed by Leeds United.

Leeds were still in a terrible condition off the pitch, but had been unbeaten in their previous five matches. This had seen them rise out of the relegation zone, and for long periods in the first half they looked a confident outfit against the unchanged U`s. At half time it was goalless, but the visitors were unfortunate not to be ahead. They started the second half as they had finished the first and it was no surprise when they took the lead with a deflected Eddie Lewis shot in the fifty third minute.

The goal seemed to spark Colchester, who at last began to show their play off credentials. Jamie Guy and Hogan Ephraim were introduced, and their energy started to create openings. An equaliser looked on the cards and it arrived in the eighty second minute when Iwelumo headed in a Duguid free kick. The U`s now smelt blood and Leeds were rocking. Another Duguid free kick in the ninetieth minute was only half cleared. Ephraim pounced on the loose ball and played in Cureton with a delightful pass. Cureton knocked on, before deftly lifting the ball over the advancing keeper. Another home win and, just like their predecessors in 1971, Leeds returned to Yorkshire wondering how they had lost.

| 1 | Sunderland | 42 | 24 | 7 | 11 | 65 | 41 | +24 | 79 |
|---|---|---|---|---|---|---|---|---|---|
| 2 | Derby County | 42 | 23 | 9 | 10 | 58 | 42 | +16 | 78 |
| 3 | Birmingham City | 41 | 22 | 8 | 11 | 58 | 37 | +21 | 74 |
| 4 | West Bromwich Albion | 42 | 20 | 10 | 12 | 71 | 51 | +20 | 70 |
| 5 | Wolverhampton Wanderers | 42 | 20 | 9 | 13 | 49 | 50 | -1 | 69 |
| 6 | Preston North End | 42 | 20 | 8 | 14 | 59 | 50 | +9 | 68 |
| 7 | Stoke City | 42 | 18 | 13 | 11 | 56 | 37 | +19 | 67 |
| 8 | Southampton | 42 | 18 | 12 | 12 | 70 | 50 | +20 | 66 |
| 9 | Colchester United | 42 | 19 | 8 | 15 | 65 | 49 | +16 | 65 |
| 10 | Cardiff City | 42 | 17 | 12 | 13 | 55 | 47 | +8 | 63 |
| 11 | Sheffield Wednesday | 42 | 17 | 11 | 14 | 64 | 61 | +3 | 62 |

Colchester rose to ninth, three points from the play offs and with a better goal difference than the teams in fifth and sixth. It had been a good Easter, and the side had returned to form at just the right time with four consecutive wins.

The U`s now had to travel to Hull City who were sitting precariously two points above the relegation zone. With players such as Ray Parlour and Dean Windass, Hull were packed full of quality and experience. Nevertheless, Colchester needed another win to keep on course for the top six. This would be no easy task in front of over 20,000 at the KC stadium willing on their team`s battle for survival. Ephraim started for the injured Watson, otherwise Colchester were unchanged.

The U`s looked to take the game to Hull right from the off and always seemed to have a goal in them. It was, however, the home side who opened the scoring in the twenty fourth minute through Nicky Forster. Undeterred, the U`s worked their way back into the game. After a number of close shaves they deservedly equalised in the sixty third minute. Cureton drilled home from just outside the box after great interplay with Iwelumo. United looked the far more likely team to force the win, but it finished level.

The feeling was that this was a match that Colchester could, and should, have won. With Hull being in the bottom five, and the next match being against top of the table Sunderland, the feeling was that Hull needed to be beaten if the play offs were to be reached. It seemed that at least seven points, and possibly all nine, would be required from the final three games to keep the fantasy alive. However, two of those games were at home, and there had been times in the past twenty one months when nothing seemed beyond this team.

Sunderland had mirrored Colchester's start to the season by losing their first four league matches and exiting the Carling Cup in the opening round. Results improved immediately Roy Keane was appointed as manager, and their rise up the table had been remarkable. They had not been beaten for seventeen matches and they had won fourteen of those. They now stood four points clear at the top of the table. They had a large, expensive and very experienced squad which had been strengthened during the season by Keane, but even so this had been an amazing turnaround. They had met and beaten everything the Championship could put in front of them. Except one thing that is. They had not experienced Old Lady Layer Road. That would be put right on 21st April.

This was a game which pitted two of the leading candidates for Championship Manager of the Year against each other. Both Roy Keane and Geraint Williams had done magnificent jobs in very different circumstances. Understandably, Keane did not want to hear talk of the spell that the Old Lady had cast over so many of the Championship's biggest clubs that season, "it's still a football pitch, I've never seen a supporter score" was his somewhat unromantic pre match verdict. Despite this, he must have had some concerns about how his defence were going to cope with the Championship's leading scorer. Jamie Cureton was a Manchester United fan who admitted to having Roy Keane's autograph.

The sell-out crowd included Olympic gold medallist Steve Cram, a lifelong Sunderland fan. In a strange twist of fate it was the game when the crowd honoured his Uncle Bobby, the former U's captain, whose death had recently been announced.

Fit again Kevin Watson returned to the centre of midfield, Hogan Ephraim unluckily returned to the bench. Johnnie Jackson, who had filled Watson's berth, returned to the left side of midfield. As the Sunderland players and fans arrived they looked around at their surroundings and wondered what diabolical crime their club must have committed to be demoted into non-league football in mid season!

Colchester started the game brightly and enjoyed most of the territorial advantage without seriously worrying Darren Ward in the visitors goal. As the Half Time interval approached, Jackson had to leave the field for treatment, and with the hosts down to ten men Sunderland started to look dangerous for the first time. It remained goalless however; that was until three minutes into the time added on for Jackson's injury. United were awarded a free kick on the right, Watson floated it in, Sunderland's expensive defenders were interested spectators as Wayne Brown powered in an unstoppable header, right in front of the away fans. The expression on his face gave away that it was his only goal of the season.

Like the champions they would soon become Sunderland were not downhearted by conceding right on half time. They came out re-vitalised and started to apply pressure. After Gerken had saved brilliantly with his feet from Leadbitter, the ball was returned into the heart of the Colchester box where Dwight Yorke rose to head a fifty fifth minute equaliser.

Soon after Yorke`s goal, David Connolly missed a great chance to put Sunderland in front. It proved to be an expensive miss. With eight minutes remaining, Ephraim forced the ball into Sunderland`s penalty area where Richard Garcia swivelled and drove into the bottom corner with his left foot.

A minute from time Layer Road was sent even further into raptures. Substitute Jamie Guy beat three tiring defenders on a surging run before playing in Cureton. He shimmied, and was sent crashing to the turf by visiting skipper Dean Whitehead. It was a clear penalty, and with Iwelumo substituted, Cureton got up and helped himself to the twenty third goal of the best season any Colchester United striker had ever enjoyed. At Layer Road there was little delineation between the technical area and the dug out, Roy Keane simply stood in the dug out and brooded, as only Roy Keane can brood.

"What a day this has turned into at tiny, decrepit Layer Road" shouted the ITV commentator. A club of Sunderland`s heritage, on such a spectacular run of results and led by a man of Roy Keane`s profile, had been brought crashing down, and it was exactly the kind of afternoon that football grounds like Layer Road had been put on the earth for.

The result set up what could be an amazing finale to the season. Two games remained. While Birmingham, Sunderland and Derby battled it out for the two automatic promotion spots there were three play off positions up for grabs. Seven clubs, separated by three points, were chasing them. Six of them were big clubs steeped in footballing tradition and achievement. The kind of clubs that the Premier League was created for. The other one was quite simply living a fairy tale. Never in the field of sporting endeavour had a club this small been so close to joining a league so voracious.

And yet it was possible. A win at Play Off chasing Stoke would set up a final day at home to mid table Crystal Palace, who would have nothing to play for. Stoke had already been beaten at Layer Road, so why not? Admittedly, there remained the small detail of navigating the Play Offs before attempts would have to be made to marry the Premier League to Colchester United, but one of the semi final legs would be at fortress Layer Road and we had a 100% record in Play Off finals. So why not?

| 1 | Birmingham City | 44 | 25 | 8 | 11 | 65 | 41 | +24 | 83 |
|---|---|---|---|---|---|---|---|---|---|
| 2 | Sunderland | 44 | 25 | 7 | 12 | 68 | 45 | +23 | 82 |
| 3 | Derby County | 44 | 24 | 9 | 11 | 60 | 44 | +16 | 81 |
| 4 | Preston North End | 44 | 21 | 8 | 15 | 63 | 51 | +12 | 71 |
| 5 | West Bromwich Albion | 44 | 20 | 10 | 14 | 73 | 55 | +18 | 70 |
| 6 | Wolverhampton Wanderers | 44 | 20 | 10 | 14 | 53 | 55 | -2 | 70 |
| 7 | Southampton | 44 | 19 | 12 | 13 | 72 | 52 | +20 | 69 |
| 8 | Stoke City | 44 | 18 | 15 | 11 | 58 | 39 | +19 | 69 |
| 9 | Colchester United | 44 | 20 | 9 | 15 | 69 | 51 | +18 | 69 |
| 10 | Sheffield Wednesday | 44 | 19 | 11 | 14 | 67 | 62 | +5 | 68 |
| 11 | Cardiff City | 44 | 17 | 13 | 14 | 56 | 49 | +7 | 64 |
| 12 | Plymouth Argyle | 44 | 15 | 16 | 13 | 59 | 61 | -2 | 61 |
| 13 | Crystal Palace | 44 | 16 | 11 | 17 | 55 | 51 | +4 | 59 |
| 14 | Ipswich Town | 44 | 17 | 7 | 20 | 60 | 57 | +3 | 58 |
| 15 | Burnley | 44 | 15 | 12 | 17 | 49 | 44 | +5 | 57 |
| 16 | Norwich City | 44 | 16 | 9 | 19 | 54 | 67 | -13 | 57 |
| 17 | Coventry City | 44 | 15 | 8 | 21 | 45 | 60 | -15 | 53 |
| 18 | Queens Park Rangers | 44 | 14 | 10 | 20 | 53 | 65 | -12 | 52 |
| 19 | Leicester City | 44 | 12 | 14 | 18 | 47 | 60 | -13 | 50 |
| 20 | Barnsley | 44 | 15 | 5 | 24 | 53 | 77 | -24 | 50 |
| 21 | Hull City | 44 | 12 | 10 | 22 | 49 | 65 | -16 | 46 |
| 22 | Leeds United | 44 | 13 | 6 | 25 | 45 | 69 | -24 | 45 |
| 23 | Southend United | 44 | 10 | 12 | 22 | 45 | 73 | -28 | 42 |
| 24 | Luton Town | 44 | 9 | 10 | 25 | 50 | 75 | -25 | 37 |

Chris Iwelumo was in no doubt that it was possible, "The management staff are making sure we take it a game at a time and are keeping us focused, but as players we do talk and there is a feeling that we can actually do this. If we make it into the Play Offs, then any team that comes up against us is going to be expected to win so the pressure is all on them".

At the start of the season one might have been tempted to paraphrase the great Father Ted and say, "Colchester United are small, the Premier League is far away". It was still far away, but it was close enough to catch a glimpse. If you concentrated and looked really hard.

It was a supremely confident U`s squad that travelled to Stoke on 28th April. They had picked up five wins and a draw from their previous six games. They travelled with only one aim, to win. They would be up against another multi million pound squad, which had been boosted by no fewer than eight new signings in the January transfer window. Stoke were unbeaten in five, and just like the U`s needed to win their final two matches in order to make the Play Offs.

Jackson would miss out with the ankle injury picked up against Sunderland, and Ephraim would start in his place. As ever, Geraint Williams was being positive, "I don`t think there`s any pressure amongst the players. The only pressure we have is the pressure we put on ourselves. All we can do is try and get seventy five points because that`s the maximum we can get this season. What we have to do is win on Saturday and make that happen". Over 1500 U`s fans travelled to the Britannia Stadium, with every belief that the team could do just that.

Colchester were quite simply all over Stoke in the opening half hour. Iwelumo, Garcia and Cureton all went close to scoring, while the hosts rarely threatened. The ball was briefly forgotten after Baldwin put in a robust challenge on Stoke`s Andy Griffin, a melee followed which involved most of the outfield players on both sides. Soon after order was restored, Hogan Ephraim broke down the left and crossed to Iwelumo. He was brought down and referee Graham Salisbury pointed to the spot.

Chris Iwelumo had said that any penalties would be going to Jamie Cureton so as to help him win the "Golden Boot" for being the Championship`s leading scorer. But this was too serious. Iwelumo was the number one penalty taker, and had never missed one for Colchester United. The familiar skip to the left, and the ball was side stepped past Simonsen`s left hand, 1-0.

United went in at half time richly deserving their lead. Scores elsewhere were not too encouraging as the U`s rivals were either winning or drawing but the dream was still very much alive. If things stayed as they were Colchester would go up to sixth, a Play Off position, with one game left.

Roared on by nearly twenty thousand fans Stoke meant business in the second half. They quickly had the Colchester goal under siege, and in the fifty third minute the walls were breached. The ball was crossed from the left, Sidibe headed back at the far post for Darel Russell to head just beyond Gerken's dive. Four minutes later the home side were in front. A swift passing movement had Baldwin and Izzet trailing and Sidibe bearing down on the penalty area. He unleashed a low drive and it was 2-1. Another five minutes on and the dream had been snuffed out as the shell shocked U's failed to defend a near post corner. Higginbotham headed in. It had been a three goal salvo in nine agonising minutes.

McLeod, Guy and Elokobi were all introduced as Williams tried to salvage something from the wreckage but the only remaining decisive act was the introduction of Chris Barker's elbow to Lee Hendrie's jaw. The U's full back got first use of the sparkling wash facilities at the Britannia. It was a jaw which had done a fair amount of talking both that day, and during the two club's first meeting back in December, and with the dream now dead it did at least give the U's fans something to chuckle about on their way south.

Although Sheffield Wednesday and Preston had lost, West Brom, Wolves, Southampton and of course Stoke all won, and that left the U's chasing a miracle. They had been holding the clouds all season but now the water they had been pushing up hill refused to go any further. The only thing that could be salvaged was that they were going into the final game of a second tier season, and it was still mathematically possible to reach the Play Offs.

Was there still a chance? Sadly, Slim wasn't just out of town, he had gone "walkabout" in the Australian outback. He'd also put on weight and developed a nasty foot condition. He was not going to be seen in Colchester any time soon.

The final matches would be played on Sunday May 6th and in order to reach the Play Offs Colchester had to beat Crystal Palace, Southampton would have to lose at home to already relegated Southend, Stoke would have to lose at QPR, and Preston would have to not win at home to Birmingham. Even then, all those things could happen but the U's would still probably miss out on goal difference as theirs was five worse than Southampton and Stoke.

Not just mathematical gymnastics were required, but also contortions around probability. Despite this, the home areas were sold out at Layer Road, as was fitting to mark the end of such a wonderful season. There was an end of term feel. Despite saying all the right things, Colchester played like a disappointed team and were never able to raise the intensity so often seen at Layer Road that season.

Southampton hammered Southend, while Stoke drew and Preston won. So not even one of those results went as it needed to and it was academic anyway as the U`s lost 2-0. Despite losing their last two games they only dropped to tenth. That was appropriate, as they had not been outside the top ten since November and they had taken points from every team above them except West Brom.

Many considered West Brom to be the best team Colchester had faced, but it was Sunderland and Birmingham who were automatically promoted. Derby went up through the Play Offs, narrowly beating West Brom in the final. And guess who the champions of East Anglia were!

Despite not scoring in the final two matches, Jamie Cureton won the "Golden Boot" with twenty three goals while Chris Iwelumo was the equal fifth leading Championship scorer with eighteen. After nineteen League seasons without anyone reaching twenty goals, it had finally been done while the club was playing at its highest ever level. The other statistical feat was that of Wayne Brown, playing every minute of every game the club played that season in all competitions.

In May 2006 the feeling had been one of total exhilaration at the attainment of a target which had been sought after for so many decades. Twelve months later the feeling was very different. It was complete astonishment to witness at close hand one of the greatest achievements in the English professional game. Would it last? Probably not, but we made the most of it while it did.

| 1 | P | Sunderland | 46 | 27 | 7 | 12 | 76 | 47 | +29 | 88 |
|---|---|---|---|---|---|---|---|---|---|---|
| 2 | P | Birmingham City | 46 | 26 | 8 | 12 | 67 | 42 | +25 | 86 |
| 3 | P | Derby County | 46 | 25 | 9 | 12 | 62 | 46 | +16 | 84 |
| 4 | | West Bromwich Albion | 46 | 22 | 10 | 14 | 81 | 55 | +26 | 76 |
| 5 | | Wolverhampton Wanderers | 46 | 22 | 10 | 14 | 59 | 56 | +3 | 76 |
| 6 | | Southampton | 46 | 21 | 12 | 13 | 77 | 53 | +24 | 75 |
| 7 | | Preston North End | 46 | 22 | 8 | 16 | 64 | 53 | +11 | 74 |
| 8 | | Stoke City | 46 | 19 | 16 | 11 | 62 | 41 | +21 | 73 |
| 9 | | Sheffield Wednesday | 46 | 20 | 11 | 15 | 70 | 66 | +4 | 71 |
| 10 | | Colchester United | 46 | 20 | 9 | 17 | 70 | 56 | +14 | 69 |
| 11 | | Plymouth Argyle | 46 | 17 | 16 | 13 | 63 | 62 | +1 | 67 |
| 12 | | Crystal Palace | 46 | 18 | 11 | 17 | 59 | 51 | +8 | 65 |
| 13 | | Cardiff City | 46 | 17 | 13 | 16 | 57 | 53 | +4 | 64 |
| 14 | | Ipswich Town | 46 | 18 | 8 | 20 | 64 | 59 | +5 | 62 |
| 15 | | Burnley | 46 | 15 | 12 | 19 | 52 | 49 | +3 | 57 |
| 16 | | Norwich City | 46 | 16 | 9 | 21 | 56 | 71 | -15 | 57 |
| 17 | | Coventry City | 46 | 16 | 8 | 22 | 47 | 62 | -15 | 56 |
| 18 | | Queens Park Rangers | 46 | 14 | 11 | 21 | 54 | 68 | -14 | 53 |
| 19 | | Leicester City | 46 | 13 | 14 | 19 | 49 | 64 | -15 | 53 |
| 20 | | Barnsley | 46 | 15 | 5 | 26 | 53 | 85 | -32 | 50 |
| 21 | | Hull City | 46 | 13 | 10 | 23 | 51 | 67 | -16 | 49 |
| 22 | R | Southend United | 46 | 10 | 12 | 24 | 47 | 80 | -33 | 42 |
| 23 | R | Luton Town | 46 | 10 | 10 | 26 | 53 | 81 | -28 | 40 |
| 24 | R | Leeds United | 46 | 13 | 7 | 26 | 46 | 72 | -26 | 36 |

It is one of the sad realities of football life that, when a small club has an outstandingly good season, ructions can be expected almost immediately the champagne has been drunk. That is what happened at Layer Road in May 2007. As the curtain came down on the 2006/07 season, the Colchester United contracts of Chris Iwelumo and Richard Garcia expired. New ones had been on the table for six months, but they had decided not to sign. Iwelumo started what became a stampede out of Layer Road when he moved to Charlton Athletic, where the Assistant Manager was one Phil Parkinson. Garcia went to Hull.

The club were unable to secure Chris Barker`s permanent move from Cardiff City, and he signed instead for QPR. Loftus Road was also the destination for Assistant Manager Mick Harford. Jamie Cureton and Wayne Brown were still under contract at Layer Road, but this made no difference. Cureton re-joined Norwich City, while Brown joined Garcia at Hull.

Money had spoken. Offers three or four times greater than could sensibly have been afforded at Layer Road had ripped the heart out of the team. The Premier League had shimmied briefly on the horizon, but it was being snuffed out. A wrench from hard reality was being felt. There had been a twenty one month party at Layer Road but it was over and people were collecting their coats and saying their goodbyes. But, oh boy. What a party!

# CONCLUSION

Understandably Geraint Williams looks back on the 2006/07 season with enormous pride,

*"One of the things I'm proud of is that during the 2006/07 season we had every player in the squad fit for 50% of the games, which is staggering when you think about it. This is a tribute to the professionalism of the players and to the way they were trained and conditioned. Donough was very important in this and so was Tony Flynn, the physio I had brought in to replace Stuart Ayles. We had some luck, as there's not much you can do about contact injuries, but muscle injuries are different. The way we trained was often influenced by the size of the squad.*

*We had to think a lot about recovery times and the type of training sessions we put on, how hard do they need to be? Sometimes we might turn a running session into a tactical or technical session so as to ensure we avoided injuries. The fact that all the players were getting regular game time also helped because it meant they often didn't need the sort of fitness training that can lead to muscle injuries.*

*The size of our squad was dictated by the size of the budget. I remember Mr Heard laughing with the Directors of other clubs when talking about the respective budgets. It was common for us to be against clubs with a playing budget around £20 million. Ours was £1.2 million! However, it was possible to turn this into a strength, and this is what we did. Everyone in our squad was either playing or close to playing. That was not the case at other clubs and this fostered a togetherness in our squad which I think was often lacking at other clubs."*

Immediately after the Crystal Palace match Kevin Watson, who was moving towards the end of a long and varied playing career and had seen most things in football said, "We have surpassed all expectations. It has been a magnificent season. Up until last week we were in with a shout of the Play Offs. For a club this size, with the money available and the players we can attract, that is amazing. At some of the pre season training sessions there were six of us training! We did not know where our squad was coming from. This was a team that was going into the Championship, so what the boys have done this year is nothing short of a miracle. The gaffer and Mick Harford deserve the highest sort of accolade."

Despite this, the Championship Manager of the Season award somehow found its way to Sunderland and Roy Keane, thus recognising that Keane had done exactly what he should have done at a club of their size with a multi million pound squad.

Williams does not allow himself to be bothered by the snub as he looks back,

*"As the good results carried on, you noticed that expectations went from zero to being through the roof. I was being asked why our away form was patchy. They were massive games every week for those players, many of whom had not played at that level before. They had to put a huge effort into every game. A tiny drop in work rate, attitude and effort, and we had results like the hammering we took at Derby. When people were disappointed with our away form, I think they forgot the step up that the players had to make from League One.*

*Dean Gerken came in to cover for Aidy`s injury. He kept his place on merit. Aidy said he would keep fighting for his place but he felt Dean was ready to take over.*

*Greg got his big move in January as I had promised. He was tremendous over the first six months of the season. We got £2.5 million but the playing budget was unchanged. I`m sure the club`s finances had never been so healthy.*

*We did look at a few players,as I felt at the time that the squad needed a bit of help to maintain its form, but although ownership had changed, the way the club was being run had not. In particular, there was a player from Stoke who had played at the top level who was available to loan. He would have cost a few thousand pounds per week for a couple of months but the board felt he was not worth it.*

*On the one hand this was frustrating, but I think the board may have been looking back to the Wadsworth era when a few short term signings came in on higher money and disrupted the dressing room. We had got there with a tight knit squad and it would have been easy to destroy the spirit.*

*We had by far the smallest budget in the division, and this was shown again when we had to bring in such inexperienced players as Hogan Ephraim and Gary Richards for a massive game like Ipswich away. Going into the second half of the season there were a lot of players carrying knocks and niggles. You have to ask them if they can get through the game. You have to make clear that once they cross the white line they are declaring themselves fit, and it`s no good them moaning when I say they haven`t done well enough. To be fair, they were very honest players who didn`t make excuses. They just didn`t want to be out of the team.*

*I`m sure there were times when players played when less than fit, which might have contributed to the drop off in our form in February and March. I remember pulling Big Chris out a couple of times. His back and hamstrings got stiff. He was a stiff runner anyway. It was a tough load for him and he really needed a rest. You had to do it for his own good because he just wanted to play every game. That was* *typical of the spirit in the squad.*

*We had a long talk in the dressing room after the defeat at Derby, which was on TV. A couple of weeks later we were on TV again at Southampton, and no-one wanted a repeat of Derby. We asked them if they had enjoyed the experience at Derby, or whether they wanted to roll their sleeves up and give a good account of themselves on TV. Were we going to coast to the end of the season and have more nights like Derby, or were we going to show people what we were really made of? We won and this re-ignited our belief. We went on another good run which put us back in the Play Off picture.*

*The Sunderland home match was the best game of the season for me. They were flying at the time. It was end to end. My philosophy is to attack. I like to score goals. I remember it was 1-1 in the second half and Mick said "it might be time to shut it down. It`s a bit open and they have strong players." I said "I think we can win it and I`m enjoying it. If we lose, we lose but I don`t want to draw." We carried on as we were and won 3-1. As a football spectacle, that was my favourite match.*

*With two games left we had a genuine chance of the Play Offs, but we had to win at Stoke, who also had to win. We were 1-0 up at half time, and then Tony Pulis did what Tony does best. He had long balls launched into our box at their two big lads and we couldn`t handle it.*

*It was a fantastic season. We were playing what were essentially Premier League clubs almost every week. To get twenty wins in the Championship was a phenomenal achievement.*

*I think we would have approached things differently under Phil. My philosophy is to go for wins because you get three points. I suspect we would have lost fewer games under Phil but I don`t know if we would have got as many points. We`ll never know that."*

We`ll also never know whether the Play Offs, or even better, might have been achieved if there had been greater investment in players. There is no doubt that form slumped over the first ten weeks of 2007 as the team seemed to hit a wall, while other clubs invested heavily in the January transfer window. Halford`s quality had been lost, while other players who had been performing so magnificently suffered the inevitable blip in form. The squad needed freshening, but the right type of players at the right price could not be found and probably did not exist.

Even if the transfer fee could be found, such players would have commanded the sort of wages and length of contract which would almost certainly have destroyed that precious team spirit, and there was no guarantee that they would have succeeded anyway. It must also be questionable if the appropriate quality of player could have been persuaded to join little Colchester, even if their financial demands were met.

It is better to dwell on what was achieved rather than what might have been. That was something truly special between August 2005 and May 2007. The amazing thing is that it was done without any real plan. The rules of the modern business world dictate "management by objectives". The closest Colchester United came to an objective was "to do as well as possible". Is that S.M.A.R.T? Is it specific, measureable, attainable, realistic and timely? Every management guru must have been baffled by what happened at Layer Road.

Colchester United is unquestionably one of the best things about Colchester. It is a unique local amenity. Even when crowds are down there is nothing else in the town which brings its people together on a fortnightly basis in such numbers. It does so in furtherance of a common purpose and in search of a holy grail. Success is relative, and for Colchester United the Holy Grail was second tier football.

With a budget that would stretch no further than clip clopping coconut shells Colchester United had emerged out of the mist and beaten all before them, and it was a wonderful thing to be around. In many eyes football had ceased to be a sport, and had become a multi million pound business. Not one which appreciated surprises either! It suits investors and the marketing industry if things follow well established and predictable lines. Big clubs losing in tumbledown stadia will do nothing for merchandising in the far east. Amongst these sentiments Colchester United had "reached for the unreachable star." Briefly the light of romanticism had been let in on professional football, and it allowed us a glimpse of what lay beyond.

It did not last. It could not last. The good ship Colchester United was holed and reality flooded in. But then, nobody said it was meant to be easy being a Colchester United fan.

# ACKNOWLEDGEMENTS

It never ceases to amaze me how many people have taken the time and trouble to write a book about such a small and unregarded football club as Colchester United. I am not even certain how many books there are, but six have a place in my house, not counting my own. All add something to being a Colchester United fan, but in my endeavours I must make special mention of "The Official History of the U`s" by the late Hal Mason, who I had the pleasure of meeting on one occasion. His detailed work has kept alive so many facts and stories which would otherwise have been lost to history. Equally, I would like to pay tribute to the excellent reporting of the Essex County Standard since the formation of the club in 1937.

I have also made copious use of the statistical sections of the books produced by Jeff Whitehead and Rob Hadgraft, along with Graeson Laitt`s amazing web site Coludata. Photographs have been supplied by Colchester United and by Glen Williams and I am very grateful to both. Thanks also to Paul Ost for the long distance view of "The Peter Heard Address". For some of the detail regarding Ron Meades I must recognise a fairly recent interview conducted with him by Rob Hadgraft and printed in "Backpass" magazine.

Despite its questionable reputation, I believe Wikipedia to be very accurate on Colchester United which has been of immense use. Indeed Colchester United are, for some bizarre reason, one of the most comprehensively reported football clubs on Wikipedia, not only in the UK but in the whole world!

When searching for inspiration for the title I consulted my friend Paul Hood. I decided against his suggestion, "Two years when we weren`t s**t" as being unfriendly to the family market. Thanks anyway Paul! For the title I settled upon I should acknowledge, and thank, Neil Peart. The greatest lyricist in rock music. Furthermore, I am indebted to my pre publication readers, John Ratford and Barry Crawford, for their many useful suggestions, not to mention, much needed lessons in grammar and punctuation!

I must say a big thank you to my three interviewees, Peter Heard, Phil Parkinson and Geraint Williams, all of whom were very generous with their time and their tea! Matt Hudson, the media manager at Colchester United, has also been very helpful.

In the Premier League age it is easy to forget how much dedication, professionalism and ability it takes to play third, fourth or even fifth tier level football in England. I pay tribute to all who have done so in the colours of Colchester United since 1937. And to all who have coached and managed them with such skill and application.

I salute all those who have striven to advance the club and keep professional football alive in Colchester, whether it be with their efforts or their money. An often thankless task, for which I say thank you.

All feedback on this book, good or bad, gratefully received at richard.blythe2@yahoo.co.uk.

I will end with a plea to the many thousands who will never read this book, in the hope that somehow the vibrations might get through. If you are from North Essex and like football, why not support your local club? It can be frustrating, exhilarating, hilarious and sometimes very rewarding. A bit like life really.

Up the U`s!

If you have purchased this book, you have made a donation to Teenage Cancer Trust and Headway Essex. Thank you. If it is complimentary, or if you wish to make a further donation, please visit my "JustGiving" pages,
**www.justgiving.com/richardblythetct and**
**www.justgiving.com/richardblythetheadway**

Teenage Cancer Trust is the only UK charity dedicated to improving the quality of life and chances of survival for young people with cancer aged between 13 and 24. The charity has a unique partnership with the NHS, working together to embed their vital services within theirs, complementing and significantly extending the care and support young people with cancer receive.

Teenage Cancer Trust build specialist units within NHS hospitals bringing young people together to be treated by teenage cancer experts in a place designed just for them. The charity wants every young person with cancer to have access to this specialist support, no matter where they live.

Traditionally treated alongside children or elderly patients at the end of their lives, young people can feel extremely isolated during treatment, some never meeting another young person with cancer. Being treated alongside others their own age can make a huge difference to their whole experience.

Teenage Cancer Trust also educates young people and health professionals about cancer to ensure a swift diagnosis and referral to specialist support. Cancer in young people is rare but Teenage Cancer Trust wants young people to know the common signs and symptoms so they can seek medical advice if they are worried.

Colchester United Football Club have been an incredible supporter of Teenage Cancer Trust for many years, raising vital funds from a variety of activities such as collections, cycling and running challenges.

**More information about the charity can be found at www.teenagecancertrust.org**

Headway Essex cares for people who have acquired a brain injury. This can be through sporting or work accidents, road traffic accidents,stroke, assault, illness or disease. Support is given through the Community Support Team and the Headway Centre.

The Community Support Team provides telephone support, information on the different aspects of brain injury, support groups, training for carers, specialist literature on brain injury, home and hospital visits and educational talks.

The Headway Centre in Boxted Road Colchester is a day centre where rehabilitation activities take place. These activities are designed to help people rebuild their lives after brain injury.

Headway Essex is a charity partner of Colchester United for 2015.

**www.headwayessex.org.uk**